The Road to Emmaus

The Road to Emmaus
Daily Encounters with the Risen Christ

An Inclusive Devotional
Edited by Joseph W. Houle

Emmaus Press
EMMAUS HOUSE OF PRAYER • WASHINGTON, D.C.

The Road to Emmaus
Daily Encounters with the Risen Christ

Emmaus Press
P.O. Box 70434
Washington, D.C. 20024

Scripture quotations contained herein are from *An Inclusive Language Lectionary: Readings for Year A*, Revised, copyright 1986; *An Inclusive Language Lectionary: Readings for Year B*, Revised, copyright 1987; and *An Inclusive Language Lectionary: Readings for Year C*, copyright 1985. Used by permission.

Those Scripture quotations contained herein which do not appear in *An Inclusive Language Lectionary* have been adapted from the Revised Standard Version of the Bible, copyright 1946, 1952, 1971 by the Division of Christian Education of the National Council of Churches of Christ in the U.S.A. Used by permission.

ISBN 0-9624901-0-5
Printed in the United States of America

DEDICATION

For Sister Marion,
who drew near and walked the road with me,
who warmed my heart to the wisdom of the Word,
who opened my eyes to see the risen Christ
always walking beside me.

ACKNOWLEDGEMENTS

Many people other than the authors of these meditations have made *The Road to Emmaus* a reality. It gives me great pleasure to acknowledge them in the beginning pages of this work.

I first want to thank Robert Dunbar for his encouragement, love, and patience over the past two and a half years as we prepared this devotional in our home.

I am also grateful to the members past and present of the Board of Directors of Emmaus House of Prayer — Philip Carolan, Sara Case, Adam DeBaugh, Sarah Fershee, Albert Hutchings, Lou Kavar, Scott Minos, and Candace Shultis — for sharing the vision of Emmaus House and for their faithfulness and generous effort in planning and preparing this devotional.

Gratitude is due to David Dagenais, who contributed so generously of his time and talent in virtually every aspect of this work, from cover design to proofreading the final text.

Thanks is also due to Bob Freitag for his great gift of time and expertise as a copy editor in reviewing with me every meditation that appears in this volume.

To Jean Gralley, for her encouragement and creative suggestions for artwork, I am grateful and give thanks.

To Sandra Jones, for the page design of the book and for her patience with me when things bogged down, I am thankful as well.

Wayne Lindsey (*Wayne Lindsey Graphic Design*, 2251 Rumson Road, Raleigh, NC 27610) — who came to see me about Emmaus House and ended up keying in part of the text, helping with cover design, and finding our printer — went far beyond the call of duty to help give birth to this book. I am deeply grateful to him.

Thank you to Virginia Miles, who offered many thoughtful suggestions about the practical application of inclusive language guidelines.

Joe Smith (*blu-line*, P.O. Box 1160, Inwood, WV 25428) typeset this entire book, including changes too numerous to mention, and provided hospitality that made working together a pleasure. Thank you for your expertise and, more importantly, for your friendship.

I am grateful to my sisters Elizabeth, De Lorez, and Ruth Ann, to my brother Ray, and to my sister-in-law Lorraine, for their savvy suggestions and kind encouragement for carrying out this project.

Finally, I thank God for the people of the Mid-Atlantic District of the UFMCC, especially our District Coordinator, Adam DeBaugh, who sustain and strengthen me with their prayer and affirmation, as we walk together the path of faith.

PREFACE

The Road to Emmaus takes its name from a story in Luke's Gospel in which two disciples were walking away from Jerusalem three days after the crucifixion of Jesus. Disappointed by his death, they were returning to their home in the little town of Emmaus to pick up the pieces of their broken lives.

As they journeyed, a stranger drew near and walked with them. The stranger first elicited from the disciples an account of the things that had been happening in their lives, helping them to get in touch with their emotions and release them. Then their new traveling companion proceeded to explain the meaning and purpose of the tragic events that they had undergone. The disciples' hearts began to burn within them as they received fresh hope for their lives from this stranger's words concerning the promises of Scripture.

Once at Emmaus, the disciples invited the stranger to stay with them for the night. And while they were at table, the stranger, who was in fact Jesus risen from the dead, "took bread and blessed, and broke it, and gave it to them. And their eyes were opened and they recognized Jesus, who then vanished out of their sight." (Luke 24:30-31)

So excited were the disciples by their encounter with the risen Christ that they hurried back to Jerusalem that very night to tell the others what they had experienced. Their hope, which had been crucified, was alive again!

Like the disciples of Emmaus, we sometimes find ourselves on a road that leads in a direction that we had not intended.

We may find ourselves walking away from a community that we had grown to love but which has somehow splintered into many pieces as it has lost its center. We may find ourselves searching for an identity, wondering who we really are, uncertain of our future, and attempting to return to a simpler time and easier questions. Then too, we may find ourselves estranged from God because the events in our lives have become chaotic and absurd, and Jesus seems to have died to us.

On the other hand, like the disciples of Emmaus, we sometimes experience moments when we are fully connected with life. We feel propelled towards others, bursting with the glad assurance of the good news we have to share. We know who we are, we know the central purpose of our lives, and we therefore know the relative value of every other claim on our energies. Most important, we know that God is good, that Christ is alive, and that nothing — "neither death, nor life, nor angels, nor principalities, nor things present, nor things to come, nor powers, nor height, nor depth, nor anything in all creation" (Romans 8:38-39) — no, absolutely nothing will ever separate us from the love and the life of God.

The Road to Emmaus is an invitation to become the unnamed disciple of the Emmaus story. It is an invitation to pause in your faith journey and give yourself the gift each day of time for recollection and spiritual refreshment. It is a resource to help you remember that, no matter what road you are traveling, Christ is walking beside you. It is a call to hear Christ inviting you to unburden yourself of the cares of the day and to allow our Saviour to warm your heart to the wisdom of the Scriptures speaking truth for your life.

Then, when you have released the burden of your heart and listened to the wisdom of the Word, you will hopefully move to a moment of deeper intimacy, inviting the risen Saviour into the home of your heart, where you will receive nourishment and strength as you feed on Christ. Finally, having encountered Christ, you will find yourself re-energized to go out again to re-connect with your faith community and to share the good news that Christ, our hope, is fully alive.

Such is our hope for the reader of this book. To enhance the possibility of this encounter with Christ, we have made *The Road to Emmaus* an inclusive devotional. This means that we have made every effort to apply principles of inclusivity in the language, tone, and content of each meditation.

With regard to language, we have followed the guidelines developed and adopted by the Inclusive Language Lectionary Committee appointed by the Division of Education and Ministry of the National Council of Churches of Christ in the U.S.A.

With regard to tone, we have made no assumption about the gender, race, or sexual orientation of the reader, thereby eliminating the need on the reader's part to "translate" what has been written in order to make it correspond to his or her unique identity.

Finally, with regard to content, we have sought to affirm the goodness of all God's children — the young and the old; the male and the female; the lesbian, the gay man, and the heterosexual; the single, the married, and the celibate; the Asian, the Black, the Hispanic, the Native American, and the White; the physically strong and the physically challenged.

In short, as an inclusive devotional, the underlying message of *The Road to Emmaus* is that the Gospel is good news for *all* people.

A related special feature of *The Road to Emmaus* is that it has been prepared by writers who are either openly gay and lesbian Christians or who actively support gay and lesbian Christians in their struggle for self-esteem and full acceptance in the world and in the church. This came about because of our experience that most devotionals either adopt a negative attitude towards gay men and lesbians, or they exclude us by making the assumption that the reader is heterosexual. We therefore felt a great need for a Gospel-based devotional that sees us and speaks to us in a positive way, without at the same time taking the kind of exclusive point of view toward others that we ourselves have found offensive. We have thus prepared these meditations in such a way that any reader, whether homosexual or heterosexual, could benefit from them without having to go through mental contortions to apply their message to his or her unique identity.

In simple terms, we wanted a daily devotional that reflects the kind of inclusivity that we believe the Gospel teaches. Precisely because it is written by people who have felt most deeply the need to feel included, this devotional has the potential to enrich the church as it brings new insight to the common ground of Jesus Christ that all Christians share, whether gay, lesbian, or heterosexual.

All of this means, in the end, that *The Road to Emmaus* is simply a resource for spiritual nurture that anyone may use with profit and without feeling excluded. In faith, the authors collectively claim the hope that it will prove to be for you what our sub-title suggests: a daily encounter with the risen Christ.

Joseph W. Houle
October 18, 1989

The Road to Emmaus

JANUARY

The Feast of the Holy Name of Jesus

Today is the feast of the Holy Name of Jesus, a name meaning "Yahweh is salvation." Yahweh, my God, you are my help, my protection in all life's situations, my salvation. In you I feel a calm security and a safety nothing can invade. No matter what constraints are laid upon me by the responsibilities and cares of life, in you I have freedom and peace.

If you cannot bring me this salvation, Yahweh, then there is no one who can, and it is foolish to expect such saving grace from any other source. You may use human and natural means to effect this salvation, but you, not they, are the source of salvation for me and for all people.

In today's reading, Jesus urges us to ask you for anything in his name, for his name is a reminder of your loving care for us. There is so much for which I need to ask in Jesus' name. Please help me to love others with a warm, compassionate heart, never measuring the personal costs of time, energy, or financial resources, but opening my heart and hands as much as you know I can. I ask for your blessings on those for whom I have promised to pray, those most in need, the destitute, the hungry, the sick, the homeless, the jobless. Give your strength especially to those who have AIDS or ARC and to their family and friends. Since I can never totally understand the mystery of suffering and death, help me to learn it through acceptance. Give me the grace and faith I need to feel your love for me. Knowing that the poor and the helpless are the favorite objects of your grace, I pray with a confidence that my prayers are answered.

Let me remember to say the name of Jesus many times throughout the day. "*Jesus, Jesus, Jesus*" will be a refrain to ask you all these things, my God, through your Child, my Friend and Saviour. Amen.

† † †

In today's passage, Jesus, you confront us with one of the central mysteries of our Christian life. You claim that you are the bread of life, a bread which imparts eternal life. If we eat this bread, we will never die.

Sometimes I wonder if there really is an afterlife. My mind has grown so accustomed to logical proofs that I gradually slip into skepticism. Because some of my church's tenets have been wrong in the past, I question even its most basic teachings, including its teachings about life after death. Thousands of deaths from AIDS, including the deaths of some of my friends, have brought me to the brink of despair. God, where are you?

Elizabeth Kubler-Ross and other authors tell us that their experiences with death and dying confirm their belief in a life after death. These "out of the body" and "near death" encounters, like your own Resurrection, are signs which bolster my tottering faith. And I remember your words to Martha when you raised her brother Lazarus to life: "I am the resurrection and the life; those who believe in me, though they die, yet shall they live, and whoever lives and believes in me shall never die." (John 11:25-26)

I believe in you, Jesus. I believe that the physical death of the body is not final. I believe that God, who raised you from the dead, will also raise us up on the last day. I believe in this fullness of life that you have promised. Help me in my moments of unbelief. Amen.

✝ ✝ ✝

You tell us, Jesus, that you are the good shepherd. In Biblical times, the nomadic shepherd's life meant traveling great distances with the flock in search of fresh pasturelands. Like the good shepherd, you have travelled with me through the changing seasons of my life. And when I strayed from the main body of your church flock, you sought me out and helped me find my way back to the faith community.

In inclement weather the protective shepherd leads the sheep to a safe shelter and, when predators lurk, defends them against bandits or beasts of prey. Jesus, I have felt the harsh and windy climate of social rejection because of being different. I have seen the bands of ecclesiastical predators expel lesbian and gay Christians from our churches, relegate women to second-class citizenship, and support government policies that oppress the poor. But like the good shepherd, you are there to gather the sheep together, to give us comfort and support in each other's presence, and to assure us that we are safe because you are at our side.

The good shepherd has a remarkable rapport with the flock, whose members recognize the shepherd's voice. With perfect confidence, the herd will follow wherever the shepherd leads. I too want that extraordinary relationship with you. When I hear your voice calling me to risk being just who I am yet another time, I wish to trust that, despite initial discomfort or tension, the end result will be a greater dignity and a sense of well-being within me.

Unlike the hired hand, who feels a diminished sense of responsibility because of a lack of ownership, the good shepherd's commitment to care for the sheep reaches the ultimate, a willingness to die for them if necessary. I am humbled and feel your love anew each time I realize that you did just that: you gave your life for me.

Help me today, Jesus, to imitate your selfless love by doing one kind act for another. Amen.

† † †

Jesus, in today's Gospel reading, you tell us that you and God are one. By knowing and loving you, we come closer to God. Today I draw nearer to you to experience the fullness of life that you offer.

You tell us that we can ask for anything in your name because of your special relationship with God. In a society whose main ambition seems to be an insatiable desire to accumulate wealth, I ask you to help me to appreciate and strive for those values that are truly worthwhile treasures.

I ask for physical and mental health for those who are suffering from AIDS, for all who are living with emotional or psychological disorders, for those handicapped in the use of their limbs or unable to fully experience the gifts of sight and sound. I ask for the grace of soundness in mind and body for myself and for those I dearly love.

I ask you for a full and meaningful life. When you determine that I am ready to be united with you through that process we call death, may I leave this world a better place than when I entered it. May I have the comfort of knowing that, in some small way, my life here has made a difference to others.

I ask you for genuine social security — not a monthly financial dole, but the continual solace of being surrounded by friends who love me despite my numerous weaknesses and limitations. May I, in turn, provide security and care to others, especially to those who seem to have no friends.

I ask for these and for other graces, Jesus, confident that a request in your name is a direct prayer to our God. Amen.

† † †

In this passage, you tell us that you are a vine, Jesus, and we are branches which will bear fruit as long as we remain in you. Your loving Father-and-Mother singles out those branches that will produce good fruit and gently prunes them. In addition to the planting, watering, and weeding needed in the cultivation of crops, a good gardener will also prune the stock to produce a heartier plant that will bear more and better fruit.

I believe that I am a worthwhile branch of our Creator's vine. Now, I don't mean to complain, Jesus, but don't you think our God is pruning me just a little too much? When I become disheartened and discouraged by the values and choices of our country and our church, is our God pruning me of my adamant conviction that I know what is best for everyone? When I feel searing disruptions and conflicts with my most intimate friends and loved ones, is our God pruning me of my dependence on human relationships? When I want so much to pray and to be connected to the holy but seem unable to find you because of the empty tomb within me, is our God pruning me of my longing for spiritual satisfaction? When I feel frustrated because so many of the ambitious tasks I have set for myself remain undone, is our God pruning me of my self-reliance and reminding me that I am powerless without you, Jesus?

Yes, I am being pruned, reduced, cut down, diminished, so that my vital union with you, Jesus, will yield an even greater harvest. I believe that you chose this branch to help make this world a better place and to lead others to the eternal joy of the next. Today, please keep this branch close to you, Jesus, our life-giving vine. Amen.

† † †

The Feast of the Epiphany

At one of his public lectures, Edward Schillebeeckx, the famous Dutch theologian, was asked how he first came to an experience of religion and God in his own life. He replied that it happened when his mother took him to the parish church and he saw the Christmas crib.

It is a strange assembly at the Christmas scene: a poor family, shepherds who were at the bottom of the social ladder, and three royal figures from foreign lands with foreign gods. It was to these different and strange visitors that God first revealed the helpless child who was later to proclaim himself light for all people. The feast of the Epiphany invites us to join this gathering of outsiders and to see the reign of God in Jesus, the outsider whom paranoid political leaders and complacent religious leaders seek to destroy.

The reign of God continues to break in upon us in the most unexpected circumstances and people. God continues to come to us as the outsider: the poor, the foreigner, the social outcast, the seeker. And when we ourselves are the outcasts, like shepherds and seekers of old, we can also be transformed by what we find in the Christmas crib of our hearts.

*Loving God, continue to reveal yourself to
me in all those whom I encounter: in the poor, in
strangers, in foreigners, in those who are different
from me, and especially in the bruised reed and
smoldering wick — even when
they are part of me.*

† † †

Did you ever wonder what happened to that couple who will always be remembered because of the honored guest at their wedding? Did they ever tire of recounting that day over and over to their children and grandchildren? Did they remember their feelings of panic when they discovered they had no wine, their surprise at the sudden appearance of even better wine than they had purchased, the whispers that went around the wedding party about this man Jesus? Did this first of Jesus' signs bring them to faith in him or discipleship? Did they ever leave each other?

Weddings and Holy Unions evoke profound feelings of happiness and deep feelings of pain in all of us — couples, singles, celibates, divorced, widows and widowers. We are happy for these two who pledge their love and faithfulness to a life that calls for the transformation of the water of selfishness, individuality, and established ways into the wine of mutuality, respectful love, and continued growth. And yet we know of so many others who have for many reasons broken commitments to partners.

Wedding and Holy Union ceremonies may also awaken in us our own deepest longing for someone who will never go away. In the light of this moment of crystallized fidelity and commitment, we may remember the lost chances, the broken commitments, the unhealed hurts of broken relationships in our own lives. At such moments we can turn to God, the one who embodies perfect fidelity to us all the way to death and beyond.

Jesus, you are really the only one who
will never go away. By your abiding presence,
you help us to transform our isolation into community
and our aloneness into intimacy. And when others go
away, you are still there at the end — the best
wine for us to drink at life's wedding banquet,
celebrating the union of our God-with-us.

† † †

In his novel of the life of Jesus, Nikos Kazantzakis describes a sunrise conversation between Jesus and John the Baptist. Sitting in the hollow of a rock above the Jordan, they are discussing the fate of the world. Kazantzakis describes the face of John as severe and decisive, that of Jesus as tame and resolute, with eyes full of compassion.

"Isn't love enough?" Jesus asks.

"No. The tree is rotten," John responds. "God called me and gave me the ax, which I then placed at the roots of the tree. I did my duty. Now you do yours. Take the ax and strike."

And Jesus answers: "If I were fire, I would burn; if I were a woodcutter, I would strike. But I am a heart, and I love."[1]

John did not recognize the Lamb of God. Perhaps he expected not a lamb but a wolf, not healing and accepting love but a purifying and destroying fire. But the only fire that Jesus kindled was the spirit of Pentecost, and the only wood he needed to have cut was the cross he mounted for us.

The images of Jesus we fashion and shape for ourselves reveal our deepest needs, our real fears, our vision of the reign of God. As with John, perhaps the image of the lamb doesn't always fit comfortably for us. The lamb reminds us even in the midst of our seeming powerlessness that we must accede to the slaughter of our preferred ways of bringing about the reign and accept God's call to us to forgive and heal.

Jesus, like John I too am tempted at times to burn and cut my way to justice and dignity and freedom. But you have made me heart, and I must love. For this is the only way that I and others around me will know that we are indeed all God's chosen ones.

[1] Kazantzakis, Nikos, *The Last Temptation of Christ* (New York: Simon and Schuster, 1986), p. 235.

✝ ✝ ✝

In two terse sentences Mark leads us into the desert with Jesus at the beginning of his public ministry. This event immediately follows Jesus' turning-point encounter with John the Baptist, in which God whispered the name "Beloved Child" in Jesus' ear as he rose up from the watery tomb of the Jordan. The psychological and spiritual experiences of Jesus in that desert are described in symbolic words like "test," "wild beasts," and "angels." In the wilderness Jesus wrestled with the demon questions of his personal identity, his mission in life, his relationship to power and prestige, and his ultimate dependence and trust in God.

In the Christian tradition the desert has always been a place to face the ultimate questions and issues of life. Those who left the cities and towns were called "ascetics" (from the Greek word *askesis*, meaning exercise), or athletes for Christ. Some left to escape persecution; others fled because they were tired of the shallowness and emptiness of urban life. They believed that, like Moses, Elijah, and Jesus, they would hear the voice of God in the desert, and that in finding God they would also find their authentic selves.

The desert is still a place where we hear the voice of God calling us to our true selves: the desert of failed relationships; the wilderness of rejection by loved ones; the solitude of unjust exclusion from churches; the wastelands of wrestling with the demons around us and within us.

Yet the desert is also a place of cool winds, sweet water, and nourishing bread, a place where we meet the one who sustains us lest we fall from the heights, dash our feet, or starve in selfishness. When we find ourselves in a desert, we can therefore take comfort in the promise recorded by Hosea: "Therefore I will allure Israel, and bring them into the wilderness, and speak tenderly to them. And I will give Israel vineyards, and make the Valley of Achor a door of hope." (Hosea 2:14-15a)

† † †

For several summers I worked at a mission church on North Carolina's Outer Banks. One year I met a Jesuit priest there who gave me a book of his poetry called *Psalms of the Still Country*. In one poem, "The Successful Catch," there is this question: "Why did I leave the security of the sea for you? Why does the line of your face excite the rattle of life in me?"

Mark's account of how Jesus called his early followers is not as simple as it might appear. Bible scholars think that Jesus and some of his disciples were originally members of John's movement. It is very likely that group tensions were generated by Jesus when he began to announce the imminence of the reign of God and members were faced with the choice of remaining with the "Baptist movement" or joining the new "Jesus movement."

In our own lives there are moments when we wonder if we really want to make a choice, times when we feel it might be better to simply stay where we are. Jesus did not call all those he met to leave their work and homes and families and follow him; some were left to continue their daily lives. To "fish" for people in the name of God is no easy task!

Although discipleship requires choices at points along the way, perhaps it requires even more a steady gaze in prayer "on the line of [Jesus'] face," in order to know where God is calling us. What to do will be shown us; and not always knowing exactly is all right, too.

My friend's poem ends this way:

> I clearly do not know
> what I want to do
> but as clearly now I know
> what I do not want to do
> and that is
> to remain here
> outside the shadow of your net
> untouched by you.[1]

[1]From *Psalms of the Still Country* by Ed Inglebretson, © 1982, Resource Publications, Inc., 160 E. Virginia St., #290, San Jose, CA 95112.

† † †

In this passage from Mark, we read about the essence of your life, Jesus: healing, praying, and preaching.

Not just Simon's mother-in-law and the man with the dreaded skin disease, but all the sick devoured you in their desire to be whole. I too run to you for spiritual comfort and nourishment. When I feel the weighty responsibilities of my work and the seemingly endless routine of my days, I seek your healing. Heal my feverish ways and empower me to rise up like Simon's mother-in-law to be of service to others.

Because the crowds pursued you, clamoring for your healing presence, you often had to flee to lonely places to be alone and quiet with God. I also need to meet our Father-Mother God in a quiet place, a space that is sacred and holy, a sanctuary apart from the world's bustling activity. Praying with you, Jesus, to our loving God, restores my spiritually depleted energy. I know I don't make enough time for private prayer. While people came constantly to you from everywhere and invaded your praying space, I seem to avoid quiet moments with my God and venture instead into the noise and distraction of outer stimulation. Enable me, Jesus, to integrate contemplation into my busy days.

And may those busy days be filled with preaching the good news that we are graced with Yahweh's love. Help me to preach your goodness by kindness to others, by affirming my co-workers, by rooting out jealousy from my heart. I do not need to be a TV evangelist or on a street-corner soapbox to preach my love for you and your love for the world. Help me to preach by the witness of a Christian life which will heal the wounds of those I touch.

Help me to walk in your footsteps today by healing someone's wounded spirit with a gentle touch, by silently preaching your love, by the way I live my life, by taking some quiet moments to move apart and pray with you. Amen.

† † †

Today's reading from Mark tells a story of faith, forgiveness, and healing. The friends of the paralyzed man must have had a tremendous amount of creative determination along with faith in your ability to cure, Jesus. They went to all the trouble of making a hole in the roof in order to let down the paralyzed man on his bed into the middle of the group in front of you.

Because I deeply believe in your power to heal, I boldly and confidently ask forgiveness of my many sins. Forgive my pride, my self-righteousness, my lack of a generous spirit. Forgive, too, the sins of our society: greed, consumerism, self-interest, and domination of others under the guise of providing aid. I too become infected in this environment of societal sin.

When some of the religious leaders heard you forgive this man's sins, they began to grumble and complain that you had blasphemed. After all, as teachers of the law, they knew that forgiveness of sins was one of the marks of the Messiah. You were claiming that you were the Messiah, the anointed one of God!

I don't have to be a modern teacher of the law or a church official to know that forgiveness is one of the marks of a Christian. In order to be sons and daughters of God, we must make the cornerstone of your teaching — love of one's enemy and forgiveness of others — evident in our lives. Just as you proved your power to forgive sins by healing the paralyzed man, I will know that I am forgiven when I feel the inner healing of my bitterness and rancor toward those who hurt me or who disagree with my views and opinions.

Jesus, I believe that you are the Messiah. Heal me of all the selfishness which keeps me paralyzed on my mat. Help me to pick it up and go home with forgiveness in my heart. Amen.

† † †

Today's reading describes your calling of Levi, a Jew, who collected taxes from his own people on behalf of imperialist Rome. Little wonder that he was despised and considered an outcast by his people.

Jesus, many people couldn't understand why you sought the company of tax collectors and other social miscreants. Nor could they understand why you and your disciples did not fast like other good and holy men and women. You did not seem to behave as many expected a religious teacher or prophet to behave.

Jesus, help me not to be afraid to associate with society's outcasts: homeless street people, prostitutes, transvestites, pedophiles, people with AIDS, or the poor who depend on welfare checks and food stamps.

And yet, just being on the underside of economic power, or not having political influence, or feeling the burdens of ecclesiastical structures — these things do not in themselves make us right with you, Jesus. We can so easily create our own caste of outcasts, people toward whom we may be tempted to feel superior and with whom we may arrogantly feel that you would never eat and drink and share your intimacy.

Just as devout Jews self-righteously scorned Levi as a greedy traitor, so we have our own pariahs to look down upon. Our Levi's are the black police officers of South Africa employed by the white apartheid government. Our Levi's are the religious leaders who enforce doctrinal orthodoxy at the expense of God's command to love. Our Levi's are the politicians, businesspeople, and scientists who perpetuate a military-industrial complex that keeps the Third World supplied with weapons instead of with food.

Help me today, Jesus, to be critical of unjust systems but compassionate toward those who are trapped in them, for you are also calling them to be your disciples. Amen.

† † †

There was a Jewish law that forbade any work to be done on the Sabbath so that one's labors could be set aside in order to pray and give praise to Yahweh. But your disciples picked wheat on the Sabbath, and you healed the paralyzed hand of a man on the Sabbath — two violations of the law which the Pharisees minutely observed.

Your response to your accusers did not show a blatant disregard for law, but a healthy and holy disposition toward it. The Sabbath (i.e., the law) was created for the good of people, not vice-versa. If the literal following of a law does not draw people closer to God or does not serve humanity, then the law simply does not apply. Jesus, give me a balanced respect for law which does not disdain civil or church law but which recognizes the times when the good of persons must supersede a slavish adherence to rules and regulations.

I pray today that those laws which do not serve people's needs and respect their dignity will be abolished. I bring to you the laws of apartheid in South Africa that demean the Blacks of that nation. I bring to you immigration laws in the U.S. which discriminate against the poor, who seek a better life for themselves. I bring to you church laws which prohibit women from being ordained to the priesthood or which bar homosexual persons from having their committed relationships blessed. As you were angry and grieved at the Pharisees' hardness of heart, so I am angry and grieved today at the stubbornness and ignorance of those who are closed to a broader vision of the law.

Yet, I am also at times like those Pharisees in my day-to-day life. I seem to make my own laws for others to follow. Jesus, please change my compulsive desire to control other people's actions and lives. I pray for a conversion of heart that I may grant others the freedom I so desire for myself.

Today, help me to respect other people's choices. Amen.

† † †

"One sows and another reaps."

After your lengthy theological discourse with the Samaritan
woman at the well, and before her return with the townspeople, Jesus, you took some time to teach your disciples the
dynamics of the spiritual life. Your disciples were shocked,
but they were afraid to ask you why you conversed with a
Samaritan whom any "good" Jew would despise more than
he or she would a pagan. And you conversed with a woman
who was supposed never to speak in public to a man other
than her husband. To cover their discomfort, they begged you
to take some food to eat. Replying that you had a different
kind of food, you began to teach them about cooperating rather
than competing, being benevolent rather than jealous.

Help me, God, not to seek or desire the satisfaction of public
acclaim. Let the accomplishment of good deeds be sufficient
reward for my labors. Help me, dear God, to be a faithful sower
of the seed, content to let others reap the fruits of my work.
Concern about gaining recognition is part of a competitive
model that is foreign to your Gospel spirit.

We are one human family, working your garden of creation.
Some sow, some till the land, some irrigate, some weed the
fields, some harvest the crop. We have different jobs, different
skills, different gifts, but none is more important or more
valuable than any other. All must work harmoniously and
cooperatively to produce a good harvest.

Though I may desire different skills or envy the resources of
others, help me to rejoice in the good fortune of others. I
believe that my petty jealousies will abate if I recognize, value,
and treasure the many abilities you have given me. Help me
today, God, to thank you again and again for making me the
person that I am. Amen.

† † †

Why is it that people of all kinds wanted so much to touch Jesus? Why is it that he himself often touched others when he cured them of their diseases or held their children in his arms for a blessing? Why is it that, after the Resurrection, Jesus urged the disciples to "touch and see" that it was really the Christ in their midst, fully alive?

A friend of mine who belongs to Mother Teresa's Brothers, the Missionaries of Charity, founded The Center in Oakland, California, for people with AIDS and their care-givers. In an interview for a Catholic newspaper Jeremy says that, because AIDS is "mixed up with so much we are afraid of, especially death," those with AIDS are "Jesus in his most clever disguise."

One of the services The Center provides is massage for those who are not helped much by drugs and from whom others have often withdrawn physically or even emotionally. Massage therapy is important for those individuals in that it enables them to know and feel that they are still in touch with others and can thereby experience inner emotional and spiritual healing, if not an actual cure of the disease.

Jesus knew well that his touch contained power that could heal on many levels. Moreover, he shared that power with his most intimate collaborators. We can still give and receive the touch of the risen Christ today in massaging the sick, in feeding the poor, in holding a lover, in embracing the unlovely — whenever and wherever our touching is respectful and reverent, neither intrusive nor manipulative.

> *People press in on me at times and, like you, Jesus, I withdraw in prayer and contemplation. Refreshed and renewed in my spirit, I can then plunge again into facing the demons around me and in me. I have so many times experienced your healing touch in my own life. As your intimate companion and friend I want to pass that touch on to others I encounter today, in such a way that it will really be good news for afflicted humanity.*

† † †

An old piece of folk wisdom defines the home as a place where the hearth is. The hearth, which housed the fire, was at one period of history the center of family life. The hearth was the place to prepare food, to feel warmth, to have light in the darkness. These experiences bonded the family together, both physically and emotionally.

Several years ago the *New York Times* reviewed a book dealing with emotional and physical conflicts, including violence, in contemporary families. The writer, in a clever adaptation of the traditional adage, titled the review "Home Is Where the Hurt Is."

No human family, not even that of Jesus, escapes the pain that certain misunderstandings can bring to family life. The family of Jesus is portrayed in the Gospel as thinking him possessed by a demon when they heard the crowd say that he was out of his mind. How ironic that the Scribes accused him of being possessed by evil forces! One of the strongest signs of his making present the reign of God was his ministry of expelling demons and breaking the bonds of evil forces that controlled others.

It is easy to sympathize with Jesus and feel his disappointment. In our lives we have also felt the misunderstandings of families — birth families, work families, church families — for one reason or another. Yet the response of Jesus is not counter-rejection or further alienation. He simply makes it clear that commitment to the reign supersedes all family ties. Like Jesus, we need family loyalty. And, like Jesus, we often find our loyalties in other kinds of families, especially among those who support and nourish our commitments to personal integrity.

Lord, you did not reject your own family
even though they misunderstood you. Instead, you
invited them and us to membership in that larger family
of God in which, through baptism, water is
thicker than blood.

† † †

In 1988, the students of a prominent national university for the deaf in Washington, D.C., reacted with several days of protest and turmoil on their campus when a hearing person was named as president. The students were demanding that, for the first time in the institution's history, a deaf person occupy that position. They wanted both a positive role model and a president sensitive to their struggles.

One scene presented on the evening news was a noisy and tumultuous gathering where a university official attempted to address a room filled with angry, chanting students. At one point she said that if the noise continued, she could not speak. Immediately the students shot back in sign language, "What noise?" There was no more convincing argument for the timeliness or justice of the students' demands!

There are more ways to hear than with one's physical ears. The deaf students were speaking quiet "words" which could only be heard by the ears of the heart. Their words succeeded beyond all expectations in producing justice as their fruit. Jesus' story of the tiny seeds producing unheard-of abundance, in spite of almost overwhelming obstacles, is a description of the fruitful abundance of the reign of God when we hear God's call in our lives with the hearing of the heart.

> *God, your reign comes inevitably and abundantly when I hear with my heart the needs of others around me for meaning and value. Your reign comes powerfully and successfully when I respond with my tiny efforts to sow the seed of Jesus in hearts that are barren and rootless, pressured or persecuted, choked with anxiety or compulsion. But, first of all, make me good soil for Jesus-seed. Amen.*

† † †

A man who had a weak heart inherited a billion dollars. His family was afraid that the good news would precipitate a heart attack, so they asked the priest to tell him the good news. The priest visited the man and tactfully asked him what he would do if someone gave him a billion dollars. When the man said he would give half to the parish, the priest had a heart attack.

Some heart attacks today come from stress caused by overwork in pushing too hard for material success. Others are spiritual heart attacks caused by pushing too hard for the reign of God. It is easy to recognize material greed. Spiritual greed is more difficult to discern, but just as dangerous.

Jesus teaches that the reign of God cannot be hurried or pushed for any purpose — no matter how good. The reign of God grows slowly in our lives and in our world. The reign-sower must be patient. All processes of growth take time. A rich harvest is not possible without waiting and hoping and trusting.

So the sower goes about living the ordinary day-to-day business of life. And the seed, slowly but inexorably, passes through the various stages of growth. Worry, anxiety, fear will not help the seed grow one bit faster. Once the seed is planted, its growth and fruitfulness are out of the sower's immediate control. Life continues through it all.

A handful of wheat, five thousand years old, was found in an Egyptian tomb. When planted, the grains came to life. The power of growth is in the seed. When I have dug and planted and watered and watched, I can patiently wait until God's power gradually unfolds, perhaps in lives and events I had not expected. I do not know *how* God works. I *do* know it is God's power, not mine, that works.

† † †

A famous painting in one of the churches in the city of Rome depicts a large ark-like boat riding atop a storm-tossed ocean. At the helm is the Pope. Behind him, crowded in the boat, are bishops and clergy and lay people. The boat rides high in the water far above the threatening waves. In the water all sorts of drowning people try to reach and enter the boat which will bring them to safety.

This image of the church is in sharp contrast to that of Mark's, who describes the boat's captain as being sound asleep, the boat itself as taking on water and being in danger of sinking, and the terrified passengers as huddled together in fear. It is hard to believe that anyone could sleep through the violent storm that Mark describes, even after a hard day's work of preaching and teaching.

Mark's account of the calming of the storm is meant to speak directly to the disciples of Jesus. The story's purpose is to encourage them to face the stresses of discipleship and to rely on a deep, inner calm that strong faith can bring. The charge of Jesus that they had little or no faith is probably a remembrance of their fears and discouragement following the death of Jesus and before the Resurrection.

As a disciple of the risen Christ called to be in the human family and not safely above it, I, too, experience the storms that break over the bow of the church. At times I fear drowning in the debates and polarization that rock the church-ark over issues of human sexuality, nuclear weapons, capital punishment, abortion, and authority. My own faith at times is "little," and I wonder if Jesus is not sleeping once again.

Today's Gospel reminds us that, in the eye of the hurricane, there is a calm, peaceful center. In the midst of the storm, the disciple can enter into the "I-am-present" of Jesus — and rest in trust.

† † †

The hills around the Sea of Galilee contain many large caves that were used to shelter cattle or other animals or to provide refuge for fugitives from war or from the law. They were also used as burial tombs. It was from one of these burial caves that a man possessed by a legion of evil spirits emerged and fell on his knees before Jesus. Having compassion on him, Jesus cast out the demons, so that the man was able simply to sit there, clothed, and in his right mind.

Sometimes I, too, feel that I am possessed by a legion of the evil spirits that permeate our culture and keep me immured in burial caves. I am buried in the caves of consumerism which urges me to spend, to buy, to satisfy my selfish desires. Loving and compassionate God, help me to break these chains by spending my money and my time on projects which enable those less fortunate than myself to gain a sense of worth and self-respect.

I am buried in the caves of a capitalistic sense of competition which subliminally urges me to compare myself with others and to denigrate them so that I can feel secure. Gracious God, smash these iron chains of insecurity so that I can compete only with myself and feel jealous only of the person I am meant to become.

I am buried in the caves of a superpower mentality of domination which always seeks to control and manipulate others. Help me, gentle God, to regain my right mind and to clothe myself and others with respect for individual freedom.

Jesus, today I fall on my knees before you and beg you to banish the mob of demons which possess me and keep me locked in burial caves. I want to go home to my family and friends to tell them how kind you have been to me. Amen.

† † †

Loving God, it has always bothered me that the man in today's Scripture reading "ratted" on Jesus. The healed man revealed Jesus's identity to the Jewish authorities, knowing well their intent to persecute Jesus for healing on the Sabbath. Little wonder that this paralyzed man had no one to put him in the pool when the water was stirred; the ungrateful wretch probably had made few, if any, friends!

When charged by the Jewish officials with an offense against the Sabbath, the healed man exonerated himself by shifting responsibility to his healer. After being cured of a thirty-eight-year illness, the ignorant ingrate did not even bother to find out the name of the person who had made him well again. He sounds like a rascal, a really unlovable fellow.

Gracious God, there are people I find unlovable and unattractive. They are often society's rejected and disposable ones: the derelicts, the sick, and the poor. Some are socially acceptable but are simply unappealing to me. Help me respond to all these people with the respect and compassion you showed. Instead of ignoring them, let me firmly suggest what might contribute to their own enhancement and enable them to claim their own dignity. Help me to befriend the friendless.

In many ways I am like that pitiful rascal at the pool of Bethesda. Often I don't want to assume responsibility for my own actions, especially when the results are less than desirable. May I not excuse my own failures or unwanted outcomes beyond my control by blaming others. Help me to be grateful for the support I receive from friends and never hurt them by any inadvertent words or actions.

Dearest God, I pray that today I may recognize the man at the pool of Bethesda in myself and love him in others. Amen.

† † †

The woman who had suffered severe bleeding for twelve years believed wholeheartedly that she would be well if she could only touch your clothing, Jesus. Mark's Gospel today tells us that she touched your cloak and was healed immediately.

Jairus, too, kneeling at your feet, begged you to cure his twelve-year-old daughter by touching her. You took her by the hand, told her to arise, and she walked.

The woman, Jairus, and you yourself believed in the power of your touch. Today your touch, through me and others, still holds the power to transform lives, to bring meaning and significance into a lonely or despairing world.

In the North American and British culture, we are so often afraid to touch, or we interpret another's touch wrongly because of the sexual overtones we associate with physical contact. In our society, people seem to have lost the willingness to be warm and human, to touch another with simple caring.

Jesus, use your power of touch once again through me. May my touch comfort another's grief and my hearty handshake say, "I'd like to know you better." May my hugs tell someone that I care and my arm around another's shoulder show that I am a friend.

Jesus, let me also experience the power of your touch through others. Help me to appreciate the feel of human skin without interpreting another's touch as a sexual message. Give me once in a while the gift of a relaxing body massage to ease my stress and tensions.

Help me today, dear God, to "reach out and touch someone." Amen.

† † †

Today's Scripture passage speaks of rejection, Jesus. You were rejected by your own townsfolk as you taught there in the synagogue. They did not believe that someone from such an ordinary background as theirs could utter words of wisdom. And your disciples, too, were often rejected as they traveled from village to village, preaching your good news of salvation.

Jesus, in many ways I am like the people in your home town of Nazareth. I reject the prophet. I am skeptical that wisdom can come from the uneducated, from those who are not politically correct, from those who do not share my ideology, from those who are "below" me in social or intellectual standing. Because of my lack of faith in those who seem "less" than I by this world's standards, you are unable to perform your miracles in me. By failing to recognize the wonder and beauty in the ordinariness of my life, I even sometimes reject the prophetic voice you have placed within me.

Jesus, in other ways I am like the disciples whom you sent out to preach about conversion from sin. I feel rejected. I preach your message of conversion of heart, but no one seems to want to listen. We are too busy acquiring status, money, power. I preach a Gospel of spiritual and corporal works of kindness, justice, and mercy, but few want to hear.

Jesus, help me today to accept the prophet in others and not to be silenced by the rejection I myself may meet. Amen.

† † †

Today's Scripture reading tells of the beheading of John the Baptist because of a foolish promise made by Herod during a drunken orgy. Because he wanted to save face before all the officials and leading citizens of Galilee, Herod lacked the courage to deny Salome's unreasonable request.

Like Herod, our modern-day political leaders also often seem drunk with power; they set policies which interfere with the self-determination of other countries and then save face by denying any covert or illegal involvement. Some make pledges to balance the federal budget and when they do not succeed, they save face by blaming an increased deficit on previous administrations. O God, give our civic leaders the moral courage to speak out like the Baptist on behalf of the poor, and to work for an economic order which would effect a more just and equitable distribution of this world's goods.

Like Herod, some of our church leaders are also so drunk with power that they seek to control the intimate, private lives of others. They save face by appealing to church doctrine, all the while failing to ask forgiveness for past and present religious intolerance, racism, and sexism. Help our leaders, O God, to preach, like John, the spiritual coming of the Christ instead of exalting their own traditions and teachings.

I, too, am like Herod, for I have locked up the holy person I am meant to become, and I say things to please the crowd. I am often unwilling to admit that I made a mistake, or to apologize for offending another. Help me, O God, to experience a true conversion of heart so that, like John, I can prepare the way for your reign.

My prayer today, O loving God, is that our civil and ecclesiastical leaders, and I, too, may overcome the weak Herods in ourselves and grow into the strength of John. Amen.

† † †

When Jesus tells his disciples, "You give them something to eat," he is alluding to both human and spiritual hungers. Fortunately, our instinct for survival reminds us when the body is hungry, and we naturally take the time to nourish ourselves. But there is no comparable instinct to alert us to our spiritual hunger. Even when we are hard at work building the reign of God, for example, there is still the danger that our good works, plans, and concerns can numb the hunger for prayer and religious meaning. Maybe that is why Jesus takes the disciples off to a deserted place immediately after a very busy and apparently successful missionary journey: to remind them that the real source and the ultimate goal of all their efforts is the one who alone satisfies the hungry heart.

When Jesus fed the people bread, he satisfied their physical hunger; when he fed them God's Word, he only increased their spiritual hunger. Prayer not only satisfies our hunger for God, but at the same time increases and stimulates it. To fill ourselves with food when we are hungry is good and natural, but it is not possible to so fill ourselves with God that we no longer hunger for God.

If we hunger for food, perhaps it is because we do not hunger enough for God. I cannot be hungry for God and try to satisfy that hunger without at the same time wanting to share my bread with the needy. My prayer must be that I become ever more hungry for God and ever more ready to help feed others — with care, compassion, support, and perhaps even at times simply a cup of coffee or a doughnut.

† † †

As the great ship Titanic went down, it is said that the band played "Nearer My God To Thee." That myth salutes the self-sacrificing courage which provided spiritual comfort to those in distress. Some people confront tragedy by drawing on their spiritual resources for courage and hope.

What a different scene emerges when the disciples of Jesus are in danger of drowning. Not only do they fail to recognize the person of Jesus approaching them, but they mistake him for a ghost! These are the close intimates who traveled with him — the followers who heard his words, saw his deeds of power and healing, and tasted the bread provided just before they set out across the lake. And yet, Mark says that their minds were "completely closed" to the real meaning of the events.

The real meaning of the events, from a faith perspective, is that even as the people in large masses were fed and cared for by Jesus, all the more are we who have chosen to be Christ's collaborators watched over and cared for by Christ.

But we are not so very much unlike the first disciples of Christ. Having fed on the bread of life, having heard the Gospel, we still think at moments of danger and fatigue that we can somehow outrun the storm and reach the opposite shore by our own efforts. At these times the ghosts of past failures, of life-long struggles with sin, of parental and family hurts, of pain from bad experiences with church representatives, all rise up and distract us. We have been rescued before from drowning in our guilt, our self-pity, and our inadequacies, rescued by the one who has fed us so often. If the ghosts do not scare us into a lack of faith, and if we can find the meaning behind the events which terrorize us, we will still hear Christ saying, "Take heart, it is I; have no fear."

† † †

A monastery's abbot had a cat that roamed the chapel during prayer. So the abbot tied the cat to a peg to prevent the monks from being distracted. When the abbot died, the practice continued. When the cat died, a new abbot purchased a new cat and tied it likewise. Eventually no one remembered why the cat was tied. Though it had lost its original purpose and meaning, the monks kept the tradition alive.

Rituals are a deep part of both human and faith life. All religions use symbols and signs (doctrines, practices, acts, objects) to externalize internal beliefs and feelings about God and human existence. The danger arises when the symbols and signs lose their original purposes and become ends in themselves. There is nothing inherently wrong with such practices as ritual meals (Eucharist), purifications (baptism), or acts of intimacy (embracing, kissing, sex); the danger emerges when these practices do not express authentically what they are meant to convey.

It is far easier to wash one's hands ritually than to clean one's heart of impure thoughts such as envy, jealousy, bitterness, or revenge. It is much easier to share in a ritual meal like Communion than to commune with the unlovable, the ungrateful, or the enemy. Jesus was the most authentic person who ever lived. The outside and the inside were one. He performed the prescribed rituals and prayed the required prayers, but in a way that illuminated their true meaning. And when they were empty and meaningless, he did not hesitate to transform them, replace them, or discard them.

"Happy are the pure of heart" is a teaching of Jesus. I need wisdom to be pure in heart. If my heart is pure, my lips will be also. And the reverence I pay to God and others in words and signs will be the most authentic kind of worship I can render to God.

† † †

Upon college graduation a young man returned to his home church for a reception. He had majored in drama and was asked by an old nun, his former speech coach, to display his skills. She asked him to read her favorite psalm. Taking the Bible, he read slowly and dramatically, "The Lord is my shepherd," in a rich, mellow, well-trained voice. The people were spellbound and applauded loudly and enthusiastically when he finished.

Then he handed the Bible to the nun and asked her to read the psalm. She took the book, laid it aside, and from memory began slowly and with deep feeling to recite the psalm. When she had finished there was dead silence in the hall and not a few wet eyes. The young graduate stepped forward and said: "Now you know the difference. I know the psalm, but she knows the shepherd."

People were amazed by what Jesus taught and by the way he spoke. Traditional rabbis quoted their teachers, passing on learned wisdom. Jesus' education came not from rabbinic schools, but from a personal and intimate relationship with Yahweh. He had no credits, no degrees, and no institutional backing. But his whole life was spent glorifying God, and from that source he drew a teaching which could not be challenged or denied. His enemies accused him of being possessed by an evil spirit. But the spirit that possessed Jesus was the spirit of truth and integrity, instantly recognizable by those who seek God with their lives.

Speaking about God is not just for theologians, academics, seminarians, or preachers. Baptized Christians can and must speak about God. Those who nourish a deep relationship with God often speak to us in direct and simple ways that reveal God to us. Whether as educated as Thomas Merton or as simple and "unlearned" as a Latin American *campesino*, their honesty and truthfulness, if we listen, speak to us clearly of the one who sent them.

† † †

An order of Roman Catholic priests called Dominicans (named for their founder, St. Dominic) is known for scholarship and orthodoxy. As inquisitors looking for theological deviations and heresies, they have been dubbed "The Hounds of God," rendered in latin by *"Domini"* (of God) and *"cani"* (dogs). An old Roman adage says the city of Rome is so hot in August that the only creatures who remain there are the *"cani"* and the *"Dominicani."* Though the insult is taken in jest by the Dominicans, it might well originally have been a rather hateful put-down.

The insulting remark of Jesus to the woman looking for a cure for her daughter may be a sign of his extreme tiredness and his annoyance that his peace and quiet had been interrupted, or, as others have suggested, it may show that even Jesus was subject to cultural prejudice against a certain group, a prejudice which he had to overcome.

What strikes us about the account is that the woman simply refused to let a painful and derogatory remark anger or distract her from her main objective. She turned it right back on Jesus. She knew her own self-worth and basic goodness. She would not accept the negativity and the oppression implied by the designation. And she is the only person in the whole Gospel who got the better of Jesus in a verbal duel!

Author Brian McNaught says that certain words we use about people suggest less than human status. "I also think they dehumanize you," he states, "regardless of who is using them."[1] Just as ethnic jokes can create false images of people, so do depreciative words about race, religion, and sexuality create false images, both for the person being subjected to them and the person using them.

May the Lord today help me to understand the truth about people and speak words that humanize and build them up. May the Lord cast out my demons of words and descriptions that limit others — and myself as well.

[1]McNaught, Brian, *On Being Gay* (New York: St. Martin's Press, 1988), p. 22.

† † †

In the first of Mark's two Gospel accounts of Jesus' feeding the crowds (Mark 6:30-48), it is the disciples who first come to Jesus. They take the initiative. They are the ones who first show concern for the hungry followers, although it never occurs to them that they themselves can do something to resolve the situation.

In this second account, Jesus takes the initiative to summon his disciples and express his deep concern. He gives some thought to sending the crowds home, the practical solution, but he knows that some of them might not make it. Yet the disciples see no other alternative.

The story has been understood in the Christian tradition as a symbolic anticipation of the Last Supper. Jesus takes bread, blesses it, breaks it, and distributes it to the people. The description is very similar to the account of the Last Supper. These same actions continue today in those communities which still celebrate the memorial meal.

These actions also encompass the daily life of the Christian. Each day brings us knowledge or personal experience of hunger, either in ourselves or in others. The hunger can be for food to stay alive, but more often it is a hunger for community, meaning, affirmation, forgiveness, and healing. Each day also brings us the bread of time, of people, and of our own individual gifts. As disciples of the Lord we need each day to pray in thanksgiving over these gifts, break them open, and distribute them to others. Every time we commune with others, we are in a position to nourish and feed them as Jesus did, rather than being paralyzed by our inadequacies and limited resources as were the disciples. Then our hearts, too, will be moved, and we will be able to work real miracles.

† † †

FEBRUARY

A strange healing story is found in this passage. Jesus lays hands upon a blind man, but the man's sight is not completely restored. A second time Jesus lays hands upon the man, and finally he can see.

The man's vision required a second touch. Often we too need a second touch. When we don't get all we expect, we need to return to the source of health and healing instead of wandering away in search of other healers, other saviors. For many this means a return to the faith which touched us once. Like the blind man, we too can receive the fullness of God's blessing by returning to Christ for a second touch.

Wholeness in life is something which grows. God works in us, then works again. God's movement in us is a continuing event through which we go from strength to strength. Do you need to return to Christ so Christ can complete what has begun in you?

Today tens of thousands of alienated and disenfranchised Christians are returning to the faith that touched them once before. If you have not received all you wanted from Christ, consider waiting, expecting a second touch, or maybe a third!

Jesus, I have always been in a hurry. Today,
however, I want to wait, because I want all you
have for me. Forgive the times I have run away, looking
elsewhere for a blessing, not trusting that you had more
for me. Forgive the times when, not seeing life
clearly, I have given up on you. I am here
now, waiting. Touch me again.

† † †

The Feast of the Presentation

"Lord, now let your servant depart in peace."

The song of Simeon begins with a profound truth: seeing Christ is enough. Simeon saw his heart's desire, the promised deliverance of his people. He could now accept death, for having seen the Lord, his life was now complete.

Simeon's truth is the same truth offered to all people of faith. In Christ Jesus everything is complete and finished. There is no need to look further for a more definitive revelation. Sometimes persons who have inhabited the household of Christian faith depart to explore and embrace the occult or popular trends in spirituality. Sometimes people abandon Christ for another "revelation" without fully exploring the depth of Christ's treasures and riches.

Like Simeon, it is possible for us to find in Christ all we need to fulfill our lives. Once we have found Christ there can be a sweet completion to our spiritual journey. Not a completion that is an ending, but one that is a fulfillment of the truth. At that point we begin to explore the depth of Christ and find the fullness of God's Word to us. Instead of a futile searching for meaning and purpose, we can now rest by the living water, drink deep, and grow to maturity.

I bid you come to this eternal refreshment place. We can live the rest of our days, be they few or many, with all we need. With the psalmist we can say, "I shall not want . . . God restores my soul . . . ." (Psalm 23:1,3)

My God, come to me. I want to know the
sense of fulfillment Simeon knew. I want the
peace you promised. Come now to your servant.
I wait for you.

† † †

*"And there appeared to them Elijah with Moses;
and they were talking to Jesus."*

The event of the Transfiguration must have been an over-whelming experience for Jesus. Throughout his life, from his childhood in Nazareth to his death in Jerusalem, people failed to understand his unique calling and his intimate relationship to God. Surely Jesus must have longed for his followers to understand his sense of mission. He was always explaining himself to his disciples, who never seemed to grasp his mean-ing. But on this day, on this mountain, something happened. God gave Christ glory, revealed power, and put Christ in the company of the patriarchs of old, Moses and Elijah. If we believe Christ was fully human, then he must have needed this moment just as much as the three disciples with him.

Remember your most mystical spiritual experiences? Remember how you felt you couldn't tell anyone about them? Just as we might do, Jesus tells Peter, James, and John not to talk about this experience until after his Resurrection. Here for a moment we can see Jesus so very much like us, private and personal, keeping a secret of this most amazing revelation of God's favor. How strange that in this moment of being set apart from others we can see how much like us our Saviour is!

Jesus asked his disciples to keep this secret until he had been raised from the dead, when they would be free to share this news with others. What about us? If we have been baptised into Jesus' death and are raised to new life with Christ, are we not now free to disclose our most intimate encounters with God? The work of Christ would surely be enhanced by our telling our stories, disclosing the spiritual dynamics of our lives.

*Jesus, not only do I want to experience the
power and glory you experienced on the mountain,
but now I want to share my experience with others
so that you may continue to be glorified. Please
give me an opportunity to do so today.*

† † †

". . . 'Why could we not cast [the demon] out?' And he
said to them, 'This kind cannot be driven out by
anything but prayer.' "

When the disciples cannot cast out a demon, Jesus tells them
they need to understand the power of prayer. Surely they
prayed, but perhaps, like us, they prayed out of habit. So often
prayer can become an empty form we use out of habit.
However, if we are growing in Christ, our prayer life will
expand to meet the greater needs which we face in life.

In today's Gospel, the disciples face a sickness they cannot
heal. The power afforded them by their spiritual lives is not
enough to cast out the demon in question. Jesus says to them
that only prayer can work in this case. The response of Jesus
becomes a challenge not only to the disciples of his day, but
also to us.

Does our prayer life contain the power to heal? Jesus indicates
that only prayer offers this power. For many modern Christians, prayer is used to discuss with God our wants and our
spiritual state and our emotional needs. When it comes to
physical needs, we have become used to going to the doctor.
What then do we do when the doctor can offer no healing?
What do we do when medicine says that a disease is incurable?
Such an illness can only be cured by prayer.

If Jesus prescribed prayer when nothing else worked, would
he not prescribe the same today? Prayer leads us into truth,
truth imparts spiritual power to its bearer, and spiritual power
makes healing possible.

My God, life sometimes seems so filled with
sickness and despair. Wherever I turn I see the
need for healing. So much sickness makes me afraid.
Help me now to stop and turn toward you. I want my
prayer to be healing for me and others. I want
your power to be manifest in my praying.

† † †

"Now is the judgment of this world, now shall the ruler of this world be cast out."

Jesus says these words after he has again taught the disciples the paradox of the Gospel — the tension between giving and receiving, between having and losing, between dying and living.

The judgment of this world and the defeat of Satan occur in the death of Jesus on the cross. This seems absurd, and yet it is the centerpiece of God's saving work. How? In death, the world has exercised its ultimate power and threat over Jesus, and yet in the end Jesus conquers. In the cross, it appears the powers of the world have won — and yet God grasps life eternal from the hands of death by raising Jesus from the dead. Once and for all, death is destroyed.

This triumph over death is meant to be so real for us that no threat of death can harm or intimidate us. Neither persecution, nor rejection, nor disease can overwhelm us, for God has already defeated death. Dying thus becomes for us only another experience of life, a mystery to embrace as we move on to closeness with God.

O God, settle in my heart this day my own fears of dying, so that I may live in the hope of life eternal. I choose today to live without fear. I trust that death has no power over me. My faith is in your victory. May your victory be visible in my life.

† † †

"And the Word became flesh and dwelt among us,
full of grace and truth . . . ."

In two thousand years the Christian church has not yet comprehended these words. We have been taught to despise the flesh. We are sure sexual and physical things are inherently evil. We are embarrassed by our bodies. We hide ourselves, even from ourselves.

Yet John tells us that the Spirit of God took on all flesh. Nor did this incarnation of spirit stop at the neck or the waist, but it filled every cell of Christ's body. John goes on to tell us that Christ's flesh was beautiful, filled with grace and truth.

God desires to fill us in like manner. God wills that each of us should be full of grace and truth. Many people have negative self-images. We look with disgust upon our bodies. A part of our salvation surely must be a new appreciation of the flesh, our flesh. When we consider that the Word of God chooses to dwell in us, we can begin to look at our flesh and our sexuality in a whole new light. God's creation is called good.

This is good news. How wonderful! What delight is mine! Just think for a moment: God created all of me, calls me good, and wants to use all of me. More than this, Jesus Christ fully understands everything about my flesh and my life in this world. God has come so near to me. This is my good news.

Jesus, take my hand. Today, more than
ever, I need to let your truth and your Spirit fill
me. Maybe some parts of the world and of the church
don't understand your being in my flesh, but I do, and
that's enough for me. I always knew that you
knew me; thank you for making it so clear
in your Word.

† † †

". . . 'Who are you? . . . What do you say about yourself?' John said, 'I am the voice of one crying in the wilderness, make straight the way of the Lord.' "

Has the church forgotten its prophetic role? Do we no longer believe that it is part of our task to prepare the way of the Lord?

No! The zeal of John the Baptist is coming back to the church. God is calling many new prophetic voices to make a path for God to enter the hearts of millions of people who have been tossed aside by many churches. Minority peoples abandoned by the church are now being brought back to the grace of God. If the Word of God dwells in flesh, then all flesh can become a testimony to God's action. That God has chosen to dwell in the flesh of diverse peoples is a prophetic word from God in our day. The movement to liberate all peoples opens a new path for God's presence in the world.

Each of our lives makes a specific and unique testimony. Like John, we are voices crying in the wilderness. Like John, we prepare the way for Christ to enter our communities. Just like John, we baptize so that Christ shall be revealed.

"What do you say about yourself?" The question to John the Baptist is also the question addressed to us. What is your answer?

Precious Jesus, I want to say yes to your using me. I want the world to look at me and see you. Let me be the highway you take into the life of my world, my relationships, my family, my home. Walk in me, my God. I am not afraid anymore.

† † †

". . . those who humble themselves will be exalted."

In the midst of the positive, self-esteem building, uplifting voice of the Gospel, there is balance. Here the Word reminds us not to elevate ourselves above others. Why? Quite simply because God chooses always to work through us, and when we exalt ourselves, we limit God's options. We become unavailable as a sign and witness to those from whom we have distanced ourselves in our exaltation. God would have us be open to all, and especially to the most despised. Sometime, in fact, it is to those we like least that God sends us.

A second truth is that if we exalt ourselves, we cannot exalt Christ. God desires our lives, our gifts, our words, and our deeds to point to Christ, not to ourselves. The channel of revelation works like this: we lead persons to Christ and Christ leads them to God; we reveal Jesus, and Jesus reveals God. By pointing only to ourselves we prevent others from seeing Christ, who desires to show them God. The chain of revelation is broken.

Healthy persons who love themselves and rejoice in God's gifts joyfully point the way to the Giver of all good and perfect gifts. God gives a promise to us: ". . . those who humble themselves will be exalted." God will exalt us in the end. We will not go without praise and recognition. Jesus showed us the way when he humbled himself and "became obedient unto death, even death on a cross. Therefore God has highly exalted him . . . ." (Phillipians 2:8-9)

My God, I know that when I have sought honor and praise, I have not found joy. My joy is you and your presence in me. Be enthroned in my life so that I may reveal you to all who look upon me. I have found your presence in my life to be exaltation enough.

† † †

"I myself did not know who it was; but for this
reason I came baptizing with water, that the one who
was to come might be revealed to Israel."

My spirit joins with that of John the Baptist when he said he baptized that Christ might be revealed. As a pastor, I experience a sense of power as I participate in God's entry into our lives. For such a long time in my life the sacraments of the church seemed like empty rituals. This was especially true of baptism. Then one day John's words struck me. When asked why he baptized, he responded that he did not know Christ, but believed he could make Christ known to others. Suddenly the need for Christ to be made known in today's world became clear to me, along with a sense of the power God offers to all Christians to help make Christ known. Suddenly, baptism became powerful: God moves through the sacrament to reveal Christ to the seeker. With that insight, I discovered a new zeal and fervor in an old faith.

I see so many people who don't know Christ, or who think Christ wouldn't want to know them. Now it is possible to offer baptism as an invitation to encounter God. I trust God to use the water I pour to refresh barren lives. The power John evidenced has become the power I expect and experience. God is present in the waters of baptism. God wills to reveal Christ today as clearly as God did when John baptized.

Do you recall your baptism? If your parents acted for you, does their action have personal meaning for your life today? Consider that God wants to be a powerful presence in your life. Are you open to God's encounter? Baptism is about identity. It is about your being a child of God and knowing who you are.

Thank you Jesus, for the power of faith. I have
a new enthusiasm. Like John, I feel I can make you
known to others. You have invited me to participate
in your revelation. Thank you for opening
the way for me.

† † †

"Jesus turned, and saw them following, and said
to them, 'What do you seek?' And they said 'Rabbi'
(which means Teacher) . . . ."

Andrew and Peter followed Jesus the moment they heard John the Baptist call him "the Lamb of God." They noticed him and followed. They did not ask him questions. First they saw, then they followed. What is it that they saw? I think the answer to this question is found in their word, "Teacher."

A teacher reveals truth, leads to knowledge, shows the way. In Jesus they saw something they wanted to follow. They saw the truth and the way of life. Faith comes by seeing Jesus clearly. A clear vision of Jesus can be attained by simply seeking to see the truth as one reads the Gospels. When the open eyes of the seeker of truth examine the Gospel story, very quickly the reader begins to see. One can see the way Christ leads, the truth Christ speaks, and the life Christ is. When Christ is seen as teacher, as guide to truth, it is natural to want to follow.

Faith is about following the right teacher. The right teacher always leads to truth, and truth always leads to God. The question is, whom do we follow? Scripture tells us to look to Christ, who is the "pioneer and perfecter of our faith." (Hebrews 12:2)

Join me in looking at the portrait painted by Matthew, Mark, Luke, and John. Look closer still at the picture Paul gives in his letters. We can expect to see Jesus and be taught by Christ.

Jesus, show me yourself.
As I read the Scriptures today, let me see you
more clearly. Teach me your truth.
Open my eyes that I may see.

† † †

The dialogue between Nathanael and Jesus begins with Nathanael's skepticism. "Can anything good come out of Nazareth?" Jesus discloses a prophetic knowledge of Nathanael by responding, "Before Philip called you, when you were under the fig tree, I saw you."

The pattern of this discourse with Nathanael is often the pattern of our experience of God. God comes to us from the most unexpected places. When truth comes unexpectedly, it catches us off guard and pierces our defenses. Perhaps this is one of the reasons why God often encounters us when we are least prepared. Perhaps it is also why God chooses the foolish things in the world to shame the wise. (I Corinthians 1:27)

In today's world, God is speaking from the most unlikely places. Not so long ago many Christians did not expect a woman to speak the Gospel from the pulpit or offer sacraments at the altar. Gay people, once thought by many to be outside the faith, have become a place of God's revelation of love and justice. When God speaks to us from unexpected places we are often called to examine our ideas about God. If God's new prophet is someone we never expected to be carrying God's Word, we are left with the need to look again at this person God has chosen to use.

When you are in places where you do not expect God to be, beware, for God favors such places to encounter us. When you hide from God, seeking to evade revelation, be prepared for a divine encounter. "Can anything good come out of Nazareth?" Something good comes from any place God comes from.

God, there are people who don't expect you to
come from me. As you prepared me to receive you,
prepare them also. I know they will be surprised, as
I was. I know they will end up being changed,
as I was. Have your own way, God.

† † †

". . . no one puts new wine into old wineskins;
if one does, the wine will burst the skins, and the
wine is lost, and so are the skins; but new wine
is for fresh skins."

So clearly, so simply, Jesus describes his message. The truth of the Christian faith cannot be added to old forms of religion any more than new wine can be poured into old containers. The faith of Christ makes life completely new.

People of faith have often resisted the newness and the radical change Christ brings. If the Gospel is to achieve its goal of bringing all the world to the saving knowledge of Christ, then change must occur. Allowing the Spirit of God to make all the changes necessary ultimately allows God to add to the body of Christ countless outcast persons.

The Spirit of God shattered the early church to make room for gentiles; it shattered the white American church to make room for persons of color; it is shattering the heterosexual church to make room for homosexual persons; and it will fracture the church again and again if we become closed to other groups of persons.

The Spirit of God descends to make life new and to make the house of God a house of prayer for all peoples. The religious forms of our faith are replaced when they no longer contain the new wine of Christ. God is a creating God; which often means we must be made over and made new for God to fill us. If we are thirsty for the new wine of Christ, then we must allow God to make us fit containers.

God, let me be unafraid of your changing me; let me
trust that the changes you make will always be for my
well-being. I want to trust that the newness I
welcome is really you, God.

† † †

"This, the first of his signs, Jesus did at Cana in Galilee, and manifested his glory; and the disciples believed in Jesus."

The story about Jesus turning water to wine at Cana in Galilee has sadly been lost to much of the church. It has been lost because it has been used mostly in an attempt to argue for Jesus' sanction of marriage. The story has nothing to do with the sanction of marriage; its purpose is, rather, to demonstrate who Jesus was: Jesus "manifested his glory; and the disciples believed."

When this story is added to the other marriage references in the New Testament, their meaning is clarified. In Matthew 9:15, Mark 2:19, and Luke 5:34, Jesus makes reference to himself as the bridegroom. In Revelation 19:9, John speaks of the end times as the coming of the "marriage supper of the Lamb." The wedding images in the New Testament are therefore not about the sanctity of marriage, but about the union between Christ and the believer. Christ bids us to come to this Holy Union and join in the wedding feast, now and eternally.

New life in Christ is about a new relationship with Christ. Faith is a dimension of growing intimacy with God. The good news is that the manifestation of Christ's glory calls all of us into new relationships. Henceforth all our unions are judged in the light of our union with Christ.

In Cana, as in every event of his life, Jesus revealed who he was. We see the special relationship he shared with God and the power God granted him. It is this special relationship which was disclosed in Jesus that God offers us. We become disciples also; we glimpse Jesus' true identity, and in seeing, we believe and follow.

Jesus, as I read your Word, let me never miss your glory or neglect to follow you. I know your miracles are for my life, and my life becomes your miracle. Let it be with me according to your will.

† † †

"Take these things away;
you shall not make God's house
a house of trade."

As Jesus sweeps the Temple clean of merchants he causes a great frenzy among the Jews. With boldness and zeal Jesus refers to himself as a temple which, if destroyed, shall be raised in three days. The actions of Jesus serve to refocus faith. Instead of a place and a set of religious practices, Jesus makes the person and the meaning of a relationship with God the centerpiece of authentic religion.

Reading this passage recalls Isaiah's promise in chapter 56:7, ". . . for my house shall be called a house of prayer for all peoples." Today the promise of Isaiah and the cleansing action of Jesus have indeed opened the door of God's house to a multitude of people who were once excluded. Christ has become the temple all can enter. This inclusive image and its open invitation to all people has become the power of the Gospel in our world.

But not only does Christ become a holy temple; the New Testament goes on to say that our bodies are temples of the Holy Spirit. (I Corinthians 6:19) Not only has Christ included us, but we have been chosen in Christ as the dwelling place of the Spirit. Christ continues today to cleanse the Temple and restore faith. But now, since I am a temple of the Holy Spirit, it is my life which is cleansed, renewed, and made the dwelling place of God.

My God, when I think that you choose to choose
me, I am overwhelmed. You make me feel desired and
worthy. In you I find a confidence I could not find from
the world. I feel both humbled at this thought and
exalted. I give you thanks.

† † †

"That which is born of the flesh is flesh
and that which is born of the Spirit
is spirit."

In teaching Nicodemus about new birth, Jesus begins to open the truth of spiritual things. Like Nicodemus, we find spiritual teaching difficult to understand; but when we receive the Spirit of God, suddenly things of the Spirit make sense.

Spiritual knowledge comes to a person when the Spirit reveals the truth. If we are to understand spiritual things we must first become open to them. We often try to analyze and comprehend spiritual truths as if they were rational and measurable facts. Thinking we can grasp the Spirit through analysis, we miss the truth, for we grasp the truth only when we are grasped by the Spirit. It is the Spirit that imparts understanding.

To me, the quest for spiritual truth is like this. First, I begin by seeking the presence of God. I want to be near God. I ask God for God's Spirit to be near me, to guide me into all truth. Then I study the Scriptures. I read expectantly, with the hope that God may speak to me of a deeper truth, and that God's will may become known. In the experience of understanding and new insight, I gain evidence of the Spirit's presence. I trust in faith that the Spirit is present, because spiritual truth is being revealed.

This quest for truth leads one beyond the limitations of the flesh into a new world of wonder, born of the Spirit. Suddenly, the human soul seems to access knowledge and understanding not gained by traditional ways of study and learning. With spiritual knowledge, ordinary events take on a new meaning. We see with a clearer vision. Jesus asks Nicodemus to let God give him this new birth in the Spirit. Suddenly I hear Jesus asking me to receive this new birth as well.

Jesus, let your Spirit lead me into all truth.
I have been looking on my own, without allowing the
Spirit to lead. I am lost. Lead me.

† † †

Immediately after Jesus' discourse about spiritual truth, John states the central spiritual truth of the Gospel in the sixteenth verse: "For God so loved the world that God gave God's only Child, that whoever believes in that Child should not perish but have eternal life." John's commentary then returns to the issue of recognizing truth by saying that many could not see Jesus as the light of the world, that many would not receive him as Saviour.

Coming to truth, coming to Christ, coming to a personal faith — these things are more a matter of "seeing" than doing. The Spirit of God shows Jesus to those who seek. The words of verse 16 have a way of stopping the reader. I know they do me. I stop and ask: "Do I believe God loves me? Does Jesus tell me this?" So often I have read the Gospel account of the life of Jesus as if I were reading an interesting story that did not affect me. But if this verse is the central truth of the whole story, I have to ask the question, "Do I believe this?"

I return to the story in a more personal way, my mind flooded with questions. It is when my feelings begin to overflow my thoughts that the truth of the Gospel starts to break through to me. I need to feel love. I don't want to perish. I want life eternal. Am I able to grasp what John is talking about? Do I not recognize who Jesus is? Do I refuse to receive Christ as Saviour?

I continue to read the Gospel, seeking to know that Jesus is my Saviour. I know that my faith begins in knowing I am the one loved by God, that God gave Christ for me. In hearing John speak to me, I must answer. Now the words are mine: God loved me so much that God gave Jesus Christ, that I might believe and not perish, that I might have eternal life. This is my faith, my testimony.

Christ, show yourself as God's gift and salvation
to all who read these words. We seek you here and now.
My words seek to reveal you. I know you want
to be known to all. Jesus, I want to add
my testimony to John's.

✝ ✝ ✝

"Christ must increase, but I must decrease."

In John the Baptist's witness to Christ, John speaks of Christ's authority, and to illustrate his point, he begins to step aside so his followers will look upon Jesus and not upon himself. John's task is done, for he has revealed Christ as the Lamb of God who takes away the sins of the world.

Spiritual maturity for all who seek to follow Christ ultimately leads to the place John speaks of: "Christ must increase, but I must decrease." In the exercise of one's spiritual gifts and ministry, success occurs. Our churches can thrive financially. Our public visibility can increase dramatically. Our ministry can grow powerful and persuasive. At such times we are naturally tempted to believe that God couldn't accomplish God's will without our achievements. In fact, however, the moment our mission begins to promote ourselves instead of God, however subtly, we have fallen into a snare which mutes the true voice of the Gospel. A way to avoid this trap is to keep John's words close to our heart: "Christ must increase, but I must decrease."

What a wonder it would be if, when the world looked at each of us, they beheld Christ. Our task, like John's, is to reveal Jesus and then to step aside so others may see Christ clearly.

Not my will but thine be done. Jesus, fill me
and make my face your own reflection. Hide me behind
your cross, Jesus, so that when others look at me,
they will see you.

† † †

"The water that I shall give will become . . . a spring of water welling up to eternal life."

Jesus meets the woman at the well, and he tells her everything she's ever done. In this conversation Jesus promises the water of life to the Samaritan woman. Water becomes the sign of God's new and eternal life. The promise of Christ is that the need or thirst of the human heart is quenched by Christ.

The second part of the promise is that this living water becomes a spring in the believer's heart. The image Jesus gives is an overflowing stream. It is an image of steady and consistent sustenance.

A third part of the promise of the wellspring is this: It is not to Jerusalem or some holy shrine that humanity must travel to meet God; rather, the journey to the wellspring is inward. It is here that God creates a place for each of us to return to for refreshment and worship. True worship occurs deep in the recesses of the spirit.

"But the hour is coming, and now is, when the true worshipers will worship God the Mother and Father in spirit and truth . . . ." In the depth of the heart God reveals truth. It is to truth that Jesus led the woman at the well, and it is to truth that Jesus leads us, too. Only in allowing the Spirit to lead us to truth do we find the refreshment of living water. As Jesus spoke to the woman at the well, so Christ continues to reveal a way to God not found in temples or journeys to holy places, but rather in the holy of holies, the heart of the believer.

As we have avoided the truth, we have kept ourselves away from worship and from God's promise of living water. I know in truth that I thirst. Does your faith refresh you, or do you thirst, too?

God, I have studied many books and traveled to many churches, yet I have neglected to return to the spring you placed in my heart. I fear my well has run dry. Flood my soul with your spirit, wash my barrenness away. I thirst.

† † †

"Here are my mother and my brothers!
Whoever does the will of God is my brother,
and sister, and mother."

There is a saying in our society, "Blood is thicker than water."
This saying is usually invoked to strengthen family loyalties.
Jesus turns these words and their message around. In fact, his
teaching about family could literally be stated as, "Water is
thicker than blood"! Water is the bonding agent of the family
of God. The water of baptism creates family ties to those who
are born of the Spirit.

Even in the church, there are many who lament that they have
been cut off from families. Christ heals this wound by redefin-
ing family. While we may have no ability to change the minds
and hearts of those who have rejected us, we do have the
ability and grace to be bonded to those persons whom Christ
has brought to us as new brothers and sisters. Where lonely
and separated souls dwell, God creates and offers family.

I have come to know my true family to be that larger body,
the congregation of the faithful whose love and truth sustain
me. Even when my relatives cut me off from communion with
them. I find my true family sustaining my spirit, giving me
joy. I am never abandoned to isolation and loneliness.

Open my heart, Jesus. I want to receive your truth
about family. Plant your teaching in me so it may bear
the fruit of freedom and joy. I don't want to feel
alone or abandoned any more.

† † †

"It is no longer because of your words that we believe,
for we have heard for ourselves . . . ."

The friends of the Samaritan woman rushed to see Jesus. Her testimony caused them to seek him out. Her testimony was that in Jesus all the truth of her life became clear and visible. Her secrets, hidden from others, had become the good news she wanted to tell. Perhaps she knew her friends held secrets also. Hidden and buried secrets often torment the soul. It takes so much energy to hide our lives. Every human heart has need to be released from holding so much in secret. Christ unburdened the woman at the well. Her new freedom gave her joy.

It was a testimony to truth that brought the crowd of friends to Jesus, but it was their personal encounter with the truth that caused them to stay. They said, ". . . we have heard for ourselves." It is one thing to keep company with Christians because of their testimony about what Christ has done for them, but unless all of us have the experience of hearing Christ for ourselves, our faith may not be lasting.

But when we have encountered Christ personally and heard the truth of the meaning and purpose of life for ourselves, then we can say ". . . we know that this is indeed the Saviour of the world." Like the friends of the woman at the well, we then rejoice that we, too, have heard the good news and been unburdened of our secrets.

God, speak to me that I may hear your truth for
myself. Then give me the courage to tell my story to
others so they will seek you out. Lord, I believe that you
work today, just as you worked in the life of the
woman from Samaria. My eyes are open
to see your wonder, my ears long
to hear your truth.

† † †

"Jesus said to him, 'Go; your son will live.' "

With a word, Jesus brings healing to the dying son of the man who pleads for Jesus to come and heal his son. Healing comes because the man believes the word Christ speaks. Jesus never goes to the boy's bedside. However, Jesus does say, " Unless you see signs and wonders you will not believe." Then he gives the signs and wonders.

Modern people of faith are like the man who pleaded with Jesus. We too seek signs and wonders. We want life to really change for us and those we love. I believe God still gives what is needed for belief. Lives are changed; physical healing does occur. But perhaps the most wonderful miracle of all is that people still take Jesus at his word. Like the father in the story, they return to their lives and their homes expecting the promise of Jesus to be real.

Belief comes through hearing. Christ's word speaks out of the Gospel and into our hearts. We can go about our life expecting Christ's word to be fulfilled for us and in us. Like the man who returned home to find his son healed, we too return to our daily lives after an encounter with Christ, in the Word or in the Eucharist, to discover that Christ has gone before us to make things new. Life has changed. There are signs and wonders God gives to our lives. Those who have eyes to see will see.

Yes, Jesus, I really do believe. I have kept my faith hidden like a secret. But I really do expect your promise to be real for me. Now I want to get up and go about life seeing your signs and wonders.

† † †

"When Jesus saw him and knew that he had been
lying there a long time, he said to him, 'Do you
want to be healed?' "

For those who lay by the pool of Bethesda there was a system for healing. The sick had to wait for the angel of the Lord to stir up the waters. The first one into the pool got the healing.

The poor man in the story never got there first. Someone else always got the healing. Perhaps he was so used to someone else getting healed that he no longer expected to be healed. After all, he'd been sick for thirty-eight years! When Jesus by-passed the process and said, "Do you want to be healed?" the man perhaps had to think about it. He tried to explain why he wasn't healed. This time Jesus by-passed his excuse and said, "Rise, take up your pallet, and walk."

This healing caused a great commotion among the Jews because it happened on the Sabbath. Jesus had once again by-passed the rules. The healed man by-passed the law as well, by carrying his bed on the Sabbath.

Jesus consistently overcame the barriers to healing. Those of us who become whole in Jesus Christ soon begin to act as lawlessly. We too can by-pass all of life's artificial barriers which keep people away from wholeness. A time comes when excuses must be laid aside. Into our pain and suffering the word of Christ comes to say, "Do you want to be healed?" To all our hesitations the Lord speaks: "Rise, take up your pallet, and walk."

Jesus, I know you broke a lot of other people's
rules to include me in your realm. People get angry
at me for considering myself included. But it's you who
did it. I want to be as bold in healing others as you were
with me. I know that you can work in me to continue
the restoration of my life. Thank you for what
you have done, and for what you
are about to do.

† † †

"Truly, truly, I say to you, anyone who
hears my word and believes the one who sent me,
has eternal life . . . ."

In this passage from John, Jesus claims a unique relationship to God. Jesus claims that it is God who is acting in and through him. Clearly a new authority is claimed by Christ. It is this authority that becomes the stumbling block to faith for many.

The very notion of authority is troublesome for many of us. Rather than giving authority to another, we tend to seek authority for ourselves. If we have experienced authority that is repressive, we may also seek to strip others of authority. This attempt is rooted in a positive effort to find some sense of power in life, but it can take on a negative aspect when we seek to diminish others in order to enhance our own position in life.

Christ addresses our ambivalence with issues of authority by saying, "Truly, truly . . . ." These words are in themselves the heart of Christ's authority. Christ speaks truth, Christ acts in truth. We could argue about notions of authority, but in the end we are left with the glaring truth of Christ's word and witness. In seeing the truth Christ presents, we become free from our own competitive reaction to power and free to participate in Christ's truth and authority. God's work then becomes ours, and we can say with Christ, ". . . whatever God does, that the Child of God does likewise."

The Gospel message invites us to exalt the name of Christ above every other name, including our own. When we do so, we find peace and freedom. We no longer have the need to struggle to assert our own authority, for we now participate in the authority of Christ.

Jesus, I have striven against many and against you.
My heart is weary. I long to yield to you that I may
know your strength in me and for me.

† † †

"You search the Scriptures, because you think that in them you have eternal life; and it is they that bear witness to me."

As Jesus asserts his authority from God, he challenges his listeners. He claims that they refuse to receive him. Jesus rightly reveals how people are willing to receive others, seeking glory from them, yet are reluctant to receive Christ. In refusing Christ they refuse the glory God gives in Christ.

We too search the Scriptures to seek eternal life. And for us, too, the Scriptures have at times become a law in themselves, restricting life and faith. As Jesus judged his listeners, so too are we judged when we refuse to receive Christ, the one to whom the Scriptures bear witness.

Christ calls us beyond the written word, beyond the Scriptures. We are called to an encounter with the living Word, the person of Jesus Christ, in whom the fullness of God dwells. Christ is the way to life. Christ is the standard of faith. Christ is our salvation. Our search of the Scriptures leads us to Christ, who leads us to God. If we stop short of Christ, we fall short of God.

Does your faith seem lacking? Do you find yourself looking for more information, eager for something new? Does your suspicion of authority keep you away from Christ? Won't you risk taking a step toward Christ today? Perhaps you have not yet met the truth and authority of Christ.

Jesus, can I receive all of you? I want to understand you, and to experience your life and love. I am tired of searching for another source of salvation. I have not yet opened my life to the things you have said. I come today to you to end my search. I come to listen to your truth and to behold your glory.

† † †

"My time has not yet come, but your time is always here. The world cannot hate you, but it hates me because I testify of it that its works are evil."

When pushed by his brothers to be more public in his ministry, Jesus responds that it is not yet his time, but that their time is always here. The brothers represent those who do not believe. They urge Jesus to be more public in order to convince the disciples of his divine mission, yet it is the brothers themselves who seem to need further proof of Christ's power and identity.

Jesus is drawing a contrast between himself and his unbelieving brothers. He says that the world hates him because he testifies that its works are evil. Jesus then points out that his brothers, in contrast, are not hated, implying that his brothers do not testify to the evil at work in the world, and may even be cooperating with it either deliberately or unconsciously.

Are we more like the brothers of Jesus than like his disciples? Do we keep asking for more proof of Christ's power before believing? Do we claim Christ's name, but not Christ's authority? We seem at times to want to follow Christ only so far, then to ask for more evidence of what has already been demonstrated. Do we fear that if we challenge the world about its evil, we may be hated as Christ was? Are we afraid we won't be loved? Is God's love too little for us? Do we withhold our witness, trying to be loved both by the world and by Christ?

We make only a partial witness to Christ. We hold back.

Jesus, sometimes hearing your word and being your disciple is uncomfortable for me; I have wanted both the world's affection and yours. Today I choose to follow you, whatever the cost. Your love is enough for me.

† † †

"And they came to Jesus,
and saw the demoniac sitting there,
clothed and in his right mind, . . .
and they were afraid."

How strange that fear should be the reaction to the healing Christ brings. When I look at the world, I begin to see the reason for this fear. Many people have become used to living among the tombs, outside of society, taunted for being different, not fitting in. They have begun to understand and define themselves by their difference. They accept not fitting in, they learn to play the role of victims.

The rest of the world has also grown comfortable with the victim's place in it. As long as people who play the victim's role remain on the outer fringes as objects of derision, they serve a certain purpose in the balance of things. These people are not taken seriously, not dealt with.

Into these fragmented lives Christ comes to restore the broken spirit. When the people saw the crazy man made whole, they were afraid. Now they had to change their way of behaving toward him. Now he would no longer inhabit the tombs. He could even come into the town, where they lived and did their business. Jesus Christ changes people and restores their relationships to wholeness.

We may be so accustomed to the way we have lived with each other that we fear the changes Christ brings. Christ nonetheless offers us the opportunity to depart from our limited lives and to live more fully. The love Christ brings with this newness will also dispel the fear we may experience at first. You or I may be one of the outcasts now included, or we may be one of those asked to embrace the stranger. In either case, Christ comes to dispel our fears and to include us all in the family of God.

Yes, Jesus, you can change me. The change you
bring is better than anything I've been used to. Come to
me, touch me, make me whole.

† † †

*"Yet we know where this man comes from;
and when the Christ appears, no one will know where
the Christ comes from."*

This passage is part of a continuing debate about the authority of Christ. Here the listeners in the Temple are sure that Jesus could not be the Christ of God. They knew him. He came from Nazareth. He was the son of Joseph the carpenter.

People then and now seem to expect God's messenger to come from some other place. There is a tendency to want revelation to be something far removed from our daily lives. God's wisdom is just the opposite of this way of thinking. It is our ordinary lives which need saving. A savior must be acquainted with our needs and ways.

Every time we seek to separate God's revelation from the physical reality of the moment, we deny the centerpiece of the Christian faith: "And the Word become flesh and dwelt among us . . . ." (John 1:14) It may seem strange at first that salvation should come in a form which is so common and familiar. Because we so often wish to escape our own reality, we look beyond the temporal. God saves us by taking on the temporal. We can transcend this flesh by taking it seriously, finding it redeemed by God. Hope and healing for the human condition is not far off, but close at hand.

The messages we find the hardest to hear are the ones that come through friends, loved ones, the familiar teacher, our pastor, even the still small voice in our own hearts.

*Christ, don't let me miss your arrival in my life.
Prepare my heart to receive you, especially when you
speak to me through the people I least want to talk to.
I don't want to miss a word you are saying.*

† † †

". . . no prophet is to rise from Galilee."

In a continuing debate, the Pharisees attempt to find grounds for dismissing Jesus. Each time they seek to brush aside his witness, someone comes forward to proclaim, "No one ever spoke like this man."

The words of Christ tend to throw people into confusion. The players in the story are divided about who Jesus is. ". . . some of the people said, 'This is really the prophet.' Others said, 'This is the Christ.' " Jesus, however, simply says, "Whoever believes in me, as the Scripture has said, 'Out of that one's heart shall flow rivers of living water.' "

Beside the questions and debate about who Jesus is and the attempts to prove Jesus could not be a prophet, Jesus' words rise like a tower of truth. All human communities with their pressing issues and arguments come to a hush and silence as our spirits consider the promise of Christ. Christ stands in our midst speaking truth, offering healing, and the refreshment of living water in the spirit. So often we join in the debate on the side of those who cannot conceive that a prophet could come from Galilee. Are we offended by Christ? Jesus did not meet the expectations of his day. Does Christ now meet ours?

In reading the Gospel we may spend a lot of time questioning Christ, as well as Christ's authority and origins. When all the questions cease, however, we are left looking at Christ's power, promise, and truth. We are left to say with the soldiers, "No one ever spoke like this man."

When we are done questioning, will we follow, seeking in Christ the living water? The test of whether or not Jesus is the one he claims to be comes when we look to see whether or not we receive what Jesus promised. When we look, there is no more need to question. Bring to Christ your need. We will find infinitely more than we had expected.

Jesus, you spoke of a river of living water
from my heart. I thirst.

† † †

MARCH

In God's Time

The other day a friend was complaining about how slowly his therapy was going. It had taken over two years, he plaintively asserted, and it seemed interminable. I gently suggested that it had taken him over thirty-five years to arrive at the emotional state he was in and, though I doubted it would take another thirty-five to sort out his tangled emotions, perhaps he was right on schedule with his healing.

In today's verses, a remarkable passage follows Jesus' controversy with the religious authorities: "These words he spoke in the treasury, as he taught in the temple; but no one arrested him, because his hour had not yet come."

In the Bible there are two concepts of time: *chronos* and *kairos*. *Chronos* is the time which is measured by the clock. *Kairos*, in contrast, is the "fittingness" of time, or as Scripture states it, "the fullness of time." *Kairos* is God's time. When we honestly try to align our will with God's will for our lives, time takes on this new dimension of *kairos*; things happen when they are supposed to.

Perhaps no one laid a hand on Jesus because he had more to do: more healing, more loving of souls, more spreading of the realm of God. Ultimately he was arrested. Ultimately he had to die. But not before "his hour" had come.

I told my friend that I felt sure that his therapy would yield good results in "God's time."

Loving God, help me when I grow impatient with the gentle workings of your Holy Spirit to remember that things happen in your time and at your speed. Help me not to uproot what you have planted in me through an impatient need to see if it's growing, but to trust that you will finish your work in me "in the fullness of time." Amen.

† † †

Radical Obedience

I remember the following conversation recurring often when I was a child and my mother would tell me what to do:

"Why, mom?" I would ask plaintively.

"Just because," she would answer.

"Just because why?" I would persist.

"Just because I say so," she would finally answer, exasperated.

She would eventually explain the real reason, but I still remember the frustration of being required by my parents, who were in authority, to do something I didn't want to do.

Many of us, I suspect, react the same way to God because of such experiences with our parents. But if we take our example from Jesus, who declared that he did nothing on his own authority but always did what was pleasing to God, we find an example of radical obedience worthy of our imitation.

Radical obedience is attempting to align ourselves with the will of God so completely that we become one with God through Jesus. It often brings us into conflict with our culture, even as it did for Jesus with his culture — conflict with what we have been taught, with the attitudes others may have about our conduct, and even with temporal authorities. But radical obedience brings its own reward. As Jesus says in today's reading, "If you continue in my word, you are truly my disciples, and you will know the truth, and the truth will make you free."

Dear Jesus, help me to know your will for me today, and give me the strength to carry it out so that I may be one with you as you are one with God. Amen.

† † †

Freedom

John Sanford writes in his book, *The Kingdom Within*, "Jesus is opposed to the Pharisees primarily because the Pharisees wear masks — they conceal themselves . . . . In terms of the sins of the flesh the Pharisees were virtuous people. In popular view they were the most perfect examples possible of what God wanted people to be like. But Jesus strips away their masks and exposes them to themselves. For this he was never forgiven, for there is no hatred more bitter than hatred for one who strips away from us the facade behind which we have been hiding."[1]

In today's Gospel reading, the Pharisees insist that they have never been in bondage, that as descendants of Abraham they are free because they scrupulously practice outward piety. Jesus insists that such outward shows can be demonic, and he condemns it.

How much like the Pharisees we can be today! We assume that because we are law-abiding citizens, we must be doing God's will. But today, as when he was on earth, Jesus calls us to a deeper walk, a walk of interior consistency in which our "walk" matches our "talk"! Anything else is hypocrisy and slavery.

Sovereign Jesus, unmask me
today. Show me the inconsistencies
in my life. Let me not be overwhelmed by
the incongruities there, but let me turn such incon-
sistency over to you so that you may make my soul-life
congruent with my outer life. Thank you for that
daily cleansing process. Amen.

---

[1]Excerpt from *THE KINGDOM WITHIN: The Inner Meaning of Jesus' Sayings* by John A. Sanford. Copyright © 1970 by John A. Sanford. Reprinted by permission of Harper & Row, Publishers, Inc.

✝ ✝ ✝

Hearing the Words of God

Jesus says in today's Scripture, "The one who is of God hears the words of God." The concept of hearing God is a strange one in our society, but people who follow God can hear the voice of God in a variety of ways.

First, we can obtain guidance for our daily living through reading the Bible. Second, we can hear God's will through the advice of men and women of faith. Third, we can hear God's voice through the community of faith, the church. We can also find direction through knocking on various doors and going through the open ones, through "words of knowledge" from friends, or even directly, as the still, small voice of our inner consciousness directs us or speaks encouragement.

It is the promise of Jesus that we can hear God's voice if we are of God. The problem may be that too few of us have been listening: we may have been taught not to expect to hear God's voice, or that we are "crazy" if we claim to hear it. Even a cursory reading of the literature of faith reveals, however, that these are only a few of the means of hearing God's voice. We can and ought to expect to hear the voice of God, who wants to provide guidance for us in even the mundane things of life. We need but listen.

Loving and Guiding Presence, open me today to hear your voice. Like a child learning to listen to the voice of its parents, let me learn to listen to your words to me. I pray in Jesus' name. Amen.

† † †

Beware of the Leaven

In today's Scripture, Jesus' disciples are guilty of a very human failing: they mistake a metaphor having a spiritual meaning for one having a physical meaning. When Jesus tells them to beware of the leaven of the Pharisees and of Herod, the disciples turn to one another in puzzlement, telling each other that they have forgotten to bring bread, and wondering what Jesus could be talking about.

Recall that just before this Jesus had been talking to the Pharisees, who had asked for a sign. Here, he is trying to tell his disciples that, when it comes to pass that they recognize him as the Messiah, they should not think of him in terms of earthly power, but in terms of a higher realm. The disciples, however, miss the point. They are able only to think in terms of empty stomachs, even though Jesus reminds them of the times that he has fed thousands.

In the modern world, too, little effort is made to see the layers upon layers of spiritual meaning that underlie the mundane surface of things. Jesus' warning still applies: beware of the leaven of the Pharisees and of Herod, the moving force that shapes one's vision so as to give primacy to temporal power. For that was the way the Pharisees and Herod saw Jesus' mission.

Often, we too believe that the way to fulfillment is to strive for temporal power. We should remember that, even as Jesus' power derived from rejecting Satan's temptation and choosing the power of the Spirit, so too must we give temporal power a secondary priority if we seek to gain the power that the Spirit can give.

Jesus, help me to see that by surrendering
myself to you, I do not lose, but gain power.
Teach me the difference between spiritual power and
temporal power, and let me seek the spiritual
power that comes from you. Amen.

† † †

There Will Be Enough

In today's world we receive the message that we are running out of everything and, by implication, that there is not enough for everyone. This "theology of scarcity" says, in the language of the street, "You only go around once in life, so grab for all that you can get."

Today's Scripture belies this attitude. Jesus takes the offering of one person, a little lad with five loaves and two fish, and feeds five thousand. In a theology of abundance, God's arithmetic is five thousand to one!

In more practical terms, when we make ourselves available to God to be used, as did the little boy, God can make our efforts five thousand times what we could have done on our own. Such is the economy of the Spirit.

Therefore, on a daily basis, I approach God and make myself — my will and my life — available to God to be used. I find not only that my life goes more smoothly, but that my inter- actions with the earth and with other people go more smoothly too.

Great and wondrous God,
help me to learn what you can do
with one surrendered and obedient person.
Today I offer myself to you to do your will.
Help me to know your will and to do it
with all my heart and strength.
Amen.

† † †

The Taming of Fear

Psychologists tell us that we revert to primitive reactions when we are faced with a threat: fight or flight. Yet in our modern times, we can only rarely react primitively, so we usually contain our reaction to a perceived threat within ourselves in the form of anger and rage (fight) or fear (flight).

Jesus' words to the disciples in today's Scripture echo one of his primary goals: to set us free from fear. Of course, when faced with a life-threatening danger, all of us feel fear; it is natural. But the fear that Christ frees us from is not only the fear that arises from life-threatening danger, but also the bondage of paralyzing phobias and irrational fears.

The disciples felt the calming presence of Jesus. Because he came walking on the water, they thought they had seen a ghost, but Jesus' calming words were, "It is I; do not be afraid."

When we face the stresses and strains of daily living, we too, if we stop to listen, can hear Christ saying, "I am with you, do not be afraid." No task is so overwhelming, no situation so frightening, that it is not transformed when Christ's presence is there. Christ is the friend who sticks closer than a blood relative.

Many are the times that I have faced new and frightening situations and have found that I could get through them by remembering Jesus' words, "It is I; do not be afraid."

Thought for today: Courage is fear that has said its prayers and has felt the presence of Jesus.

† † †

Food for Thought

In today's world, we hear a great deal about eating disorders and alcoholism. These obsessive-compulsive disorders may result in part from an emptiness deep within, an emptiness which the person is trying to fill with "the food which perishes."

Jesus speaks in today's Scriptures of an imperishable "food which endures to eternal life." In recovery programs for eating disorders, spirituality is sometimes emphasized in order to teach the food addict other ways to fill the void that he or she has been attempting to fill with "the food which perishes." Jesus urges us to work instead for the food which does not perish.

Jesus goes on to make an astonishing statement: "I am the bread of life; whoever comes to me shall not hunger, and whoever believes in me shall never thirst." This is, of course, an obvious reference to the Eucharist, but I believe that this passage also suggests a connection between the promise of Jesus and the affliction of persons who suffer from eating and drinking disorders.

What we are talking about here is our need to satisfy the inner emptiness that every human being probably experiences at some time: the need for a sense of self-worth and for others' respect of our right to exist. When that need for self-worth and respect is thwarted by faulty upbringing, childhood trauma, or pain, Jesus, the resurrected Christ, can guide, re-parent, fill, and restore us.

Who among us in today's world, replete with its stresses, strains, and challenges, does not need what Jesus offers here: a chance to experience nourishment, peace, and harmony?

Risen Jesus, when I am harried and hurried by the world, when I feel the need to fill the resulting emptiness in my spirit with food or drink, let me stop and feast instead on your accepting love. Amen.

† † †

Drawn by God

In today's passage, Jesus addresses the misunderstanding of the people of his native Galilee, who do not see how he could have come from above. "Is this not Joseph's son?" they ask. "How can he be from above?" Jesus asserts that, in order to understand his heavenly origin, one must be "drawn" by God. Further, to be drawn is defined as learning from God.

Today, as then, we are drawn by God into a deeper spiritual journey, into an exploration of a deep, subterranean river missed by those who travel on the surface. It entails breaking through the surface and being willing to be led to the "springs of living water" that lie below superficial religious practices.

God calls each of us to that journey through Jesus. Many are afraid to start, afraid of the unknown. Others are afraid of the introspection demanded by such a journey. For in order to make this journey, we must confront and work through our many buried hang-ups, the mental logjams that block the path. These mental logjams, obstacles to experiencing the presence and power of God, are the result of our past attempts to reconcile the religious rules, school teachings, and family and peer group mores that conflict with our own experience and deepest sense of who we are.

God draws us into confronting these obstacles, the remnants of the wounded child's old ideas about God and the world we live in. It is an exhilirating journey — a journey with great rewards if we are willing to pay the price of self-knowledge: the sacrifice of the ego.

Loving God, I know you as the one-who-calls. Help me not to resist your call, nor to be afraid of what that call entails. Draw me nearer to you and give me the grace to be completely yours. Amen.

† † †

On the Christian Eucharist

Today's passage centers on the Christian Eucharist. Jesus uses ordinary things in the Eucharist, ordinary bread and fruit of the vine. But by faith, they become Christ's body and blood. This spiritual transformation illustrates another transformation which happens when we receive the Eucharist: God consecrates ordinary, mundane daily lives. As the bread and wine become a means of grace for us at the Eucharist, so our ordinary lives become the focus of God's grace in this world.

The Eucharist, then, is a meeting between heaven and earth in which the eternal, invisible sphere and the temporal world join together. We experience our complete dependence on God and God's abiding faithfulness to us. We can be completely who we are; we can be vulnerable.

There is, then, a sacredness in the meal itself. Jesus promises eternal life and resurrection to the one who participates. This is available to each of us by faith. In experiencing this eternal life in the Eucharist, we need not experience anything but the present moment. In the words of theologian Paul Tillich, it is a moment of grace:

> . . . at that moment a wave of light breaks into our darkness and it is as though a voice were saying, "You are accepted, accepted by that which is greater than you, and the name of which you do not know. Do not ask for the name now; perhaps you will find it later. Do not try to do anything now; perhaps later you will do much. Do not seek for anything; do not perform anything; do not intend anything. *Simply accept the fact that you are accepted.*" If that happens to us, we experience grace.[1]

Thought for today: In the Eucharist I experience eternal life simply by abiding in the present moment.

[1]From *THE NEW BEING* by Paul Tillich. Copyright 1955 Paul Tillich; copyright renewed © 1983 Hannah Tillich. Reprinted with permission of Charles Scribner's Sons, an imprint of Macmillan Publishing Company.

† † †

Where Can We Run?

When I was a little girl, I got mad at some fancied injustice and ran away from home. I packed my little toy suitcase, walked out the back door, and hid under the bleachers at the football field across the street from my house. The time wore on, and my mother did not come to get me. Eventually, as I got hungry and nature called, I gave up and went home. Years later I learned that I was being watched the whole time by my mother, who knew my every move but had decided not to come and get me. Sometimes I think our attempts to run away from God are like that.

Perhaps you have known people who tried to run away from God. Usually, if they've been honest with themselves, they've found, as the psalmist did, that there really isn't any running away from God:

> Where shall I go from your Spirit?
> Or where shall I flee from your presence?
> If I ascend to heaven, you are there!
> If I make by bed in Sheol, you are there!
> (Psalm 139:7-8)

The disciples in today's reading evidently realized that there wasn't any running away from Jesus, either. Jesus, hurt at the desertion of many of the disciples, turned to the twelve and asked plaintively, "Do you also wish to go away?" Their reply indicates that they had contemplated running away, but had realized that he alone had "the words of eternal life."

We, too, may have experiences that test our commitment to the spiritual path we have chosen. Far from finding the way all roses, we discover that it also harbors thorns of persecution and misunderstanding. But we also discover that running away would mean deserting our only hope for security and meaning in this life.

Jesus, help me to stand with you and not run away
when adversity comes. Amen.

† † †

Gain the World — Forfeit the Soul

A friend came to see me the other day. Sobbing, he poured out a tale of abuse and arguments with his spouse. He had lost all confidence in God, in his relationship skills, in himself. "Pastor, I feel like I've lost my soul," he wept.

I recalled the last time I had seen him. He had been attending church regularly, learning a great deal, loving Jesus. But because he was lonely, we had prayed for God to send him someone special with whom he could share his life. And God answered our prayers. A beautiful partner for him came along, and they entered into a relationship with each other.

But then my friend forgot Jesus' words about seeking God's dominion above everything else. Suddenly the new partner was taking all of his time. Instead of bringing his spouse to church, he stayed away. He made his partner the center of his life, and thereby began the painful process of gaining the world but losing his soul.

How like that young man we are prone to be! So many voices compete for our attention that it is easy to ignore the one voice that says, "For those who would save their life will lose it; and those who lose their life for my sake and the Gospel's will save it."

How different life could have been for my friend if he had prayerfully led his young spouse into the knowledge of God. Failing that, he himself could at least have remained faithful to God. As it was, he had made his partner his god and had suffered the consequences. The solution to his problem was to place his spouse in the proper role, that of a human being created by God. With this change, he began to rediscover his own soul.

Gracious God, help me to put you first in all
that I do. If I begin to wander, I trust you to gently
call me back. Amen.

✝ ✝ ✝

As Jesus Passed By

The blind man sat by the roadside near the Jerusalem marketplace. Although he couldn't see, he could smell the marketplace, with its pungent odor of live animals, aging meat, ripe fruit, and that particular smell of fresh-woven cloth.

He had heard that the rabbi from Galilee was in town. It had only been whispered about, but because of his acute sense of hearing he had picked it up. He had heard that this rabbi had actually healed the blind. He wondered . . . .

Just then he heard a noise. A large crowd was passing by. He heard someone mention the name Jeshua. Why, that was the name of the rabbi he had heard about, the one from Nazareth who had healed the blind men! He held his breath as the crowd approached. He tried to call out, but found the words sticking in his throat. Oh! Could it be . . . YES! They had stopped right in front of him!

Someone asked a question: "Who sinned, this person or the parents, that the child was born blind?" The rabbi dismissed the question with some strange talk about the works of God and about day and night. Then he said he was the light of the world! It was all too much!

While speaking, however, the rabbi applied some sticky stuff to his eyes and told him to go wash in the pool at Siloam.

He did, and praise to God, he could see!

Jesus, heal the broken parts
of my life today, even if I do not see you as
you pass by. Amen.

† † †

Once I Was Blind, But Now I Can See

When the blind man of yesterday's reading came back healed, the religious authorities angrily refused to believe that Jesus had anything to do with the healing. "Give God the praise," they said; "we know that this man is a sinner," to which the healed man could only reply, "Whether he is a sinner, I do not know; one thing I know, that though I was blind, now I see."

Like the healed blind man, few of us are theologians, and there will always be those who challenge us to give an acceptable explanation of the kinds of things that happen in such simple and powerful encounters with Jesus. In his book, *The Taste of New Wine*, for example, Keith Miller tells us about a woman who, after experiencing a deeper walk with Jesus, also found healing from a depression, a condition for which she had been taking medication for years. He notes that, when she tried to tell her pastor about this unsought blessing, she encountered only hostility and suspicion, probably a result of the pastor's inability (or unwillingness) to see the experience from her point of view.[1]

In such circumstances, we would do well to follow the example of the healed blind man by simply sharing our experience and our joy in it, without attempting to formulate dogma or generalize from our personal experience. The testimony of a changed life speaks far more eloquently than any theological treatise or dogmatic proof could ever do.

Thought for today: I will be happier and more effective if I simply introduce my friends to the Jesus that I have learned to know from my own experience, rather than insisting on their assent to specific creeds or religious dogmas.

[1]Miller, Keith, *The Taste of New Wine* (Waco, TX: World Books, 1965), p. 105.

† † †

Abundant Living

Someone has said that Christians have just enough religion to make them miserable! And far too often, that may be so. It is said that Ghandi explored the Christian religion and admired Jesus, but was disillusioned by the fact that Christ's followers did not really follow Christ! In that respect, we may be missing what Christ has promised: the abundant life.

It is a tenet of the Jewish religion that it is a sin to be offered the opportunity to enjoy life and not to do so. How different from the Puritans, who felt that if something was pleasurable, it had to be a sin. Jesus was Jewish, so it is not inconsistent with his upbringing to say, "I came that they may have life, and have it abundantly."

Does abundant life mean doing just as I please, indulging every whim? No, for that is merely self-indulgence. Abundant living is living life to the fullest. St. Augustine put it this way: "Love God, and do what you please." He could say this because, if we love God, what we will want to do will be God's will for us. We will live increasingly for others and for the world. Abundant living means seeking first God's domain and God's "right-use-ness"; then all the other things we need in life — food, clothing, shelter — will be given as well. (Matthew 6:33)

*Jesus, so align my will and life with your
will and life that I become one with you, as you
are one with God. Let me know the abundant life that
comes from knowing and doing your will
on a daily basis. Amen.*

† † †

Security

Many religions, including Christianity, promise an afterlife of eternal peace and happiness. Often, however, certain conditions are attached to the attainment of this eternal life, conditions having to do with striving to achieve a state of perfection that will make one pure enough to be one with God.

But Christ promises us that if we will but follow and trust the good shepherd, we will have eternal life." "My sheep," Christ says, "follow me; and I give them eternal life." It is important to recognize that the emphasis here is not on the character of the follower, but rather on the asssurances of Christ. We don't have to achieve perfection, since we can rest secure in Christ's absolute trustworthiness.

In today's reading Jesus promises that he will not abandon us to the "wolf" or to the "thief." In our lives, many "wolves" — trials, bitterness, resentment — try to devour us. The "thieves" of deprivation, worry, and loss try to rob us of our peace of mind. But Jesus promised to be with his disciples in these times and to lay down his life for them.

And this is precisely what Jesus did: he laid down his life to destroy that which would destroy us — fear, guilt, anger, resentment, sickness, and ultimately, death itself. With such a Saviour watching over us we have nothing to fear.

Gentle Shepherd,
I confess I have looked for the security
I need in my mother, father, spouse, friends, and
even my church. Today I realize that no one else can
give me the security that you provide. Help me to
relax, secure in the knowledge that you call me
your own and that I can experience life more
abundantly by simply following you.
Amen.

† † †

Living Even If You Die

In today's Gospel, Jesus does a seemingly callous thing: he waits two days before going to the sickbed of Lazarus, called "the one you love" by Mary and Martha. Sometimes we may wonder why Jesus delays answering our prayers when we specifically send for him, just as Lazarus' two sisters worried when it appeared their brother would die. In this case, the worst happened. Lazarus died. But Jesus showed how faith could bring greater glory out of adversity, even out of death itself. In the case of Lazarus' death, it was the glory of Resurrection.

Later, Jesus would undergo an untimely and cruel death himself. But again, *"Christus Victor!"* The defeated one, surrendering to the will of God, would become victorious through the power of God even unto resurrection!

A full theology must include an understanding of death as the ultimate healing, wherein the dying go on to live forever in the presence of God. Jesus' affirmation that he is the resurrection and the life, and that those who believe in him will live even if they die, underscores the ultimate good news of the Christian faith: death is not all there is. We will go on living! Even if we are not sure just what kind of life it will be, the example of Lazarus, and then of Jesus, assures us that it will be glorious.

Jesus, help me to understand that because we live in
a world that is not yet fully redeemed, death is a part of
human existence. Help me to rejoice today that because
we believe in you, we and those we love will live,
even though we die. Amen.

† † †

Our Weeping Lord

Consider this interesting phenomenon: Jesus wept so profusely at the death of his friend Lazarus that onlookers remarked, "See how Jesus loved him!" Yet only moments later, Jesus raised Lazarus from the dead. One would think that his message to Mary, Martha, and the mourners would be, "OK folks, don't cry! God's going to raise Lazarus in just a few minutes! Hang on just a moment and you'll see!" Yet this was not Jesus' message at all. Instead he wept. We wonder why.

Perhaps Jesus felt such empathy for Mary and Martha that he wept for their sorrow. Perhaps, as the onlookers assumed, the death of his friend moved him to tears. Just as likely, however, and just as consistent with the actions of Jesus recorded in other parts of the Bible, he was weeping over all the sin, death, and corruption that he saw in the world.

The central message of today's passage, therefore, is this: God weeps with us in the midst of our need. God weeps for the systemic sins of society, for the greed, the pollution, the child abuse, the sexual abuse, and all the other things that weaken our families and corrupt our planet. God weeps as well for the personal pain in each of our lives.

The Bible says that Jesus is our high priest, the one who has endured everything we endure on earth, yet without sin. So Jesus can empathize and weep with us even though he knows the outcome will renew us and glorify God — just as it did in the case of Lazarus.

Loving God, let me not allow grief or pain to drive me from you, but help me to know that you weep with me in my pain and work within my grief for my good and your greater glory. Amen.

† † †

On Praise

The word "criticize" comes from the Greek word meaning "to tear flesh." It presents a violent image with a powerful negative connotation. In contrast, praise edifies and builds up, contributing to the positive side of life.

In today's reading, Jesus encounters the realities expressed by both words. First, those who were being healed were praising Jesus, saying, "Hosanna to the son of David." Then there were the indignant religious authorities, criticizing Jesus.

Criticism or praise. This is often the choice for us. Will we be a presence that tears down, or one that builds up?

The Bible tells us that God inhabits the praises of the people. The reason for this is that when we allow others to speak positively, we align ourselves with the creative spirit of the universe — the God of the Bible and of Jesus. When we criticize and speak negatively, we align ourselves with all that could, and often does, destroy our spirits.

Jesus says that God so cares for the positive power of praise that God brings forth praise out of the mouths of babies and infants. Here, infants and babies may well be an image of the childlike part of ourselves. Elsewhere, Jesus commands that we let the children come unto him. When we come to Jesus like children, allowing the child inside to be open, free, trusting, and creative, we find ourselves on the positive, praising side of life.

Dear Jesus, let me concentrate just for today on trusting you, enabling the inner child in me to express itself in natural praise and joy. Amen.

† † †

On Signs

In today's Gospel reading, John portrays Jesus entering Jerusalem shortly after raising Lazarus from the dead. It is part of the drama of the Gospel that the writer has the multitude going after Jesus because he had given this sign, the raising of Lazarus.

Jesus himself, of course, warned his disciples not to follow others simply because they perform signs: "And then if any one says to you, 'Look, here is the Christ!' . . . do not believe it. False Christs and false prophets will arise and show signs and wonders, to lead astray, if possible, the elect." (Mark 13:21-22) Clearly, then, the Gospel imperative to us is to stand firm and believe in Jesus no matter whether signs are present or not.

Certainly we can be misled by following signs — we can grow to love the signs and forget the one they point to. The crowd following Jesus allowed Jesus' raising of Lazarus from the dead to deceive them into thinking that Jesus was a temporal Messiah who had come to liberate them from temporal darkness. Their misunderstanding led to Jesus' crucifixion. The irony, though, is that the crucifixion, coupled with the Resurrection, provides the greatest sign of all of Jesus' true identity and trustworthiness.

Dear Sovereign, let me
carefully discern what kind of spirit is being
manifested when I encounter a wonderful sign. Help me
not to look for you in signs and wonders, but in the
fruits of the Spirit. Amen.

† † †

Dying to Live

The other day, a friend made a painful revelation to me. She was being discriminated against in her office in favor of a male who had less experience and seniority than she. She had almost enough time in her company to be vested in her pension plan, and if she pursued the discrimination complaint, she risked being fired. What to do, she wondered. "Pastor," she said to me, "it seems to me that I have a clear and frightening choice between doing what I know I ought to do — not only for myself but for every woman in the company — and saving my own skin."

Jesus' words in today's reading encapsulate one of the deeper mysteries of the spiritual life: those who try to save their lives will lose them; those who give up their lives will save them.

We seem to be confronted again and again with choosing between what we know is a right course of action and an easier path of less resistance. Doing what we know is right rather than taking an easy way out involves a death, of course — the death of our own ego. It is a painful choice, one that may not turn out all right in the short run. Hurling ourselves at the forces of injustice in life may result initially in a tragic defeat, but ultimately success is sure to follow.

This is what I believe Jesus meant when he said, ". . . unless a grain of wheat falls into the earth and dies, it remains alone; but if it dies, it bears much fruit." Jesus himself provided the example: he was crucified after a mock trial, but the end result was a greater glory — triumph over death itself, and eternal life for us all.

Jesus, when I am faced with a difficult moral choice,
help me to die to myself so that I may, with your help,
make a difference in the world. Amen.

† † †

The Love That Draws Everyone

A story is told about a man who, during World War II, accepted a dare from his buddies to enter a confessional and do all the priest told him to do. If he was able to complete the penance assigned by the priest, he would win a bet.

The priest, evidently having a wisdom from above, prescribed that the man approach the crucifix and say, "Jesus, you did all this for me, and I don't give a damn."

The young soldier approached the crucifix and tried three times to say the words. The third time, he was so overcome by the realization of what Jesus had done for thim that he broke down and cried. Not only did he lose the bet, but he eventually entered the priesthood and became a cardinal in the church.

Jesus said, "I, when I am lifted up from the earth, will draw all people to myself." His crucifixion, while still a mystery in its cosmic significance, remains the greatest act of love in human history. It is the love that draws everyone.

The power of what Jesus did at the cross is demonstrated in his later words to his disciples, "Greater love has no one than this, that one lay down one's life for a friend." It is precisely Jesus' laying down of his life that draws us to Christ today. For the one who called even Judas "friend" at the time of his betrayal, also called us "friend" while were yet at enmity with God. This is the love that draws us to the cross with the message, "Friend, I will always love you. Nothing you can ever do or say will stop me from loving you. *You are loved!*"

Oh, Jesus, my reaction to such love as you displayed at the cross is one of simple awe. I love you because you first loved me and gave yourself for me. Amen.

† † †

One With God Through Jesus

Some have questioned the validity of Christianity, saying, "How can Christianity be *the* true way when even the followers of Christ cannot agree on what the true way is? Is not the divided body of Christ a proof that Christianity is *not* the only true way?" A valid question.

"Holy God, my Mother and Father, keep them in your name . . . that they may be one, even as we are one." This was Jesus' prayer in the garden. His last thoughts, the true "Lord's prayer," were of his disciples and of those who would come after them. And he prayed for unity among them.

While the skeptic may look at the various denominations within Christianity and see factionalism, there is another way to look at Christianity. The vast majority of Christians exhibit "unity within diversity": unity under the dominion of Jesus Christ, diversity in mission and emphasis.

The Bible describes the church as "the body of Christ," and even as a body has various parts, so, too, does the body of Christ. Thus it can be that Catholics, Lutherans, and Episcopalians, for example, offer a beautiful Eucharistic ministry, while Presbyterians, Methodists, Congregationalists and ethnic churches emphasize Biblical justice and righteousness. Baptists and Evangelists bring new believers into the body, while Pentecostals and Charismatics function as healers and prophets. What a diverse and beautiful body, with one head, Jesus Christ!

Lord, help me to see your church not as a collection of splintered and quarreling factions, but as the beautifully faceted diamond that it is. Amen.

† † †

An Inward Look

In today's Scripture, Peter stalwartly avows his loyalty to Jesus, declaring that he will die for him if need be. Jesus predicts that Peter will deny him three times before the cock crows. And indeed, that's just the way it happened. Peter did deny Jesus, and when the cock crowed, he realized what he had done and went out and wept bitterly.

There is no doubt that Peter's intentions were good. He probably believed that he *would* die for Jesus. But Jesus had spent three years with Peter. He had seen something that Peter did not see in himself, a weakness that, at the moment of crisis, would cause Peter to deny Jesus rather than die.

Like Peter, we can often be deluded about our inner faults and weaknesses. Perhaps for Peter, fear was the motivation which caused him to deny Jesus in the crisis. Or perhaps it was the need to be a part of the crowd. Maybe it was a sense of helplessness over his inability to prevent Jesus from being arrested, or anger over being rebuked by Jesus for cutting off the soldier's ear with a sword. Whatever the weakness, Jesus seemed to have known in advance that it was there. But he loved Peter anyway.

Fortunately, that is not the end of the story. Peter had plenty of time for introspection during the days that followed the crucifixion. And Jesus' love, during the days that followed the wonder of the Resurrection, transformed Peter. Jesus had said to Peter, "Satan demanded to have you, in order to sift you like wheat, but I have prayed for you that your faith may not fail; and when you have turned again, strengthen your brothers and sisters." (Luke 22:31-32) When the strengthening of Peter was completed, he became the leader of the early church, and he was able to die for Jesus.

Jesus, help me to take an inward look to be sure my faults do not sabotage my intentions. Amen.

† † †

The Feast of the Annunciation — Favored of God

The angel announced to Mary that she had found favor with God, and she humbly acquiesced to the Annunciation. Through the Annunciation, womanhood was blessed, and the chattel status of woman was forever changed. Christianity continues to evolve this theme of women's equality.

But it is to the question of having "found favor with God" that we look today. Looking at her own life, Mary might very well have wondered just what the favor was. She was subject to rumors that her child was illegitimate; she was subject to the rigors of an uncomfortable birth in a strange place; because of Herod's paranoia, she had to flee to Egypt to save her child's life.

Then there were the years of his growing, and the loss in early adolescence of his earthly father, leaving Mary a young widow, with all the hardships that widowhood implied in first-century Nazareth. Worst of all, she had to be present when the Romans crucified her son. Looking at all of these events, she might well have wondered just what the advantage was in being favored by the Most High.

So, too, with us today. We may believe that the measure of God's favor lies in money, property, ease, success, or fame — and sometimes even churches tell us this. Had Mary measured her status with God in this manner, though, she might well have concluded that she was not favored at all.

The measure of God's favor often comes in the form of strength of character to endure great hardships, especially the hardships of the spiritual path. And it is often those who tread this path who give us the courage, strength, and hope to meet our own trials.

Mary came through her moment of trial to see her son resurrected and the Christian church formed. Tradition has it that she, together with one of Jesus' brothers, for many years pastored the church at Jerusalem. She was truly favored of God!

Thought for today: If I have too much of the world's favor, I may not have enought of God's!

† † †

Shalom! The Holy Spirit is Peace!

In today's Scripture, Jesus says, "Peace be with you . . . receive the Holy Spirit."

Someone has said that in order for people to be at peace they need someone to love, something to do, and something to look forward to. Jesus employs that very formula in these verses. First, the disciples showed that they loved Christ: "The disciples were glad when they saw the Lord." Secondly, Christ gave them something to do: "As God has sent me, even so I send you." And lastly, Christ gave them something to look forward to: "Jesus breathed on them, and said to them, 'Receive the Holy Spirit.' " Christ gave them the formula for peace even within the inner turmoil that they were experiencing because of their fear of the religious authorities who were seeking their lives and, supposedly, the body of Jesus.

We, too, can experience the peace that Jesus gives. Even in the midst of storms, we can experience that peace. The "storms" in our lives may arise from inner turmoil or outer stress. They may occur within ourselves or they may involve others. But Christ enters our lives, just as with the disciples, and says, "Shalom! Peace be with you!" Christ promises peace, not as the world gives peace, but the peace that passes all understanding.

Gentle Shepherd, give me peace in the middle of the storms of my anxiety. Give me the peace of loving you, of doing your mission, and of looking forward to your rewards. Amen.

† † †

Freedom From Anxiety

It has been said more than once that we live in an age of anxiety. Historians point out that never before in history have human beings been subjected to so much fear and uncertainty. Stress- and fear-related heart attacks abound. We yearn for peace, but we are confronted by wars and rumors of wars.

In today's Scripture, Jesus addresses the basic anxiety, lack of trust: "Let not your hearts be troubled; believe in God, believe also in me." Do not be anxious, only trust.

Trusting in Jesus is no mean feat. All of us learn before the age of two that a good many aspects of the world around us are untrustworthy. As children, we are born with anxieties as basic as fear of falling and fear of loud noises. Then, many of us learn that even Mommy, Daddy, teachers, ministers, and other caregivers cannot always be trusted. Anxiety seems to be one of the givens of our lives. How, then, are we to believe that God really cares for us?

Fortunately, Christ is there personally for each of us — to teach us that we *can* trust God. When we have really learned this, we can relax, let go, and experience freedom from anxiety.

*Saviour, release me from my lack of trust and anxiety
into a joyous trust in you. Amen.*

† † †

The Subconcious Mind and the Holy Spirit

Have you ever found yourself vowing never to do a certain thing again, only to find yourself repeating it? Have you even prayed about it, only to find that you seem to be in bondage? I certainly have. When confronted by my failure to control these manifestations of what has been variously termed in the Christian faith as "doublemindedness," "the war in my members," or "the old sinful human nature," I have often berated myself for that failure.

Then I discovered that I was in good company. The Apostle Paul experienced this same struggle, as do many contemporary authors. But a noted theologian's commentary that relates well to today's Scripture shows us how the Holy Spirit can uncover the roots of these problems, which are hidden deep in the recesses of our subconscious.

E. Stanley Jones, the great Methodist theologian and missionary to India, had this to say about such problems:

> The area of the work of the Holy Spirit is largely, though not entirely, in the realm of the subconscious. There the Holy Spirit works — purifying, redirecting, and dedicating age-long driving instincts. [The Holy Spirit] refashions the depths of [humans] and unifies [them] at the center, so that the conscious and the subsconscious speak the same language, understand each other, drive for the same goals, and own a common Lord.[1]

In other words, it is the Holy Spirit's job to take care of these thorny problems. My job is simply to cooperate with the Holy Spirit. When I do this, I find that eventually I discover the root of these problems in some early trauma, of which I can then be healed — and the old habit disappears. What a relief!

Holy Spirit, make me willing to be cooperative with your work in my subsconscious mind. Amen.

[1]Jones, E. Stanley, *Abundant Living* (New York: Abingdon Press, 1952), p. 152.

† † †

Fruitful Living

Driving down the freeway the other day, I saw a bumper sticker that read, "LIFE IS HARD; THEN YOU DIE." In today's world, one of our deepest longings is for a sense of purpose. Many have succumbed to ennui, a boredom with our Western abundance. Others suffer from loneliness, a haunting sickness of the soul. Still others experience a lack of connectedness, an alienation from self, from other people, and from the world. Many would say, with the psalmist, "As for human beings, their days are like grass; they flourish like a flower of the field; for the wind passes over it, and it is gone, and its place knows it no more." (Psalm 103:15-16)

In today's verses, the metaphor of the vine and the branches is used to emphasize the point that fruitful living begins with life intimately connected with the life of Christ.

Aligning our wills with the will of God through Christ is the first step in finding a purpose in life, which leads in turn to fruitful living. "Apart from me you can do nothing," Jesus said. When we get ourselves grafted properly into the source, Christ, we are like a branch connected to the vine. We receive the nurturing we need in order to continue our spiritual life, just as the branch receives the sustenance that keeps it alive. We receive many other gifts too: wisdom, joy, and not least, a sense of purpose and calling that fulfills us to the very core of our being.

Conversely, when we do not abide in Christ, we ensure that our spiritual being will dry up in today's highly stressful world. So, we have a decision to make each day: to abide and flourish in Christ, or to waste away in the narrow confines of our own egos.

God, help me to make the daily choice to abide
in Jesus, so that my life may be filled with purpose
and meaning. Amen.

† † †

Love One Another

The early Christian church was renowned for its love. People seemed drawn toward Christianity, not because its followers had superior philosophical insights, but because of the love they showed toward each other.

Jesus says in today's passage, "This I command you, to love one another." But how do we do this? So many of us have found this passage, and many similar ones in the New Testament, almost impossible to understand, let alone to obey. How can we feel warmly about people, including some of our brothers and sisters, who just don't arouse that feeling in us — some of whom, indeed, we just plain don't even like? It's frustrating!

Strangely enough, a careful reading of the New Testament gives a clue to the answer. For one thing, it becomes clear that even Jesus himself often didn't show any warmth of feeling toward those whom he said he loved. If his use of the word didn't have to imply warm feelings, what is the meaning of agape, the Greek word which underlies the term "love," as Jesus uses it here?

Agape, as used in all but a few places in the New Testament, means "love of the other person for the sake of the other person," a meaning for which we have no equivalent in English. To love, in the sense of agape, doesn't require me to have the kind of warm feelings that we usually associate with "love." All that it requires is that I act in a caring way, a way that clearly shows my real concern for the other person's well-being.

Surely, I can act this way no matter how I feel about the other person. It is simply a matter of doing it.

Jesus, help me to practice your kind of agape love for other people — to simply act in a caring way, no matter what my feelings about it may be. Amen.

† † †

The Work of the Holy Spirit

Jesus promised, "When the Spirit of truth comes, that Spirit will guide you into all truth." But how does the Spirit do this?

First, each of us has an innate sense of right and wrong that is not culturally conditioned. Our sense of justice and the universal human thirst for freedom are examples of this sense. Surely our awareness of such ultimate meanings and truths is the work of the Holy Spirit.

It is also the work of the Holy Spirit to "convince the world concerning sin and righteousness and judgment." The "world" of John's Gospel is the whole world system that operates without reference to the precepts of God — in today's terms, multinational corporations that pollute the earth out of greed, or government bureaucrats who steal food from famine victims in order to sell it for their own gain. The Holy Spirit works within the hearts of these perpetrators to convince them of their sin.

If the Holy Spirit does not reach their hearts, the Spirit will often work through people of conscience in the community to convince them and us about the "right-use-ness," or stewardship, of the earth's resources.

Finally, the Spirit works to convince the world of its judgment whenever nature rebels against damage to natural resources — damage brought about, for example, by industrial activities that produce acid rain; by agricultural and economic practices that reduce human food supplies; and by hunting and land use practices that lead to the virtual extinction of plants and animals.

As Jesus promised, the Holy Spirit speaks convincingly to us today in our hearts, in our communities, and in nature itself, so as to guide us into all truth. Will you open your heart to hear that Spirit?

Holy Spirit, open my heart to your work today, and give me courage to act on what I hear you saying. Amen.

† † †

APRIL

Following the Effort

In summer, my son squatted round
Over an ant. Watched the creature
In painstaking silence
Lift, drag a scrap of sandwich
Over inches, inches of sidewalk, sidewalk,
To a (final) nest where others came to break it
Up and pull it underground.
His wonder turned to realize my company,
In his eyes, love for the courage of the
Small one's brave, relentless effort.
Suddenly, he knew his strength and smiled at me,
And I knew the feel of rough and wearing sidewalk
Under foot. I laid a hand along his cheek
In blessing.

Dear Creator,
We move, in life, covering an ant's distance across what seems
a never-ending course of rough and discouraging ground,
carrying the burden of learning and becoming everything we
can. Then, suddenly, what felt so torturously long is over, and
the sojourn ends. The work and effort seem secondary, the
passage, momentary. Remind us of the one who trod the path
before us, who learned so well the high price of his journey;
who left us for a moment, then reappeared and gave us his
name to take to you on our own behalf.

† † †

Companion

He seemed a picture. (Postcard, really.)
Fishing, embraced by sunrise.
He startled to the footstep of a child.
I startled to the suddenness of
Finding him on the bank.
I said my father spent Saturdays at work.
He said his Dad had taught him how to fish
And play the banjo.
(The banjo, wow!)
He thought I'd probably like his Dad.
(The banjo. Wow!)
I was four, and years have only
Crystallized the privilege.
Spending a morning
With the gentle conversation,
Humor, calm, and welcome
That he offered.

Dear Creator,
Please help me recognize in Jesus, and in others I find around
me, the gentle touch of your hand and the wisdom of your
voice. I know that there is always room for me in your world
and that a place has been prepared for me. May I approach
it one day in humble expectation, as one who believes gratefully what has been promised.

† † †

Daycare

You leave them — you know —
With people who mean well
And hold them.
But still there are all those
Electrical outlets and steps. And grapes
To choke on.
Even so, you go to work having found
The safest arms you can.
You rock them in the sunset —
Tired, both. And hungry
For each other.
Silent about why
You weren't together
All along.

Dear Creator,
When Jesus had finished his task, he asked your protection
for those he left behind. He did not do this without careful
thought and agonizing decision. He took precautions as best
he knew how: he prayed for our comfort and safety in a world
of spiritual danger. Help us to keep sight of the price he paid
and to be grateful for your generous protection. Too, may we
be eager for the warm reunion with you after so many weary
days of managing this life.

† † †

Messenger

The boy belly-crawled
The muddy, numbing field
Knowing one small sound
Would bring a wall of foreign bullets.
Too, that the words in his jacket
Meant freedom to the rest.
He held his breath and moved again,
Wished with every boy-like cell
That tomorrow this would be a soccer field
Again, with more boys who were not boys
(Anymore or ever).

Dear Creator,
You have given us your word and asked us to carry it,
sometimes at personal risk, to others who seek to know it.
Please protect us in the task. More importantly, help us to
remember that it *is* our task, and there is much at stake in the
carrying. I forget sometimes that I express your word more
powerfully with my actions and responses in the world than
with my tongue. Give me, please, a silent tongue and loud,
loving conduct to carry your intent, lest my own words change
or spoil the message.

† † †

Essence

I knew my grandmother, loved her,
Not because I'd met her (though I had),
But from the stillness of my
Mother's warm and fragrant
Breast.
The locket with Grandmother's picture
Waited there, warm and young and
Smelling of perfume,
For me (delighted) to find and open
As I sat in Mother's lap.
I rocked, remembered with her
Another mother's
Comforting embrace.

Dear Creator,
We come to know you not because we "meet" you (though
we *have* met you), but because we see in others your reflection. Please remind me from time to time that knowing Jesus,
or knowing your earnest followers, is my best chance of knowing you myself. While I am free to approach you on my own,
you have given me pieces of yourself through every person
in my acquaintance. To know them *is* to know you, and to
know you is to live.

† † †

Aura

You know a migraine long before the pain.
First you cannot see,
Except at the sides.
Slowly, there is no way to read
Or drive or smile.
As sight returns, relief heralds
The next nauseous hours.
Dark Torture that closes out
The world.
You understand a little
About hell.
Then you wake. It's over,
And it's time to find the others
Who held vigil through the nightmare.
Who were faithful through the pain.

Dear Creator,
It is never an easy job to be the scout, to go ahead of the others
and prepare the way and anticipate the dangers. John the
Baptist had a message that some received with eagerness and
commitment, and that others received with anger and hatred.
I must remember that not everyone is ready to understand the
truths that keep them from your grace. Do, though, help me
be the sort to hear those messages for myself and prepare my
own life to receive your constant, loving Spirit.

† † †

Sorceress' Apprentice

> I hate it
> When people think I am she.
> I have to tell them (and me)
> That I am not.
> Or when we do our act together —
> She makes her magic find them
> While I hear *my* lines fall empty.
> My tricks, hollow deceptions,
> Imitations of the real.
> And still, my wounded magic,
> Small and waiting,
> Glistens in the dark.

Dear Creator,
Taking a back seat is such a difficult thing. I'm sure that John the Baptist must have felt the burden of his ministry and the humility of knowing his own limitations. Help me to see that the "magic" I offer, while it may not be earth shattering, could help bring people one step closer to you. And that to be anything but humble in my offering of it is to invite those same people to find me lacking, and therefore to walk further away. I know that I have a special touch, but that it is best displayed in the shadow of the master.

† † †

Pastor

When I took this job
They never said
About Mrs. Talbot's seductive
Overtures.
Or what to say to Julie Wilson
When she lost the second baby
(By her boyfriend).
What about David Martin,
Who can't (?) keep his hands off his niece?
No one questions my discretion
With discretionary funds
Or suspects my midnight visitors.
Is there someone
Who would hear my own confession
And re-subscribe to trust?

Dear Creator,
We deal every day with our own temptations no less than with those of others. My prayer is to be delivered from my own, of course. But even more, I pray that *my* struggles not blind me to the chance to help others learn from their own. And that my struggles not cause some to walk further from you than they already were before being in my company. Please, protect people from any mistaken advice or influence I may offer from my areas of blindness.

† † †

Inheritance

We haven't been close, you know,
Not like before.
When the will was read, embarrassed, I heard,
"My possessions and estate to go
To my second son, William."
They hated me then. I guess
I might have too.
My father's face rose behind my eyes,
Grey against the hospital sheets. "I'll leave it to you, son.
Make it fair. I love you all. Please tell them."
I tried to divide it up, to give the others theirs.
They were caught in hating.
Couldn't hear how much he'd loved them.
They never took their shares,
You know, and we haven't been close.

Dear Creator,
I get lost sometimes. I forget that my job is to follow you, to keep my own heart on track. It's so difficult to look at the gifts of others — material and spiritual — and not be envious or imitative. I need to remember that my walk with you is unique, that my relationship with you is formed by the particular combination of personality/spirit/mind that I am. You speak to me in a way that I recognize, and I must answer in a voice that is my own. It is so easy for me to misunderstand that which others have and want it for myself. You have given me so much, I must see that and be grateful.

† † †

Counselor

I don't buy it.
Where does she get off
Telling me my family stinks.
If my boyfriend hits me
Sometimes
That's between him and me.
And the pills. Big deal.
How the hell am I supposed
To get up in the morning?
What does that have to do with
Crying in the dark?
Or playpens? Eh?
What kind of garbage will she push at me
Next week?

Dear Creator,
Why is it always so hard to think about where we come from?
And we can't really go back, yet there is that need to keep
trying. Those things, places, and people who helped us come
to where we are (or aren't) are so difficult to understand. Why
would it matter if Jesus wasn't loved in his own home town?
And yet it did. It mattered enough for him to warn us that
we can't expect to be appreciated by the very people who
should be most proud. Now that I buy it, give me the grace
to accept it.

† † †

Spirit of the Law

Eight years I've watched it. Starts about November.
Huddled kids at the back of the courtroom watch
Their mamas plead guilty for taking dolls from K-Mart.
In Harrison's court they get the same sentence.
"Yes, sir, I knew what I was doin'.
But I couldn't let them see another
Christmas without no toys."
"Three months in the workhouse."
Their frightened eyes move wide,
Children whimper at the back.
"Suspended."
Relief.
He pays the clerk to see they get the toys they took.
Some, too, find an envelope — a turkey maybe,
Or a pair of shoes.
In eight years
I've never seen Harrison so much as smile.

Dear Creator,
I get so rule-bound that I sometimes lose my perspective on
the reason we make rules to begin with. I walk a mental line
between being principle-bound and being flexible, all too often
letting others' opinions determine my stance. Please show me
a middle ground that allows me to respect the rules in this
life without sacrificing the higher principles on which they
are founded. Give me a clear vision and sure footing that will
take me with each step more surely in your direction.

† † †

Request

So much depended on the
Very shape of that pile of dry sticks.
His hands trembled as he sparked the tinder
And watched the fire grow and swallow
Each new piece of wood.
His agile body, small for twelve years, brown
And shined with oil,
Rocked, and his chant wound loud and louder,
Asking for his sister.
Asking what she could not even know.
Then, the answer. Tiny drops, then a soaking rain.
Rain that took the fire into smoke, carried it
Upward with the prayer.
Somewhere within him the chant
Became a joyful, shouting clamor and his feet
Led him to dance.
"Thank you, Great One. Thank you."
Miles away, near other waning embers, his sister
Stirred in feverish sleep.
And made the noise of one whose soul has
Decided to rejoin her after all.

Dear Creator,
This business of faith is difficult. It grows too slowly and
steadily. It makes me know not only that anything is possible, but that many things are probable. It defies my efforts to
explain to friends how it is that I believe. I am grateful for
it, and yet I hardly know how to describe my certainty to those
who ask. There is no question in my heart that I have found
a way to connect with you and that you walk beside me in
everything. Please, let me believe in you always, as you have
always believed in me. Thank you.

† † †

Student Teacher

She found me tired
And read my journal in my eyes.
Picking up my lesson plan, said
"How'd it go?"
My eyes filled, and she looked over
The plan and the twenty empty seats.
Resting chin on hand, she smiled—
"They like to laugh you know."
(Yes, how well I knew.)
She held my shoulder, whispered,
"Tomorrow it will go better."
She had surely forgotten the sweaty agony
Of facing 20 demons once again.
The next day, cartoons and stories
Cleared a path. Grammar in disguise.
Laughing, the demons filed out,
Except one straggler, who stopped shyly for chat.
Then, alone again, she found me, whispered,
"How's it feel to finally get your balance?"
Her invisible magic
Held me while I chatted shyly, loving, being loved.

Dear Creator,
Give me the same appetite for learning that I seem to have
for "teaching." Please give me enough humor to make the
teaching painless, enough love to make the learning stick, and
the faith to keep on trying.

† † †

HIV Positive

The three sat staring at the
Patterned oriental underfoot.
Terror inched through the boy
Like poison from an unsuspected dart.
From the knees, up the back, under his neck, it left his
Paralyzed gaze on the carpet.
"Are you sure?", his voice the quiet monotone
Of the unbelievingly condemned.
"Yes. We'll do what we can." An empty second.
"It starts, son, with forgiving yourself."
(Later) "This, doctor, is a clinic, not a confessional."
The younger man sat silent, letting the angry one finish.
"What the hell is this 'forgiving yourself'? Since
When are doctors priests? Is that how
They taught you to deliver a diagnosis?"
Too directly for the elder's comfort, the
Younger man met the fury in his eyes.
With unsettling calm, his clear reply,
"Sir, it's the only real medicine we have."

Dear Creator,
Whenever I get caught up in the "right" way to do a thing,
please remind me that what is done in love and with
forgiveness is done "right." Please don't let the lessons of
humans blind me to the lessons of the Spirit, nor the emotions
of the moment to the truth.

† † †

V.A. Hospital

His dry, fleshless finger
Touched her face — fresh, lineless cheek —
And bade her
"Get out of here. You're young.
There are so many babies and young ones
To hold your time and trouble.
Find them.
Leave us here to smoke and laugh and cough.
We have many old jokes among us.
Find the children. There
You may work your magic to cure,
Or grow sad and weary
Beside them."

Dear Creator,
Help me to invest carefully, wisely, and generously. I know
that it does no good to spend my resources on those who cannot grow or will not hear. The trouble is that I can't seem to
tell the difference between those who will someday use what
I offer and those who cannot accept anything. I want to give
the benefit of the doubt, but I want to do it without emptying
my coffers to unreceptive people, and then dying myself. Generosity, energy, kindness and discernment. I know it's a pretty
tall order, but I think I'm short on all of them. Thank you.

† † †

Bastard

Son,
She slapped my face.
Stopped me right there on the street and slapped my face.
She saw me holding you and loving your brown, golden
Laugh. I kissed you and put you back in the
Carriage and she strolled right up and slapped my face.
Them other ladies laughed behind their hands,
And she stood there like some righteous dragon,
Smiling down at me.
Her boy went to prison. (I heard *that* from Mrs. Freeborn.)
I thought to send her your diploma,
The one sayin' you're a lawyer now.
I thought to stand over her and laugh and show
Pictures of the house you bought me.
(Can I ever thank you, Boy?)
But I kept them and my smile to myself.
I couldn't slap her face
Knowing what a right smart sting it leaves.

Dear Creator,
There are so many lessons I could stand to learn. Among them,
that my actions are speaking loud and clear, whatever my words
might be saying at the time. However healthy a tree I might
appear to be, people know a sour fruit when they taste it. Please
guide me to humility and a pure heart so that my fruit will be
worth sampling. Thank you.

† † †

SocialWorkerNurseAidWoman

I fired her. Yes, I fired her.
It may seem small —
That she lied about that sick time —
But she never did belong
In this job.
Too involved. She just got
Too involved. Downright odd she was.
I mean, really. Used her days off
To visit clients. Imagine.
I hear she gave them money
Sometimes. On her salary? Imagine.
Watched their kids. Gave them rides.
On her days off, mind you.
I took my chance when I saw it.
Yes, I fired her.
A woman like that doesn't
Belong in the business of
Caring for people.

Dear Creator,
I struggle with this business of helping. Sometimes, it seems,
I give more than I can afford. Those times leave me tired and
angry. Then there are times when I see my contribution really
make a difference, and my enthusiasm carries me along further than I knew possible. There is so much reward and so much
frustration. It's difficult for me to know where you would have
me pour my energy. I'll try to listen for your guiding voice.

† † †

Soup Kitchen

Been comin' here for
Goin' on five years.
Been here longer myself
Than most o' them vollinteers.
Somebody said they're gonna
Tear it down.
Build a high-rise, maybe,
Or a 24-hour store.
What the hell we need that for?
That's just a lot of neighbors
Raisin' dust. They don't want
Their children to see us in here.
Or want to walk by us "dangerous types."
This year we're lucky.
This year we're "The Homeless,"
So they'll prob'ly just relocate this place.
Years ago we were just "bums"
And got run outta everyplace
But here.

Dear Creator,
Please show me my responsibilities toward the truly unfortunate. I know that you bless the poor, the hungry, the
weeping. While I may at times be any of those, or none of
those, I owe them my respect and attention. Help me to
recognize the opportunities for reaching out, and give me the
strength to keep at it. Thank you.

† † †

State Hospital

Hannah and Myra. Both survived
The Jewish camps.
Both used bony fingers to
Pick away the lice
On other thin companions.
Tattooed numbers on upper arms remind.
Hannah visits Myra
In this place of endless
Mumbling, wasted souls.
Hannah, so strong, resigned.
Forgiving; forgiven of the torture,
Never (no, never) forgetting.
While Myra, eyes turned inside,
Smoking cigarettes and humming childish tunes,
Forgets in her rancor
How to move among souls
Who mean you no harm.
But Hannah knows the saving craft
Of walking next to hatred
Without ever being stolen.

Dear Creator,
I'm not sure what makes the difference between a real learner
of your truths and one who only appears to be listening.
Whatever be my lessons in this life, I ask your patience as you
teach them to one who is nearsighted, and perhaps a little deaf,
but who hopes to compensate with persistence.

† † †

Neighbor

It was all he could do not to slap that child.
Impudent little bastard.
He had heard the children fighting in the alley —
Such a racket —
And had pulled them, arm from shoulder,
Away from one another,
Carefully explaining how to share a
Ball and glove. (Actually,
Quite a patient lesson, he had thought.)
And the child asked to play in his yard.
"No (politely), that would not be possible."
Who *were* this child's parents to let him
Learn such impudence?
The child almost spat the words:
"How do you know about sharing a glove when you keep
Your big fat green grass yard to yourself?"
It was all he could do not to slap that child.

Dear Creator,
I want you to be always forgiving and generous with me. I am not inclined to be so with others. It would serve me right if you were only as generous with me as I am with others. Always you offer before I ask, and more than I imagined. Help me imitate your example and memorize your generosity.

† † †

Sentence

I held the letter, shaken
And wondered how many
Of my own careful markings
Had so soundly,
Blindly moved a reader.
How often had I held the pen
In passion to be honest
And pierced a gentle soul?
Or poured the warm of loving
On a distant friend?
Allowed a pencil and some minutes
To change the thought or heart
Of some remote comrade,
And never seen the tears?

Dear Creator,
Words are so powerful. And thoughts. They can shape our
direction for life, cure misunderstandings, reframe trauma into
growth. When I send my words ahead, either deliberately or
carelessly, give me the grace to accompany them with love.
Let them not arrive without thought on unprepared ears. Help
me to correctly estimate the power of my words and thoughts
and to use them only as a way to greater light.

† † †

Knitting

It was her first time
To make a thing.
But her face informed
A careful watcher
Of tender plans
For the wearer of
This clumsy effort.
In smiling thought, she remade knitted
Tangled sections. Worked again and again the piece,
Until it lay perfect across her hand.
No child ever came as
Eagerly loved
As the one who would sport,
In mother's hungry arms,
The pale green sweater with the seed stitch cuffs.

Dear Creator,
In the wake of Jesus' life on earth, I struggle to realize that my
life is no less a preparation than was John the Baptist's. Though
I am not always clear about what I am preparing and being
prepared for, there is a constant sense (for a careful listener)
that I must continue to be ready. Some days this means just
getting through the day safely and harming no one. Sometimes
it means pouring energy into another's struggle or problems.
Now and then it may be training myself in some new skill. And
the days that I love most are those when I need only celebrate
what already is and what is to come. Thank you.

† † †

Admit One

The letter fell
Out of fingers numbed
By the chance to hold
Again a daughter.
The angry echo of insults,
Hatred.
Aching, dull knowing
That freedom would teach,
Or break forever,
The lesson of forgiveness.
Seven years from those
Young-blurred visions of perfect.
(Would they ever know each other's part?)
Careful not to dare expect, she'd waited.
Now, this letter.
Careful not to dare expect, she wrote reply.
"Yes. Come." She cried. Careful not to dare expect.

Dear Creator,
How many times have I moved away from you in anger or
frustration, not seeing the whole picture clearly, only to return
in sheepish apology sometime later and ask for another chance?
How many times have I received an open-armed response and
gifts beyond my vaguest hopes? When will I learn the patience
and generosity that you have modeled so often? Maybe this
time. Thank you.

† † †

Parole

She prayed like that
For hours.
Third pew from the back,
Head resting on the rail.
Then a candle to the virgin
And another prayer by
The side altar.
What sin could need
Such fervent prayer?
Hard to think this small woman
Transgressed large in anyone's eyes
But her own.
And yet the look, as she passed
Down the aisle to the outside sun —
Unmistakably,
Gratitude.

Dear Creator,
Even though I know the relief of forgiveness, I find it difficult
(impossible?) to forgive the very ones who could most use the
freedom my forgiveness would afford them. Why do you suppose I cling so tenaciously to my righteousness in the face of
my owned checkered history? Please give me the generosity
of spirit to let go of the anger and unforgiveness I harbor. You
know better than any the huge debt I have to those who have
offered me reprieve.

† † †

Artiste

They were her passion.
Exquisite pieces of vision —
Tiny chips of spirit
Fashioned of time and pain.
Flowers, birds, clouds, stars
To an untrained eye.
Agony. Tracings of courage
Poured millimeter by millisecond
Through the stiffness of a brush
Held in clenched teeth.
Held to tell a springtime story
Or a roughened tree bark truth
All but forgotten by the stiffened
Limbs so motionless at
Her side.

Dear Creator,
I waste a lot of time thinking that if I were *really* talented or
brilliant I would be a better instrument for your use. It is, I
think, my excuse for not putting my energy into the many real
and meaningful contributions that I *am* capable of making.
Then I experience someone whom I would have thought to
be "poor soil" blooming and brightening some small corner
of the planet. And those that I would have considered "fertile ground" making no contribution at all. Since I have some
control over how "fertile" I am as soil for your garden, help
me rid myself of some of the rocks and begin to produce richly
the fruit of your love.

† † †

Nightlight

The child startled, woke
And dragging blanket, bear, and fear,
Slow carefully peered the hall.
Saw that blessed light
Reach from under (parents') door!
"Did the thunder wake you?"
He hardly hears, but burrows narrowly between
Familiar smells of grown-up PJ's
And doesn't catch the smile pass between them.
Nor they the look of untold safe and grateful
That leads him back to sleep.

Dear Creator,
Help me to know precisely where to place this lamp. Not under a bushel. I understand that part. But to shine it in the face of those who have lived long in the dark, wouldn't that be showing off, not to mention cruel? Better than that, help me to remember the times I have been grateful for a light shone at my feet, so I could better see the path. And in those times when the path seems more muddy than clear, when it seems impossible not to give it up, remind me that once there was one very like myself whom even the winds and the seas obeyed. He walked the path on darker nights than this, and held his light behind so others could see to follow.

† † †

American Legion

I worked detox that night
And watched a man named William T. Jacobs
(at least that's who he said he was)
Pick *some*thing off his clothes all night.
All night, eight hours, one little thing
After another. Pluck, pluck, pluck.
"God*dam*" he'd say, "God*dam*."
He fell asleep toward morning,
Just in time for us
To wake him for a shot of valium.
Succumbing to its sterile absolution
He left his clothes alone.
I understand he died a few weeks later,
But they never knew if it was
Suicide or what.

Dear Creator,
I know there are a hundred obstacles between me and the person I'm hoping to become. Show them to me one at a time, and I will be grateful for each chance to grow. And when we have slowly, quietly overcome my legion of personal demons, let me celebrate with you and rest freely in the clear, warm light of your loving Spirit.

† † †

Prophet

We left the church
Vaguely unsatisfied
With that "healer"
Who is so famous on TV.
As we moved forward,
Awash in the crowd,
I was suddenly weak
And dizzy.
"I knew!" She smiled up
Excitedly from her wheelchair.
I realized she had touched me.
"I knew you were a healer," she repeated.
She gently squeezed my hand and we were separated
By the many trying to leave.

Dear Creator,
Help me to recognize the healer that is a part of my sacred
self. If I may touch other souls in a way that makes them
stronger, show me my part of it and give me the courage to
try. Show me, too, those who can help me become my best
self. I know you work so often through people I might not
suspect are your special healers. Open my eyes to know them.
This world could be so richly compassionate if, by the light
of your serene and healing grace, we could discover our gifts
for making each other whole.

† † †

Since Wen

"Since wen," she said,
"Did you be God?
Since wen do you know how
It be to see yo' baby die of a fit in the 'mergency room
Wif his brother lookin' on?
You white woman wif a pencil
In yo' hand.
You go back and tell them kids
Thet they ain't gonna be no food
In the kitchen. Just bugs.
No food cuz the govamint
Think we got too much money ahready."

Dear Creator,
So much around me seems unfair. I look for some "bureau"
or "center" or "office" where I can direct those who need
so much. Next time I try to refer them on, please say to me
as you did to the apostles, "You give them something to eat."
Remind me that I have every chance to multiply the portion
that I have. Give me your hand and your permission. Oh, and
send someone with baskets for the leftovers.

† † †

Baking Bread

Together we worked the dough,
Her tiny hands roundly invisible
Under firm forgiving bread.
Little wrists rising from a sculptured mound.
I (grown-up) explained,
"It is the yeast that makes the bread bigger and bigger,
And yummy so that we will want to eat it and be strong."
Open-eyed, she held my jaw in puttied gentle palms.
"I love you like yeast, Mommy."
A loving worship filled my soul and
I (aching) wondered how she so young
Knew completely what was only now
Coming clear to me.

Dear Creator,
I must admit it's difficult for me to have the kind of faith that
I often see in people I admire. Your parables of mustard seed
and leaven make perfect sense, knowing as I do your generous
Spirit. It is my own little step toward you that I have such difficulty taking. Although you have never failed to love me, there
is a part of my frightened, childish self that's always scared
to make the move. I ask for the freedom that would daily make
me as eager to seek you as a child running to meet a parent
at the end of a day.

† † †

MAY

You stand before me, eyebrows arched in a question. "And who do you think I am?"

Defensive and unprepared, I reply, "I know what I've been taught."

"Ah, yes. But what do you believe?"

Glancing up, I'm ready to attack. But there is no sarcasm in your eyes. Rather, they reflect genuine, intense interest. Clear and open, they draw me in . . . . I swallow the lump forming in my throat — why do I want to cry?

"I simply asked who you think I am. What has that triggered in you?"

Somehow, looking into your face, I know I can risk honesty. "It's your words, Jesus. Your words about denying myself to follow you. I've spent years establishing my identity. To ask me now to surrender the self I've found — to even consider that I would let someone else control me . . . ."

You sigh, and I must look away. I've offended you, I'm sure. Maybe even lost my soul. But you asked!

"My friend," you whisper, "do you think I haven't watched you climb your way to health and self-esteem? I've been there beside you, enabling, celebrating your very life. Why would I crush it now?"

"But you said . . . ."

"What I said was, what will you gain by winning the whole world, at the cost of your true self? It's only your false self you must deny if you come with me."

I step to the very edge of my theology and recall the symbols of my faith. Cross. Lamb. Crown. Manger. Mystery unfolds. I choose to understand. You are not merely a man; you are God incarnate. Friend. Liberator. Redeemer. It is safe. I will follow.

† † †

With a sense of risk and adventure, I joined the leadership of a two-day retreat for moderately retarded adults. God's love was our theme, and the program included not only nature walks and crafts, but also an introduction to silence and contemplative prayer. When it was announced that we would hike to the meadow, sit quietly among the grasshoppers and cornflowers, and wait for God, everyone was excited. Everyone, that is, but Margaret. With a loud groan, this assertive, frustrated child-woman reluctantly fell into line.

The cheerful band trekked wooded paths, delighting in the sunlit morning. Then, just as we stepped into the meadow, Margaret screamed, "No!" and fled as fast as her short, chubby frame would carry her.

A look of understanding flashed from my colleagues. I raced into the woods and eventually found Margaret perched atop a picnic table in an abandoned shelter. "Now I don't have to be quiet!" she grinned triumphantly.

Exhausted and impatient, I replied, "We can have our quiet time here." A powerful debate ensued:

"We can't, God's in the field!"
        "God's big enough to be in both places."
"But it's dirty! Look at all the dead leaves!"
        "God made the leaves, and loves them."
"But there's somebody's muddy boots!"
            "God doesn't mind muddy boots."
"But lady, I've been bad!"
            "God loves you just as you are."

Silence. Then a small, amazed voice. "Yeah? Then I'll be quiet." And she was — voluntarily — for ten minutes, after which she whispered, "Jesus is our Saviour. Amen."

Do you, like the disciples, yearn for a deeper prayer life, or are you running? What are your dead leaves, your muddy-boot excuses? Can you meet God when you've "been bad"? Take courage from Margaret. Choose to be quiet. Begin with the simple good news: "God loves you just as you are."

† † †

Tiny butterfly, you're brand new, aren't you? You fold your dainty yellow wings up and down repeatedly. Who taught you that? I've never observed the birth of flight before. I feel exquisitely honored.

But I wonder — can't you rest a bit? You look so strained. So anxious about your new life. I know you want to fly more than anything else, now that you know you can. You were a long time in that cocoon, weren't you? And even longer in the caterpillar state. Now you feel life's going to pass you by if you don't hurry and spread your wings. I know, because I've felt that way before. I feel it today.

I want to break forth and soar — free — all at once. I know I have potential for flight, for beautiful dance on the wings of the Spirit. But I'm afraid. Afraid of falling. Is that your dilemma?

I'm growing impatient. I want to see you lift your wings and move. Then perhaps I could gain courage for my spiritual journey. But you're not ready, are you? You just keep moving your wings up and down, making shadows in the sunshine. Could this be your meditation? Forgive me for intruding.

Suddenly you jump as if you've heard the word. Silently and purposefully you lift your soul — and resettle in the gravel. You bounce and flutter. It's not too comfortable, is it? But it's a beginning. A fine first landing station. You explore for a time and decide it's not for you.

Then into the grasses you plunge, sailing from bush to tree to cloud. There you go, my little friend. I love you. And I'll catch up with you later, after I've exercised my own wings. In the meantime, God's blessings! And — hooray!

> *Be not anxious . . . consider the lilies*
> *(and the butterflies) . . . .*

† † †

A divine appointment with the resurrected Christ! What could be more glorious? Yet as the disciples trudged up the Galilean mountain, at least one felt the pangs of an anxious heart:

> What am I doing on this path? I don't even know if I believe he's alive, and I'm on my way to a meeting supposedly called by Jesus! I wonder if he'll look the same. What will he ask of me this time? Will I be up to it? John's already around the bend . . . always ahead when it comes to faith! If I turn around now, I can be home in time for lunch — but what if it's true? What if Jesus really is going to be there? I must keep going.

At the dawn of the twenty-first century, little has changed. We are still called to meet Christ for instruction and challenge. We still respond with uncertainty:

> What am I doing on this one-way street in a city not my own? I don't even know what I believe about life after death, and I'm called to the bedside of someone with AIDS. I wonder how he'll look. What will he ask of me? Will I be up to it? Others know how to do this, why aren't they here? If I turn around now, I can be home before dark. But what if it's true? What if it is really Christ who waits in that bed? I must go in.

> *Jesus Christ, unique Child of God,*
> *have mercy on us. Forgive our ambivalence,*
> *our sluggish pace, and restore our confidence*
> *through the good news we already know. Steer us away*
> *from competition with others who minister in*
> *your name, and grant us a perfect balance of*
> *peace and adventure as we go forth in the*
> *light of your constant presence.*

† † †

It was a holy moment and Peter wanted it to last forever. Impulsively, spontaneously, and no doubt with reasonable confidence in his own handiwork, Peter suggested that he, James, and John construct tabernacles for the great prophets of God. He imagined booths that would protect and preserve the profound — booths that would house the miraculous, that would ensure that the sacred would endure. To Peter it seemed a splendid idea!

The booths were not to be. Before Jesus could respond to his passionate but naive friend, God's own presence descended. A thick cloud rolled in, enveloped the frightened disciples, and commanded their attention. The voice of the Almighty spoke the only words needed: "This is my Child, my Chosen; to this one you shall listen!"

Ponder this passage, allowing your imagination to settle where it will. With whom do you identify? If you had been on that mountaintop, dozing between prayers, how would you have reacted to the sudden transformation of your teacher? When Moses and Elijah joined Jesus, would you have believed your senses, struggled for rationale? Perhaps you were fatigued, hungry, or simply in need of air.

Read on, noting the contrast between life atop the mountain and life at its base. How would you have experienced re-entry?

Now consider your own life and present circumstances. Recall faces, scenes, and conversations of your past week. How does the holy intersect with the ordinary?

Sometimes my days seem so flat, God!
So uneventful! Yet I tremble when I think of
standing in the cloud of your presence. Resolve my
ambivalence. Transform it by your refreshing power,
that I might seek, recognize, and embrace each
holy moment. Forgive my schemes, my foolish
attempts to control your Spirit. When I
lose perspective, center me once again
in your unique Child, Jesus.

† † †

How the disciples must have tried Jesus' patience! They wanted to be effective ministers. They seemed generally committed and, when pressed, said they longed to be instruments of heavenly healing and restoration. At the same time, they often operated out of fear, dependency, competition, judgment, and pride. As a result, their ministries were sometimes impotent.

How tempting it must have been for Jesus to consider walking away and doing a one-man show! Or raising up a structure that would permit only the most docile devotees! These options must have seemed attractive, even efficient, given the little time Jesus knew he had.

Jesus also knew that God is not a God of isolation and autocratic power, but rather a God of partnership, covenants, and co-creativity. And so, risking the possibility that some might not be healed, that others might be offended, and that God's work might be at least temporarily diluted, Jesus elected to live out his call in the midst of a very human community. Although disappointed and frustrated, he continued to instruct and encourage his friends, showing faith in their leadership potential. As his term on earth drew to a close, Jesus steadily and thoughtfully placed his beloved earth and all its inhabitants in the hands of amateur lovers.

> Consider your own life and ambitions. Where do you strive to hold the reins of power and control? When do you feel most frustrated? Judgmental? Impotent? Competitive? Now reflect on the patience and presence of the resurrected Christ. Imagine the two of you sharing, friend to friend, over a pot of tea. Believe that Christ cares about the details of your story, and allow yourself the luxury of absolute honesty. Relax. Listen. Receive perfect respect, perfect understanding, perfect instruction, perfect love.

† † †

Sitting in a booth at the airport coffee shop, I nurse my third glass of iced tea. With every passing minute I grow more restless. Sure, I agreed to meet Gina's plane with you, on behalf of the church. But I thought we'd just slip into the crowds, claim our charge, and disappear into the safety of my car. How was I to know Gina's plane would be late?

Your face is so calm it annoys me. Perhaps you don't comprehend our predicament. Maybe you haven't been in this country long enough to fully understand the risks of transporting an illegal alien.

When I can stand it no longer, I whisper sharply, "How long can we wait?"

"As long as we're asked to. What is your fear?"

Defensive and unprepared, I mutter something about respecting the law. You are unimpressed. "My friend, " you gently scold, "we are exactly where God called us to be. Should we leave this woman to the mercy of the laws of unjust rulers? Don't you understand?" I shake my head. For the next hour, you teach me through your own story. I learn new words for human suffering in Central America. I gain insight into divine love and compassion. I discover that you, a physician, were arrested and tortured because you gave medical aid to the "enemy." With eyes glistening and head held high, you confess, "I had no choice! The love of Jesus in my heart made me bind their wounds."

An anonymous voice announces the arrival of Gina's plane. I hesitate, not out of fear, but rather to scrawl a message on the back of my paper placemat. Then, falling in step behind you and Christ, I hurry to the gate and raise my sign for all to see: "BUENAS NOCHES, GINA! WELCOME!"

*Jesus Christ, unique Child of God, have mercy
on us. You ask us to follow you, and we want to.
But sometimes, even to give a cup of cold water in this
society requires a moral, ethical, political decision.
Where's the right? Where's the wrong? Dear Jesus,
hold our hands and show us the way.*

† † †

Sullen, angry, and confused, I hurry down the dusty Palestinian road. Events of the past hour have left me exhausted, yet I summon enough strength to forcefully kick a few stones out of my way.

Your long, healthy legs keep up splendidly; you waste no time with small talk. "Perhaps you wish you were kicking me."

After nearly three years, I'm still startled by your candor and insight.

"What is it, my friend? Where does your anger come from?"

I am both annoyed and relieved by your persistence. How painful it is to be in discord with you, my beloved teacher! Without missing a step, I glance sideways into your waiting eyes. I am steadied. Encouraged.

"It was your words, Jesus! Your words and your manner back there! Those men wanted to follow you, but you were so . . . so . . . ."

"So stern? Yes, I was. I wanted them to take seriously their claims to commitment. I wanted them to realize that partnership with God requires one's fullest attention. There is no time for ambivalence. No room for excuses."

"And no room for loved ones?" There. I've said it.

"So that's the source of your storm! You think I'm tightening my requirements. You suspect my disciples are no longer permitted homes and personal loves!"

I blush and glance for more stones to kick.

"Oh friend, I do not deny you the goodness of intimacy. Rather, I call you to boldly proclaim that *all* God's people are entitled to compassion, justice, and love. I simply ask that you allow nothing — no one — to stand in the way of sharing that good news. Do you see?"

I pause from my flight. For one precious moment, we share a common vision. "Yes, Jesus, I see. And because I do, I will journey alongside you to Jerusalem and beyond."

† † †

Grandpa Fershee was dying. His family knew it. The hospital staff knew it. Most important, Grandpa knew it. After eighty-seven years, there was nothing to do now but rest, allow the medication to ease the pain of a congested heart, and wait for transition into the glory of God's presence.

Taking a break, one of Grandpa's nurses joined my mother in the visitors' lounge. "Such a remarkable man!" she glowed. "Your father-in-law served in how many lands?"

Mother was startled. "I think you've misunderstood!"

The nurse's face fell. "But in the last few hours, he's told me all about his hospital in Nigeria! He described the climate, the food, the natives' clothes, even the layout of the compound. I could almost smell the anesthetic!"

Mother shook her head. "I'm sorry to disappoint you. Mr. Fershee was not in Nigeria; his daughter was. Several of his children served as foreign missionaries."

"And India? China? Australia? Are they just an old man's fantasies?"

"Oh, he would have loved to travel. To be formally educated, to serve his God professionally. But life took strange turns. Nine children, the Great Depression, a chronically ill wife. The best he could do was keep food on the table and coal in the stove, and raise a family rooted in the Word of God."

"But the details!"

"He must have memorized his children's letters. And after retirement, he read and studied faithfully at the public library. We knew he talked daily with God regarding 'the work,' but we had no idea that . . . ."

"That he really was a missionary?" The nurse laughed. "I knew he wasn't confused!"

> Relax, child, My world thrives on love, not guilt.
> Let faces, names, and scenes flow through your
> prayers. You will recognize your passion. You will
> discover your work.

✝ ✝ ✝

I adjusted the blanket over Zeb's three-year-old feet and slowed the pace of our rocking chair. It had been a delight for me, a single, childless woman, to spend the evening with my neighbor's son. After sharing animal-shaped sandwiches, racing dump trucks, and reading half a dozen stories, we rested silently, nourished and content.

At last I rose to slip Zeb into his bed. Stirring in my arms he announced clearly, "God could've made your face black."

Startled, I settled both of us back in the rocker. "Why, yes," I replied, "I suppose so." To myself I added, "The poor boy's dreaming! I'll keep still; he'll go back to sleep."

But my tiny blond friend was wide awake. Peering deep into my eyes he asked earnestly, "Where does God keep the pile of faces?"

I could so easily have laughed! Instead I chose to listen carefully to a three-year old's perspectives on heaven. I was asked to consider a land where the once-lame now dance in pools of chocolate pudding . . . where children have forgotten what guns look like . . . where diversity is celebrated . . . where harmony reigns.

Stroking my cheek with his soft, pink fingers, Zeb concluded, "God knows we're coming back some day."

I nodded through my tears and recalled the many sermons, books, and Bible studies along my spiritual journey. How I had struggled to understand God's value system and its link to my own salvation. Now, through a sleepy child-prophet, God had revealed what ultimately mattered. Relaxing my grip on sophisticated theologies, I rocked to one rhythm: "God knows I'm coming back someday."

God, you have hidden these things from the wise and revealed them to babes. I ask only to understand what it means that my name is written in heaven.

† † †

Hoping to soothe his own conscience, a busy, sophisticated Christian asked his pastor, "Just who is my neighbor in this fast, complex society?"

The pastor replied, "Last week an elderly woman walked down a neighborhood street. She was returning home from the market when she was attacked by a gang of drug dealers who stripped her of her coat, snatched her purse and groceries, threw her to the ground, and ran off, leaving her half dead.

"It was twelve-thirty in the afternoon and the street was crowded. But no one paid attention to the woman. Stepping right over her, a seminary student rushed across the street to catch a bus. 'Can't be late for my exam,' she reminded God. Likewise, a politician glanced at the old woman, then crossed the street. 'There might be cameras around,' he rationalized. 'Besides, I supported funding for women's shelters in this city; I've done my part!'

"Rose-tinted streetlights replaced the sun's natural glow, and another workday surrendered to city night life. Making one last attempt to rise from the frigid concrete, the new street person fell back and cried with pain.

"It was a prostitute who heard the cry, saw the woman at her feet, and was immediately flooded with compassion. She quickly wrapped the victim in her own fur coat, hailed a taxi, and rushed her charge to the nearest hospital. There she spent the night negotiating on the patient's behalf, paying cash to a system that did not care about a stolen medical card.

"So, you think Christian neighborliness is outmoded, do you?" Receiving no reply, the pastor looked up. His guest had vanished.

Still, the question remained, leaving the pastor to ponder his own busy, sophisticated life.

> *Grant me the courage today, Lord,*
> *to slow down and love.*

What distracts you from a richer worship experience? What captures your attention and prevents you from moving deeper toward that holy center where Christ resides?

> Perhaps it's fear. Fear of being alone with the Divine, especially when you're feeling self critical and inadequate.

> Perhaps it's fatigue — maybe even burn-out. Maybe you feel you need an extra hour's sleep in the morning to offset the late night meetings that you're expected to attend.

> Maybe you're procrastinating, thinking you'll struggle through the current month's obligations and then you'll establish a schedule of daily prayer and meditation. In the meantime, your calendar pages for next month are beginning to fill — and you prepare for another ride on the modern scheduling merry-go-round, promising yourself that next month you'll dismount and make retreat.

> Could it be that another has taken the place of Christ in your life? Have your boundaries faded? Is your spiritual path overgrown with weeds because you neglected it for so long?

> Perhaps you, like Martha, are caught up in the whirlwind of service — doing good works, God's works, yet ignoring your own spirit's cries for another drink of living water.

Try to identify the things that are blocking you from worship. Give them names and imagine their shapes. Permit them to move into focus in your mind and acknowledge them — not with embarrassment or disdain, but with respect and tenderness. Let the blocks themselves become your prayer. Release them into the hands of the waiting Christ, and simply wait in the silence for the one who fashioned you and set you free to speak of Christ's love.

† † †

*". . . the people marveled. But some of them said,
'He cast out demons by Beelzebul' . . . while others, to
test him, sought from him a sign from heaven."*

Such a diverse crowd it was that gathered around Christ and
the newly healed man! If you had been there, what would you
have done?

Would you have been able to discern the movement of "the
finger of God" and recognized divine healing when you saw
it? Would you have found the courage to voice your praise
despite hostility, scorn, and seedy plots?

Perhaps you would not have openly accused Jesus of devilish
tricks, but would have merely stood by watching the confron-
tation, silently relieved that the strange carpenter from
Nazareth was at last being held accountable for his actions.
You might have been amused. Anxious to see more "heavenly
wonders." Curious about Jesus' spiritual prowess and ability
to pass certain tests.

Spend some time reflecting on your own life and present
circumstances, and try to identify a specific area in which you
need a miracle of healing. Be aware of your cynicism, your
doubts, your temptation to test the power of God.

What would your healing look like? What would it take for
you to know that you had been touched by "the finger of
God"?

You might wish to illustrate with colored pens or modeling
clay. Pray your way through to the answers, relaxing under
the guidance of the Holy Spirit. Allow colors, words, forms,
and symbols to emerge. Await the moment when you will be
ready to add visual prayers of trust, marvel, and thanksgiving.

† † †

"Peace, Jesus? Your parting gift to humanity was peace?"

"What do you think would have been a more fitting bequest, my friend?"

"Well, courage. Courage to face the trials ahead. It must have been frightening to remain in Jerusalem without you."

"I could have imparted courage, it is true. But courage without peace soon becomes aggression. Aggression is not the way of our God."

"Well then, wisdom. Why didn't you leave the disciples with an extra measure of wisdom? Perhaps then the Gospel could have been spread more rapidly, more efficiently."

"Wisdom is a virtue. But wisdom by itself often leads to arrogance and pride. Only when it is combined with inner peace does wisdom — even heavenly wisdom — remain humble and effective. My friend, I am willing to answer more questions; I will gladly discuss other gifts I might have given. But I wonder — what about your own life? Are you not curious about my gift to you?"

"Your gift of peace, I presume."

"Yes, peace. Are you disappointed with your inheritance?"

"Perhaps. In these days, peace seems so flimsy! So nebulous. So impossible."

"And so it is, when designed by human hearts. My friend, I give you another peace. Mine is the peace that transcends earthly understanding. It is the peace that is stable when all around you is collapsing. My peace accompanies wherever you go, strengthens and nourishes in the very face of death. My peace equips you to build strong bridges over hostile waters. It calls you to view all of life thoughtfully. It encourages harmony. It highlights truth."

"Jesus, I want this peace! What must I do?"

"Simply open your heart, my friend. Touch the peace that lies within. Unwrap the gift already given."

† † †

The junior Sunday school class which I taught was making window ornaments from dried seeds and flowers. Pressed between colored tissue and popsicle sticks, they would provide some early spring cheer for the children's bedrooms.

Nearly everyone was busy creating. Brad, however, wandered the classroom, jabbing elbows, refusing to work, yet mocking the others' products.

I sighed and started across the room, gearing up for one more reprimand. For months I'd struggled to find something that would soften this boy's resistance, something that would help him understand that, despite his hostility, I loved him.

As so often happens, God used a child to begin the breakthrough. Before I could reach Brad, he was engaged in a most profound dialogue with Heather, a doe-eyed, sensitive child who was in touch with the values of heaven.

"Huh! What's that s'posed to be?"

"I don't know yet."

"I'll tell ya what it is! It's nothin' but a pile of junk! Dead weeds and crackly old seeds! Y'know, you're gettin' your dress dirty!"

Heather paused, stared at her lap, then said decidedly, "Yeah, but it's worth it, 'cause I'm helping something that started out nice become even more beautiful!"

"Oh yeah? Well, I'll ask ya again, what's it s'posed to be?"

"An' I'll tell you again, I don't know yet! I won't know 'til I hold it up to the light!" Then, very softly, Heather added, "Brad, you are like these dead seeds and flowers. Go sit in the sunshine, and see what you become!"

It was a holy turning point. Responding literally to Heather's challenge, Brad sat daily at his bedroom window and soon flourished in the warm love light that flowed from parents, teachers, friends, therapists, and God.

God, what would I become if I sat daily in your light?

† † †

Jesus, when we invite you into our homes to dine at our tables, we expect you to follow the common courtesies of proper washing and polite conversation. But you come in and insult us! You confront us with our hypocrisy, our injustice, our failure to love. When you treat us this way, we don't want to invite you any more. We don't want your truth to expose us that way. We prefer our little deceptions. Why must you be so honest?

We prefer to think that your exposure of human failing should be directed out there against those who practice injustice against us. But you come into our homes and say to us, "You are the ones! You have failed to love!"

You are right, Jesus. We have so often neglected your Gospel commandment to love our brothers and sisters as you have loved us. We have neglected the poor. We have despised those who do not measure up to our standards. We have not reached out to the sick or to those in prison or to the homeless. We have so often failed to live out your Gospel calling.

Forgive us for our neglect, Jesus, for we have chosen to follow you. We continue to sit at your feet in our homes and learn from you. You have called us to a new way. That way is hard, but it is the way of redemption and healing for our wounds and for the suffering of our world.

Enter our very being, Jesus, so that your Spirit may empower us to live out your love within our human family. Touch us so that we may heal our world in your name.

† † †

My child, do not flee the darkness. Do not fear the grave. I see even the nesting sparrow with my eye. I have numbered each hair of your head. I hold you in my hand. How could I not know your dwelling beneath the earth?

The body dies. The persecutor and oppressor are limited by the grave. Their power is exhausted. They slip beneath the vast sea of forgotten pain. But you shall be with me in paradise. I have gone before to prepare for you a dwelling place.

Therefore, do not be afraid to stand before judges and presidents and legislators who dare to condemn those whom the Lord has redeemed. I shall teach you what to say before them in that hour. Their prisons and weapons shall not constrain you from your truth.

Yes, my child, you must confess your faith in me before those who cannot believe that you are mine. You must proclaim my love to all the little ones who would come to me, whatever their acceptability. Let no one prevent them, for my realm belongs to these. The hypocrisy of those who would deny them entrance shall be revealed. Their cloak of righteousness shall become a tattered rag, unfit to cover their nakedness. My little ones shall walk in love, unafraid.

Remember that I have said the first shall be last, and the last shall be first. Those who have been despised and rejected shall stand redeemed and glorified in places of honor in my house of many mansions. So you need not fear the darkness. The grave is but the gateway into your eternal home.

† † †

There was a certain gay man in America. He was a commercial artist in a company where he could be open without discrimination. He was respected and rewarded well for his work. His home was located in the best part of town. It was furnished in the exquisite taste of the true artist. He often hosted lavish parties to which he invited entertainers, politicians, and social leaders of his elite class. He was content with his life style and enjoyed his position as a social trend setter. He was greatly admired and everyone hoped to be invited to his next event.

One day he sat planning his next party, trying to decide what theme he should use as a focus for the entertainment. He began to feel very tired and feverish, and he remembered that his energy level had seemed sluggish recently. So he made an appointment to see his doctor the next day. Within several weeks he was diagnosed as having AIDS.

Suddenly, his world seemed to collapse. His friends called him less often. His co-workers seemed nervous when he stopped by to chat. Quite a few invited guests were busy the night of his last party. His days felt long and tiring, and his bills began to pile up. He began to contemplate his life, and it seemed empty to him, even as he touched his prized antiques and stared at his beautiful works of art. His spirit grew weary of its weight.

He considered his impending death. What did it mean? As his spirit moved beyond the grave, what hope would draw him? What God awaited him? Slowly, unsteadily, he began a journey into the depth of his spirit. He began a search for God.

✝ ✝ ✝

Where, my child, have you stored your treasure? Where have you committed your heart during your journey through life? Have you sought riches and power and prestige among the nations of the world? Or have you cast your lot with the poor, the homeless, the drug addicts of your community? Have you used your riches to keep mental patients out of your section of the city? Or have you spent time seeking political support for the task of sheltering and ministering to those cast out into the streets who have fallen through the bureaucratic cracks in human services systems? Where is your treasure, dear child?

Jesus gave up the power of his lineage and his authority as rabbi to identify with the powerless in Hebrew culture: women, children, lepers, sinners. We become his followers when we are willing to make our home with the humble, to use our power in the service of the powerless. In the humility of low estate we become like Jesus. He so identified with the tax collectors, prostitutes, and sinners of his time that he shared their humiliation, even to the extent of exposure on a cross of shame. He gave up his life to redeem the outcasts and criminals who needed his healing touch.

Are we less than our brother Jesus? Have we placed our treasure at the disposal of the political powers, the economic giants of finance, the military-industrial complex — of those powers that seek to dominate a world in which the rich get richer and the poor get poorer? If we have been given abundance, we must remember not to hoard it for ourselves. We must give it away, so that our treasure may lie in our heavenly abode. If we have been given much, much shall be required of us.

† † †

Jesus, we have been told that you are the prince of peace. When you were born in Bethlehem of Judea in the days of Herod the king, angels sang glory to God in the highest, and on earth peace among all. We thought you preached nonviolence, peace, and justice for all people of earth. And now you tell us not to suppose that you have come to bring peace on earth, but rather that you have come to bring division and dissensions in the family. Father and son, mother and daughter shall be divided against one another. The family shall be torn asunder. Jesus, we do not understand.

My children, you are not bound by an old morality that withholds my love from those who cannot meet its liberating demands. I have called you to freedom. I have called you to a new way. My way offers love to all. Only my love can heal the wounds that have condemned the sinner and the outcast to a lesser place. The community of the so-called righteous resists my love because I seek out the lost and offer them healing and restoration into a new wholeness that cannot be known by those who refuse to suffer.

So I do bring division and dissension to a world bound in a decaying ethic that enforces the rights of the privileged over justice for the little ones who call upon my name. Those who follow my Gospel will turn the world upside down. They shall come before authorities in my name. The world will hate them. Their families will reject them. But my little ones need not fear, for I have chosen them to enter into my realm. They shall rest in my peace.

† † †

O Yahweh! Once you came in the darkness of Mount Sinai. Your cloud covered the mountain where only Moses approached to speak with you face to face. We, the people, were afraid and did not comprehend your glory. We refused to hear your truth and follow your commandment because we stood in awe of your majesty and judgment. We saw only your darkness and we feared your presence.

O Jesus! Now you have come to us again. This time you walked in the light where we could see your face, where we could behold your glory. You came to be one of us, so that we did not need to fear your mysterious darkness any more. You spoke plainly to us so that this time we could comprehend your grace and truth.

O God! We still hide from you. We still wonder whether you really do receive us, for we have heard too often that we cannot be your children. We still fear your judgment. We still hide our faces from you. We push you behind a cloud of anxious doubt concerning your offering of love and acceptance. Grant us the courage to take hold of your promises, for you have come to dwell among us. We are your own, and your outstretched hand beckons us to come to you and receive the right to become the children of God because we dare to believe in Jesus' name. Out of the darkness has come a great light, and your light has touched our hearts with the joy of your salvation.

O God of both darkness and light, we have become your children. You have carried us in the darkness of your womb. You have birthed us into the glorious light of day. We revel in the life you have given us. We have become your beloved ones.

† † †

Were you there when Pilate spilled the blood of the Galileans and mingled their blood with the sacrifices? Were you there when European settlers slaughtered the Native Americans so as to possess free, undivided land? Were you there when the slave traders kidnapped and murdered African peoples for the sake of commerce in sugar, cotton, and rum? Were you there when the Nazis slaughtered Jews, gypsies, and gays because they were not members of the super-race? Were you there when Americans of Japanese descent were herded into concentration camps for fear that they might aid the enemy? Were you there when violence was done to those who were "different" or "inferior" or "impure"?

Yes, we were there, because our land, our government, our resources were built on the altar of a violated humanity, sacrificed for the sake of Western culture's success. We are of Rome and of Europe and of the United States. We despised those who were less than we were, those who were greater sinners, because they suffered this fate. Because we succeeded, we thought we were better. After all, we know the immutable law of the survival of the fittest!

Dear Jesus, you have said that we must repent, or we shall likewise perish. But how are we to repent of our sin? We are caught in the web of a system that sometimes violates our dignity, as it has violated the dignity of so many others. We would repent, but we don't know how. We would change our world, but it seems so monolithic, so huge, so immutable.

Dear Saviour, you showed us the way long ago — the way of love, humility, and nonviolence. Show us again today how your way redeems our souls and the soul of humanity.

† † †

We all know the rules. You shall do no work on the Sabbath. You shall not murder. You shall not commit adultery. Not only do we know them, we embellish them. We multiply them. Then we judge those who fail to abide by them. We blame the persons afflicted with AIDS for their tragic condition. We condemn the incest victim who aborts her father's baby. We jail the prostitute who solicits the politician's wealth. We are so sure that we would never fall prey to the human weaknesses that lead others to fail in fulfilling God's commandments.

Jesus, why do you insist on breaking the rules? Why do you heal on the Sabbath? Why do you accept the adulterous woman? Why do you forgive the murderer and the robber? Don't you know the commands of God? You should support the rules. You should stand for law and order, lest the destructive acts of the mass of humanity overwhelm our systems of righteousness and justice.

Twenty centuries later, Jesus weeps — alone, weary, and sad. We have not yet learned compassion for the old woman bent double from eighteen years in spiritual bondage. We have not yet learned to touch the leper with healing hands. We have yet to offer alternatives to those who turn to crime because they cannot house and feed the children. We have not yet learned that there can be no justice when there is no compassion; that there can be no healing without risking; that there can be no peace when domestic violence destroys our children.

*Jesus, you taught us that we must
sometimes break the rules. Love must supersede
the law. Justice and peace must flow like a river.
Grant us the compassion of your healing touch
as we reach out to our sisters and brothers
in your name.*

✝ ✝ ✝

O Lord, what is this realm you keep preaching about? You say it is a mustard seed which grows into a shelter for the birds. It is leaven that fills three pecks of meal. It has a narrow gate, and when the door is shut, even those who have heard your Gospel cannot enter. Abraham, Isaac, Jacob, and all the prophets will be there. They will come from the east and west, north and south, to recline at the table.

We are anxious to enter into your realm because we have always wanted to partake of the good things of life. We want to recline at the feast and take pleasure in your company. We thought that we should be first. We have always lived a good life. We have gone to church and prayed and given our tithes. We have paid our way and worked hard to get ahead. We should be first. We deserve it.

But you say that the last will be first and the first will be last. What kind of realm is it that does not reward those who have labored hard for achievement and recognition? Your realm is upside down, and we don't know how to get in.

Dear Jesus, teach us the way of humility. Help us give up our pride and our striving for competitive status. We have difficulty learning a new way. We are afraid we will lose everything if we give up one inch of hard-won gain. We need your word of assurance that in your realm there is enough for everyone — that no one will be left in need, even those who enter last.

† † †

O Jerusalem, Jerusalem, the city that kills the prophets! Jesus wept over the city that had killed the messengers who went before him. He knew that he, too, had to go up to Jerusalem to stand trial and be murdered to satisfy those who refused to hear the message of God's love. He knew that he would join his brother and sister prophets who had also called for repentance, justice, and faithfulness. He was going up to Jerusalem to die.

He wanted to gather his children together, like a mother hen who protects and nurtures her brood of chicks. But the priests and elders of the nation would not humble themselves and seek God's redemption. They cared only for their survival and power. They chose to sacrifice the common people, the poor, and the radical young prophet who called the people to healing and love. They refused to accept his blinding truth.

We always kill the prophets who are sent to us. We martyr them. Then we saint them. Finally, we ignore them. Once they are safely dead, they no longer challenge our comfortable hypocrisy, our indolent charity. We can settle down once more to our daily routine and recall their fine words in celebration of their birthdays.

O Jerusalem, you killed the prophets of ancient Israel. Together, we crucified the Hebrew prophet, Jesus. In our day we sacrifice our prophets: Martin Luther King, Gandhi, Oscar Romero. We cannot hear the truth. We cannot see their vision of justice, a vision that would heal our land. We cannot bear their love, a love that enfolds the wounded and helpless little ones into their embrace.

O Jesus, when will we learn the lesson
of Golgotha? When will we learn to love? When will
we learn to see your face and hear your voice in
the prophets you send into our lives?

† † †

He came and sat among his enemies on the Sabbath to eat bread. They would not let him eat in comfort. They had to confront him. They watched him closely. He was on public display even on the day of rest. They hoped he would do something shocking. Purposely, it would seem, in order to test him, they placed a man suffering from dropsy directly in front of him. They held their breath to see what he would do, since he was so intent on his healing ministry. It was as if they had invited a physician into a hospital in order to criticize his commitment to healing.

He refused their demand for conformity to the law of the Sabbath. He reached out, touched the man, and healed him. He would not bow to public pressure or censure. He committed himself to love in action. They could make no reply. When confronted with such love, confidence, and integrity, there was no satisfactory answer but silence.

How does one stand firm in the face of hostility, simply being who one is and acting with integrity, in love, toward those who suffer? How can one act in confidence and humility when under attack from the "morally" aggressive? How did he maintain his balance while they watched him so closely?

Perhaps it was by always taking the lowest place. He had no pretensions to power. He sought no place of honor. He claimed no allies in positions of authority. He walked with the poor in spirit, the outcast and beggar. His confidence lay in his refusal to seek the praise of his contemporaries. Humility was the cloak of his perfection. Its silence evoked no reply.

† † †

Dear Jesus, we were invited to your dinner. You sent your prophets to call us at the appointed time. You made all necessary provisions for our enjoyment. But we were so busy. Our demanding careers consumed all our energy. Our financial commitments and consumer drives claimed all our resources. Our social calendars demanded all our time. We begged to be excused from your invitation to celebrate and relax in the warmth of your love and generosity. We just did not need your gifts. We were content with what we already had. So we refused to come.

In anger you turned away from us. You rejected us in our wealth, self-satisfaction, and comfort because we were too proud to accept your free gifts. We had other agendas. We had everything we needed. Nothing could be withheld from us. We dominated the world. No one could refuse us.

Except you. We had no hold over you. Our economic and military power could not affect your realm. Your realm knew no economic indicators, no pride of position, no force of arms. Our markets and missiles could not penetrate the power of your love. You turned your back on us because we did not believe we needed you.

So you called on those who did not deserve our notice. You invited the homeless, the battered housewife and child, the AIDS patient. You drew the alcoholic and drug abuser, the criminal and robber, the sick and disabled, into your home. They expected nothing from you because they had received nothing from us. You welcomed them. You healed them. You loved them. They became the citizens of your realm because they were humble enough to accept your invitation. They knew only that you had received them.

† † †

Why do you look at us with those sad and penetrating eyes, Jesus? Do you know that it is Russia and Cuba and Iran who embody Satan today? They are the evil ones who would destroy the values of our family and democracy. They are the people who deny you.

Do not look at us so intently. We believe in you. We claim your salvation. We know your words. We follow your way. Do you not recognize who we are? We are your disciples. Did you not hear that we are a Christian country? Your values are our values. There is no evil in us. It belongs out there, to somebody else, not us.

Why do you look for evil in our hearts? We paid our taxes last year to support democracy and capitalism in every part of our world. We invested in the stock market. We supported police efforts to curb drugs and crime in the streets. We worked hard in our jobs. We deserved our vacation at the beach last summer. We did not deny anything to the homeless family on the street corner last week.

We are not evil. We do not murder or rob or rape. We are good, ordinary citizens, just trying to make a decent living in a competitive culture. You do not really expect that we can change anything, do you? We are not responsible for the evils of our world.

Your sad eyes reproach us. You say that we are responsible. The good bring forth good treasure out of a loving heart. We are called to make a difference, you say. How can we? We never received a sign, teacher.

> *"An evil and adulterous generation seeks for a sign;*
> *but no sign shall be given to it, except the sign of the*
> *prophet Jonah."*

† † †

The multitudes loved him. They followed him wherever he went, clamoring for his attention, hanging on his every word. They delighted to hear him destroy the Pharisees' tedious questions. Their hearts warmed to his words of love and acceptance for the poor, outcasts, and sinners who filled the streets. His miracles of power and healing excited their imaginations as they began to call him "Messiah." The crowds followed Jesus with joy.

We also join the multitudes, singing aloud in the wonder of his moving words. His message of God's love deeply stirs our hungry spirits. We cry out in joy as our Messiah goes before us.

But then he turns to us. "Have you counted the cost? Do you know what I am asking of you? Unless you are willing to give up your home and family, your dearest possessions, you cannot follow me. Unless you take onto your shoulders a heavy cross, you cannot be my disciple. I call you to a difficult mission, an awesome service. Do not follow me with careless intent. My way is hard. Those who follow me must take up my cross of humility and suffering. For I have come to redeem the world!"

O Jesus, how can we possibly pay the price? A total commitment demands too much. We only wanted to join the crowd. It seemed so inviting to follow an excited crowd. Now you demand discipleship. Now you call us to join you in redeeming our race. How can we pay this price? Besides, the world will never listen to us. After all these centuries, it still fails to heed your voice. Why do you think it will hear us now?

Then you said, "My child, there is no other way. I am calling you. Come, follow me!"

† † †

Dear Jesus, we understand the angels' joy when one lost sheep is returned safely to the shepherd's fold. We rejoice when you have found the one who went astray. We happily join you in reaching out to those who have wandered away and need the strong shepherd's hand to lift them out of a pit or rescue them from the bramble bush. We will help seek out the lost and bring them back into your care, as you have asked.

But sometimes we feel neglected. We have not wandered away. We have faithfully remained near the flock. We have heard your voice and followed wherever you led us. We have joined our brothers and sisters in prayer and worship. We have stayed with them in sorrow and sickness. We have served in the ways we could and walked along with you. Do you love us, too?

My little ones, how dearly I love all of you. What would I do if all my sheep ran away at once? If you were all scattered, surely the wolves would devour you, and I would mourn the loss of many sheep. Of course, you are precious to me. I want you by my side always. I feed you the greenest grass and give you the purest water. I nurse you to health and comfort you when you are afraid or lonely. All of you belong to me.

Do not be afraid, little flock, for I will never neglect my own. You will all be safe. You will all come home with me. I will never leave you alone, even in the midst of plenty. I know you need to be held in my arms sometimes, and I will not deny you. For you are my beloved ones.

† † †

The Feast of the Visitation

From that time on all generations have called Mary blessed because God entrusted Jesus to the womb and arms of this woman. She first loved him and nurtured him in her arms. This woman saw his first smile and enjoyed his infant's laugh. She taught him to walk and say his early words. She watched him grow into youth and manhood.

Her woman's anguish saw him to his grave. Her tears watered the earth as his blood flowed down to Golgotha's hill. She suffered with her son as no one else but God could suffer because her own body knew him. Her womb retained his memory. Her arms recalled her embrace of child and youth and man. As her son hung dying on a Roman cross, her mind and body cried out her love. Mary bore his pain in birth and in death.

If God honored the woman Mary in this way, why have we so dishonored woman? Why has responsibility for sin been laid on her when God chose woman to bear God's sinless one? She transmitted no taint of sin upon him as he lay enveloped in her womb. There was no sin in bearing him. Her mother's blood was shed to give him life, a human gift to God.

*O Holy God, Immanuel, you have come to us
in human form through the woman Mary. You have
blessed our lives and given us a place in the creation
of a world where peace, justice, equality, and compassion will reign. Call us forth once more to participate
in the new life born into our world in Jesus Christ.
Together, men and women, joining in your
creation, we journey into our future
in your love. Amen.*

† † †

JUNE

"Well, my friend, you are in hot water this time for sure."

"Stand back, conscience. I'll handle this without your help. Let's see, now. What can I do about this? If I just ignore the charge, maybe it'll go away. But, maybe not . . . . I could pray for God's forgiveness, then confess and ask my boss for mercy."

"That's a good idea. The boss is known to believe in God. Certainly your prayers will be heard."

"But no, what if my boss discharges me anyway? I'll still be without a job. What good is forgiveness with no food on the table? Too risky. I can't entrust these important decisions to God. I'll handle this one myself. After all, who's in control here?"

"Here we go again. You handled the last one and look at you now."

Leave me alone, conscience. I have the perfect plan. I'll just siphon off some funds and give them to the other workers. A regular Robin Hood they'll call me."

"My dishonest friend, you're a crafty fellow, very cleverly thinking and scheming. You use the gifts of the world to great advantage for yourself. Now learn to be as clever in matters of the Spirit."

Jesus commends the dishonest servant, not for his dishonesty, but for his shrewdness. Are we as astute in making use of our material and spiritual riches as the children of darkness are? Do we use our talents and gifts to find seemingly impossible ways to advance the reign of God?

Such riches you possess from your Parent in heaven. Use them today, cleverly, creatively. Watch the nearly impossible take shape before your eyes.

† † †

God has entrusted to us the riches of the world. So often we seem to hoard and squander those riches, ignoring the needs of the poor in our midst.

Are we serving two rulers in our quest for the comforts of life? We are the bearers of God's Spirit on earth, yet we often waver, serving two rulers, lukewarm, neither hot nor cold.

But what if God is calling us to take sides? Perhaps there is no longer time for us to sit with the Pharisees, justifying ourselves before humanity. The poor of the world cry out to us from afar and from next door. The oppressed cry out for freedom, and the disenfranchised cry out for justice.

Have we divorced ourselves from our commitment to love God first and our neighbor as ourselves? Have we wed ourselves to mammon?

My friend, imagine a new way to answer God's call to justice. Imagine yourself as God's Spirit-bearer on earth. Imagine yourself standing beside the poor, before God's altar, promising to love, honor, and cherish. Imagine all humanity in committed relationship before God . . . .

Holy Spirit, you are my vision. Open my eyes
to the many ways I can stand in commitment with
the poor and oppressed of the earth. Clear my heart
of any need to collect and display the world's wealth.
Show me myself before the mirror of your love. Let my
self-esteem be in my nakedness, my vulnerability. Let
the nakedness of the oppressed of the earth be my
mirror image. Holy Spirit, unite us in God's
work on earth, God's purpose, love.

† † †

How often there seems to open up a chasm of misunderstanding between me and you. The fires of Hades burn in my bones as my pride and hurt and longing all battle for attention. I find no bridge over which to cross the gulf. I call out to you, but you seem to be no longer listening. I cry out to God to send you over that my thirst for relationship might be quenched.

But God will have no part of my scheming. The chasm only widens, protecting you from my projections of irresponsibility and need. I look across the gulf at you lying in the bosom of Abraham. I feel abandoned. My hurt becomes anger and rejection.

Surely you have brought this upon us. How many years have you lain outside my gate, not complaining that I have not asked you into my house and my heart? I have watched as others knelt to feed you from the fruits of their plenty, from the depths of their own need. Our eyes have met as you glanced my way and happened to catch me staring. Your smile moved me.

All the day long I lie about waiting for time to pass, but time seems to stand still in my emptiness. Am I lost forever in the fires of my struggle? Where are you, my friend? Why haven't you come by now to bridge the gulf, to quench my thirst, to mend our broken relationship?

Could it be that the chasm of struggle is my resistance to your need? Could God be calling *me* to build the bridge, to open the door to my heart?

Holy Spirit show me the building materials
of relationship that I may open wide my gate, that
I may tear down my door, that I may render my house
the temple of God. Help me to build relationship
out of the rubble of my walls.

† † †

Hidden treasure buried in the dirt. Nourishment concealed in a net full of all kinds of fish. Value is revealed only by sorting and sifting, digging and examining, saving and discarding. Such is the process of discernment.

God considers the whole valuable for the treasure concealed. God, slow to discard and careful to search out hidden worth, values the whole catch, in all its variety.

We are called to do the same. We are called to consider carefully the whole of our walk with God before casting out what seem on the surface to be useless events. Like the householder, we are to examine what is old as well as what is new, for the old holds the story of our journey. Remembering what is now old tells us how far we have come and enables us to appreciate our life, seen now from a new perspective.

Consider Jesus. To his childhood neighbors he was only a carpenter's son. Unwilling or unable to search out the hidden treasure, they focused only on the field of dirt, considering it of little value. But some were able to look upon Jesus and discern God in their presence.

Dig out of the field of your mind the memory of an event. Think back to the time when it happened. Focus on the persons, sights, smells, and feelings surrounding your memory of it. Find the hidden treasure in it. This is your story. It is what has brought you to today. By valuing it you will find God in your presence as you walk forward into the future.

† † †

Being right is not important. Being in right relationship is all important. Right relationship is faithful relationship. In right relationship, I do God's work on earth without harm to my brothers and sisters, for who can knowingly cause another to stumble, being bound to them in unbreakable spiritual communion?

I say to the mulberry tree, "Plant yourself in the ocean." I say to a friend, "You are wrong." I say to God, "Let me come in and eat with you. I am tired of doing the work assigned me." I say these things without recognizing the nature of the spiritual bond between me and each of them.

And so the mulberry tree stays planted, the friend distant, and God weeps at my spirit's unwillingness to recognize faithful relationship with God and all creation.

Could faith the size of a mustard seed possibly be enough to satisfy God's desires for me? The tiny seed contains growth for a lifetime. But the shell of the seed is very hard. Responding to the sun's warmth, the seed's shell must crack. Responding to God's love, my shell must crack too, leaving me vulnerable as I open to God's movement in my being. When I can allow the mulberry tree to stand where it will, allow my friend to be wrong or right, say "yes" to God's direction for my life instead of asking God to say "yes" to my own, then faith-full growth can happen and right relationship flourish.

Imagine yourself as a seed, a small seed with a hard little shell. Imagine God watering you. Feel nourishing sunshine on your body. Begin to open. Feel your shell cracking. Allow the outside to get in. Allow your inside to get out. Your faith grows today as you seek out right relationship with God and all creation.

† † †

" 'Healed!' he said. He said we are healed! 'Go show yourselves to the priests.' That's all it takes. So many years of suffering and being outcast. 'Healed!' What a wonderful thought!

"I can get a job, find a spouse, go into stores and pubs. I'll be normal like other folks. 'Go show the priests,' he said. Let's show the priests. I wonder who that Jesus was who told us go?

"Where are you going, Benjamin? He said to go show the priests. You're going back! Why? Don't go, Ben! To be pronounced clean we must show ourselves to the priests. You're disobeying the one who commanded us to go. Ben, the priests! Oh, well. What do Samaritans know of God's ways anyhow! Poor Ben."

All the lepers have been healed; they are free to go their own ways. But one is turning back to seek out Jesus and to thank and praise God. This man is truly healed, for he is seeking to begin relating to God rather than hurrying off to seek pronouncement from the priests. Not only has his body been healed, but his eyes have been opened to the source of this blessing.

As I am created in body, mind, and spirit, so my healing takes place not only in body, but also in mind and spirit. The direction my life takes is far different if I do not relate to God when my body is healed. I can choose to go my way, or I can choose to go God's way.

Think about the leper who turned back toward Jesus. Imagine yourself turning back from your plans for today. Take a moment to thank God and give praise for the healing you have experienced at all levels — body, mind, and spirit — as you start off on today's journey toward deeper relationship with God.

† † †

I look into the starry night, into the sunlit day. I seek in my neighbor, in the cards. Somewhere I'll find signs of the presence of God. I search for signs, yet I don't know what I expect to find. How will I know when I have found God's presence?

I look everywhere. Exhaustion and defeat set in and I retire in despair. There may not be a reality of God. All around me seems to be in chaos. Life goes on. God could not be here.

I retreat and wrap myself tightly to protect my faith from those who would lead me astray. They phone me and say, "Look here, I have found one who has God. Come with me tonight." I hesitate, and yet I have nowhere else to look.

I turn to prayer. I ask for assurance. Does God really care? How will I know when I have found God's presence? Some seem so spiritual. Is that God's presence? Am I unsaved if I don't feel spiritual? God, I need a sign. I want to know.

And surely God gives me a sign. I begin to pray. I let go of the outside world. I stop comparing my spiritual state with that of others. I pray. Relaxation comes over me. I pray. God's presence comes over me. I begin to feel myself in relation-ship with God.

Try it today. Get comfortable. Relax. Let go of your anxiety. Open yourself to God's presence. Allow signs of God's love to flood your being. Experience the reality of God right here in your own presence. Your very life is a sign of God's presence.

Bow your head, release yourself to God. Experience the presence of God and feel the reality of God within you . . . .

† † †

The faithful pray persistently. But do the persistent pray faithfully?

Sometimes prayer yields answers that we don't recognize. One who has much prays for more and does not recognize in the loss of material wealth the providence of God. One prays for health and does not realize that in sickness God teaches many things.

Jesus encourages us to pray persistently and then wonders if there will be any of the faithful left to greet the reality of God. Will there? If I know what I want from God and don't recognize the hidden blessing in God's answer, I will not be faithful to the end. I will instead begin to delude myself with the thought that, because I have not had my way with God, God could not be on my side.

It is only through reflection that we discern the answers to our prayers. Look back over your day, week, month, year. Think of the prayers you have spoken aloud and in your heart. Have your prayers been answered? Did God's response match your request? When it did not, what did you learn from God's response to your request?

We humans are so finite. We see so little of God's realm. The possibilities we can foresee for our lives and our world are so very limited. Fortunately for us, God answers our prayers out of God's own wealth of possibility for us, not out of our limited awareness.

Go to God in prayer today. Seek God's presence. Let go of the cares of your world. Let go of the responses you want from God. Let God come up with the response which can best draw you into God's faithfulness and truth. Trust in faith that God knows the best answer to your need. Surrender your prayer to God's care. God answers prayer faithfully.

† † †

My doctor has told me how sick I really am. I can't believe my ears. As the doctor leaves my bedside, I find myself talking to God about my condition. "Now God," I begin, "you know I've always been faithful to you. I go to church every Sunday and I pray. We have some great conversations, you and I, don't we? And you remember the friend I brought to church last year. Why, I'm one of your greatest witnesses . . . Now God, about this illness . . . ."

From across the room, from somewhere in the next bed I hear the soft sounds of muffled weeping, the voice of someone, as though calling out to a parent. "Oh, Lord, have mercy. I'm lying here sick and in pain. The only thing I have to believe in is your love. Oh, Healer, your will be done in this body. Work out your love in this spirit. Help this sinner, Lord."

Hearing this prayer, I cannot help but wonder about my own need for God. Will God listen if I admit that I'm feeling scared, weak, and helpless? I had never thought so. Yet now, in the face of my sickness, the good deeds that I have relied on to give me a sense of self-worth seem so trivial, almost pathetic. Who will come to show me the way to empty my heart of its self-righteous deeds that it may be filled instead with God's merciful love?

Recall today the condition of your life when Christ first came to you. Remember the pure mercy and tender love that entered your heart that day. Now breathe in God's love. Breathe out the vanity of self-righteousness. Re-experience God's grace as you continue your faith journey today relying on the tender mercy of God's love to give you a sense of self-worth.

† † †

Each time I move from one home to another I throw out my possessions and start over again. At least that's what I vow to do, and try to do, and fail to do. Actually, I examine my treasures, contemplate their importance in my life story, and pack them up again, vowing to examine them again in the new place.

Sometimes letting go of my treasures feels like letting go of my identity. Who am I without my possessions? Who am I without the comforts and conveniences I have worked hard for and gathered around me?

But God desires to see my identity clad only in the glory of God's love for me. God desires to love me for who I really am, rather than for my career titles, prestigious address, fancy car, or family heritage. If I use these to tell the world who I am, then my allegiance will surely be to my possessions, and the eye of the needle will not be big enough for all of me to pass through.

Come to God this morning clad only in God's love for you. Stand in front of a full length mirror. Experience yourself as you see yourself reflected. Take in the beauty reflected in your mirror, a human who is a beloved creation of God, the one who makes no mistakes.

Tell yourself that God loves you just as you are. Affirm yourself again and begin to believe it. Appreciate your uniqueness, your completeness as one created by God. Give yourself permission to feel God's love for you. Realize that anything you put on, add on, or hold onto does not enhance your stature one bit in the eyes of your creator. Keep that image today as you move through your world, affirming that "God loves me just as I am."

† † †

In today's Scripture passage, Jesus pointed out to his disciples that the people gathered together had a problem: they had had nothing to eat for three days.

> As I open myself to God today I allow the Holy Spirit to point out problems which exist right under my nose, problems I can't seem to solve using my natural resources.

The disciples couldn't help the people. They had only seven loaves and a few small fishes, hardly enough to feed them all.

> Often I find myself saying to God, "I don't have the resources to take care of this need. There doesn't seem to be anything I can do."

Using the resources the disciples provided, Jesus took care of the problem by the power of God.

> The Holy Spirit responds to needs right under my nose, using whatever resources I have.

The disciples had been with Jesus for many days, witnessing miracle after miracle, and still they felt limited by the few resources at their disposal, helpless to respond to the need of the people. Jesus had to point out the need and the answer.

> I have witnessed the Holy Spirit performing miracle after miracle as long as I have known God, and still I find myself all too often responding to the Spirit's promptings by saying, "I don't have the resources to answer that need." The Holy Spirit continues to show me that, with God as my source, my resources are all-sufficient to fill every need.

Have you experienced this sequence of events in your life? Can we grow beyond our limited perspective into God's vision? Use the resources at your disposal to ask for God's transformation and direction today.

† † †

The disciples have been in Jesus' presence for years now, but their eyes have not yet been opened. They fail to grasp the truth. And yet a blind beggar, not seeing Jesus, not having known Jesus, grasps the truth.

It's very difficult to take in the meaning of Jesus. We want to make Christ ruler of the world, without fully grasping the source of Christ's authority. Jesus wrapped in scarlet is far more appealing to us than Jesus the leper or Jesus the blind beggar.

Walking the streets of the inner city helps me to grasp the other, less familiar Jesus. I pass the woman with her filthy hand extended toward me. Could she be my Lord? Or that man over there passed out in the gutter, could he be Jesus? Does Jesus live in tenement housing, in a crack house? Is he lying in the hospital, abandoned by friends and family to the scourge of disease?

Jesus will have to suffer and die for our redemption and we will line his path with palm fronds — but will we be able to look upon his suffering and grasp the meaning of his pain?

"Lord, let me receive my sight." Only in God's mercy, only with opened eyes, are we able to comprehend the magnitude of Jesus' gift to us. What will we see with opened eyes?

"Lord, let me receive my sight." An awesome prayer. Do we really want to see the world as Jesus experienced it? If we do, we will never be the same again. We will glorify God in a whole new way. Think about praying that prayer. What feelings rise up within you?

Your growth is right there, and your faith will make you well.

† † †

Zacchaeus knew how to live. He had taken advantage of Roman rule to further his political and financial career. Yes, he was born a Jew, but since the Romans were going to be in power anyway, why not play the game by their rules? By collecting the Roman taxes from his people for them, he could gain favor with the government and get the "perks" he wanted.

Zacchaeus felt no need to make a choice between the God of his people and the gods of the Roman empire. He shaped his ethical behavior to conform to the political situation of his day. When Jesus came to his town, he was curious, of course. Who wouldn't be? But curiosity may have been all that prompted Zacchaeus to climb that tree.

Sometimes I find myself acting like Zacchaeus. I watch the parade of life going by from the safety of my tree. Seeing unemployment, starvation, drugs, and homelessness, I feel saddened, but I go on collecting the perquisites of the system which oppresses. I deafen myself to the call of Jesus to feed the hungry, heal the sick, house the homeless.

I wonder what it would be like to just once stand up for God as if I really believed that God would want me to get involved. What if Christ called me down from my tree and bade me serve Christ as my house guest?

Imagine yourself this day being called by Christ to come down from your tree to escort Christ through your life. What would you want to throw out before Jesus arrived at your door? What would you save? Where do your allegiances lie? Could you choose sides?

† † †

When my spouse goes away for a few days I relax my vigil over the house and myself. I leave shoes in the living room, dirty dishes in the sink, and the bed unmade. And sometimes I don't even get out of the bed at all.

When my spouse goes away I am left in sole custody of what is ours. The responsibilities are mine, the pleasures are mine. It's up to me alone to keep the home fires burning. I'm not alone forever, and my spouse is not "the head of the house," but there is something in me which labors harder when she is present in the space which is ours.

I find that I treat my space with God the same way. When all is right with my world and I feel that "God is away," I get lax. I let some of the little things go. I'm not so attentive to my prayer time. I get caught up in my life in the world. I forget to talk with God as I go through my day. Yet God "comes back" when I run into trouble that I can't handle and need to be extricated from a difficult situation. It's then that I remember the talents God gave me to manage my life.

I see that some of my friends use their talents whether they experience the presence of God or not. They seem to go on even when they don't feel that God is right there with them. They seem to know that they have been charged with responsibility which doesn't end just because "the head of the house" is away.

Think about your reaction to the feeling that God has "taken a trip." Do you leave your spiritual dishes lying dirty in the sink? Or do you spiritually vacuum an extra time in case of an early return?

What do you do when "the head of the house" is away?

† † †

Some people want a savior dressed in robes of purple, gold shoes on his feet, and a jewel-studded crown upon his head. They want to bow in homage to one who truly looks the part, to one who looks as if he deserves their respect and homage.

What would people think of me if I were seen worshiping one who looked like someone who lived in the streets? Would my friends come to church if the head of the church did not appear in business suit and tie, or in splendid clergy robes, but in the dress of the poor? Could salvation really have come through someone who looks like that?

But his followers, his disciples, never questioned Jesus' attire. When he asked for an unbroken colt, they did not insist on a carriage and fine horses. They spread not a red carpet but branches and their own coats before him as he rode into Jerusalem.

God's gift to the world came and went in humble surroundings. The wealth of Jesus' life radiated through the love he brought to humanity and, indeed, to all of creation. And yet to this very day we who follow in Christ's footsteps have insisted on cloaking Christ in scarlet, worshiping Christ with golden altarware, housing Christ behind stained glass windows, protecting Christ from the street rabble who would tanish Christ's image and ours.

Who is the Christ in my life? Would I recognize Christ if Christ walked down my street? Would I be seen in public with Christ? Would Christ be seen in public in the surroundings I ascribe to Christ?

Perhaps today there is something Jesus would have me change in my image of Christ. Perhaps there is something Christ would have me change in my image of myself as one of the disciples.

† † †

Jesus begins the last leg of his journey toward the cross as he enters Jerusalem. His ministry is almost complete. But just before he enters the city, Jesus weeps. He predicts the destruction of Jersualem: ". . . they will not leave one stone upon another in you; because you did not know the time of your visitation."

Jersusalem was in fact reduced to rubble by invading armies several decades later, and the resulting desolation was so widespread that the nation of Israel never fully recovered. But there is something more here than the fulfillment of a prophecy, something that speaks to us today.

Jesus wept not for the destroyed buildings, but for those who did not recognize the coming of Christ. Jesus wept for all those who could not see the transforming power of God's love. Jesus wept for those who had closed the door against God and did not see how little it would take to open it. Jesus wept not just for the city of Jerusalem, but for us and our world today.

Jesus is longing to come into your life more fully today. Bring Christ into your heart in a special way during the moments of your day. Open yourself to the powerful ways God wants to work in your life. Let Jesus' triumphant entry into Jerusalem be a joyful journey toward a closer relationship with you.

† † †

In the passage that precedes today's reading, Jesus boldly enters the Temple and drives out those who are using religion as a means to enrich themselves. (Luke 19:45-46) In so doing, Jesus demonstrates a personal authority that is a threat to the status quo, a status quo in which the authority of the chief priests, scribes, and elders has been accepted as supreme.

In today's Gospel, the chief priests, scribes, and elders challenge Jesus to explain the source of his authority. They are, in effect, challenging Jesus to justify his right to cleanse the Temple as he has done. Moreover, they issue their challenge in such a way as to create a no-win situation for Jesus. If he maintains that his authority has come from God, they will charge him with blasphemy for claiming an authority that he cannot prove. If he states that his authority is from himself, they will charge him with over-stepping his bounds in cleansing the Temple.

Jesus therefore does not answer their question. Instead, he asks another question that places them in the same situation into which they had attempted to force him. When they answer that they do not know the correct response, he simply replies, "Neither will I tell you by what authority I do these things."

The example of Jesus in this situation teaches an important lesson: it is not always wise or necessary to disclose information about ourselves to people who are likely to use it against us. This does not imply that we should adopt a defensive posture toward others, but it rather encourages us to develop an attentiveness to the voice of the Holy Spirit which reveals to us when "the hour has come" (John 12:23) and when "the hour has not yet come." (John 2:4)

As with God's self-revelation, our own self-disclosure is a gradual process that requires a preparation and readiness that come about through the movement of the Holy Spirit. In being attentive to this movement within our lives and responding to it faithfully, we find an increasing authority emerging in all we say and do. Further, we learn when to speak and when to keep silent in response to the challenges of our world, our neighbors, and our lives.

† † †

I fought with my spouse this morning. The misunderstanding exploded as we were caught up in ourselves, unable to see and know one another. She sizes me up based on external signals such as body language and tone of voice. I approach her more intuitively, sometimes all but ignoring the sights and sounds. We seem so different, so separate as we pass each other this way, never touching the real one within.

There is healing for us and all our relationships in the story of Jesus and Nathanael. Jesus saw him under the fig tree, recognized the truth that lay within him, and chose him as a disciple even though Nathanael had no comprehension or appreciation of the vision Jesus held for him. Nathanael was deeply touched and full of awe that he was not only recognized but understood for who he was.

Receive this same touch now. Call forth the unintended misunderstandings, slights, and hurts that sometimes fill your days. Let yourself experience the pain so that you can release it. Allow Jesus to affirm the truth that lies deep within you. Take the time to feel this affirmation so that you can recall it when you need it. Like Nathanael, you are seen and known, respected and loved simply for who you are.

Take time today in prayer to receive and accept fully the affirmation that Jesus has for you. Pray, too, for the freedom to see and know, to love and respect the truth that lies within your sisters and brothers, however different it may be from your own.

† † †

The Parable of the Tenants

I sometimes find that I have made many assumptions about my life that, because they are echoed by others around me, are difficult to let go of. These assumptions often concern ownership of the fruits of my work and claims on the results of my labors.

It is so easy to forget that the abilities that allow me to work and grow and achieve are gifts. I look instead at the hardships I've worked through, the pain I've endured, the aloneness I've felt. I focus on the effort I have expended to come to where I am. Allowing my justifiable pride in the results of my labors to grow into self-righteous pride is so easy that I forget the gratitude I owe for the gifts that I've been given and for the opportunities I've had to apply them.

At times, my pride even leads me to strike out at those who remind me of the tenuous nature of my tenancy of life. I hold on tightly to my life, rejecting the claims of others and denying God's absolute ownership of all that I am and all that I do. I chafe at the "distraction" of the small, nagging voice that tries to get my attention. It is then that I feel the least joy in my life, and then also, in a moment of grace, that I realize that I am caught up in an ever more fright-filled attempt to cling to what I have never really owned.

God, help me to turn over to you the
ownership of my life, to stop struggling so
hard to hold onto things that have been freely given,
and instead to offer gratitude for the many
gifts with which you shower my life.

† † †

Paying Taxes to Caesar

"So they watched him, and sent spies, who
pretended to be sincere, that they might take
hold of what he said, so as to deliver him up to
the authority and jurisdiction
of the governor."

This particular story is one that is often described as having a very clear message about the laws of governments versus the laws of God. Today, however, the part that strikes me is the part about the spies who were playing dirty tricks on Jesus.

The chief priests and teachers of the law sent spies to Jesus. Their intentions were apparently very clear: they wanted Jesus out of the way. Their fear and insecurity prevented them from really listening to his message. Instead, they wanted above all to protect their positions.

As I reflect upon their actions and attitude, I realize that in many ways I, too, ask God a lot of "trick questions," devising little tests to try to make sure that there really is a God and that God is what I want God to be. These trick questions go: "If there really is a God, how could — happen?"; or "I didn't get what I prayed for, so how do I know God really cares about me?"; or "If there really is a God, then let God give me a specific sign."

There is nothing wrong with asking questions about life and addressing questions to God, of course. Today's Gospel, however, challenges us to examine the sincerity of our hearts and to recognize that trick questions will not bring us into God's presence. Knowing ourselves and opening ourselves to the impact of God in our lives — these are the things that will bring us closer to a full knowledge of God.

Holy One, I ask you with a sincere heart to
show me yourself as you are, not as I would imagine
you. Quiet my mind that I may open my spirit to
the experience of your abiding presence.

† † †

Children of the Resurrection

There are so many laws, regulations, rules, and customs governing our lives that it sometimes becomes difficult to maintain any clarity about what is truly important. We can easily get caught up in these rules, as though they were the only standards by which to guide our lives and actions now and in the hereafter. Like the Sadducees, we tend to think that life as we now know it is all there is. Like the Sadducees, we tend to impose upon our notions of the afterlife the limits of our understanding, limits which are based entirely on our experiences in this life.

One such limit in our understanding has to do with death. It is true, of course, that our life as we now know it will come to an end. But it is equally true that in God we never die. That is why Jesus teaches us in today's passage that those who are in God "cannot die any more, because they are equal to angels and are children of God, being children of the resurrection."

In Western society we tend to fear death, a fear that may have its roots in the limits of our human understanding. Since we have never actually seen and experienced the afterlife, we naturally fear that death is the end of life.

Jesus assures us that death is but a doorway to a new kind of life, one that we cannot experience in our present condition. Today's Gospel is therefore an invitation to open our hearts and minds to the possibility of a new age in which we and the ones we love "cannot die any more," an age in which neither AIDS, nor heart and lung disease, nor murder, nor starvation can touch us, in which the only law is the law of love. Therefore we can proclaim with Paul: "O death, where is your victory? O death, where is your sting?" (I Corinthians 15:55)

Holy One, take away my desire to ask questions about issues that are not really very important. Help me to recognize the important questions, give me the courage to ask them, and give me the grace to listen to your answers so that I may receive the full measure of your teaching.

† † †

The other day I saw an Indigo Bunting on the stop sign off Blunt Road where the new townhouses have been developed. Even as I delighted in spotting the bird, my heart was heavy, for I knew that this bird had been dispossessed. The trees that had provided both shelter and food had been cut down by the hundreds to make way for the "Winchester Homes" that are now for sale in a neighborhood that has been transformed from wildlife habitat into suburban community. I think of all the other creatures similarly removed from this small area of the county alone: the bobcats, the foxes, even the frogs and water creatures have lost their homes and their lives as the land was leveled for shopping centers and suburban living.

Land development, we call it euphemistically, as we convert more and more of the wild places to human use without stopping to consider how much of them is really our fair share as humans. As we destroy the most vulnerable of God's creatures — the birds and animals and insects, the trees and grasses and wetlands — we are truly "devouring widows' houses," to use the phrase that Jesus coined.

Today's Scripture calls us to recognize within ourselves not only the "giver," but also the "taker" — the one who, while enjoying a flowing robe and an important seat, also devours widows' houses.

As you meditate on your own "takings" and the impact they have on all of creation, bring to conciousness a specific way in which you, being only one of God's creatures, are taking more than your share. Invite Jesus to teach you the balance between giving and taking, the balance that represents reverence for God's most precious gift of life.

† † †

"By your endurance you will gain your life."

In today's passage, Jesus describes the end times. He explains that the material things we hold dear in this life will all be taken away at the end of the age. In referring to the Temple, he says that "the days will come when there shall not be left here one stone upon another that will not be thrown down." In other words, "Have fun with your cars, cameras, and computers, but keep in mind that they are all temporary toys that will break. In the process of enjoying them, don't forget to play also with the toys of the heart, with faith, hope, and love. The toys of the heart will never break. They are everlasting."

When asked when the end times will be, Jesus is very clear about being unclear. He says, "Take heed that you are not led astray; for many will come in my name, saying, 'I am the one!' and, 'The time is at hand.' Do not go after them." He goes on to talk about nations rising against nations. There will be earthquakes, plagues, and famines. People will be persecuted and even be put to death. But even then, Jesus says, "The end will not be at once."

So where does that leave us? With the wonderful verse at the end of the passage: "By your endurance you will gain your lives." The Greek word that Luke uses for "endurance" is *hypomone*. It means patience under trials, or steadfastness. It means having a spirit that is strong enough to overcome the trials of life. It does not mean sitting back and waiting for trials to be over; it means getting up and doing what is right, even in the face of fierce resistance.

Hypomone calls us to fully embrace the values Christ taught, regardless of how popular or unpopular they may be at the moment. It urges us to develop in our hearts the most indestructible of toys — faith, hope, and love. There is no better way to play and win the game of life.

† † †

"And then they will see the Human One
coming in a cloud with power and great glory."

Christ will come again. Jesus will indeed appear in a cloud.
But until he does, our eyes need to focus on this earth, not
on the clouds above it. If we spend our lives waiting for a *deus
ex machina* to deliver us, we may miss the "power and great
glory" of Jesus that is ours to share today, right here, even
before our eyes reach the end of this sentence. For it is only
by being fully present to the moment that we can experience
eternity in time.

Jesus reminds us in the Sermon on the Mount: "And which
of you by being anxious can add one cubit to your span of
life? . . . Therefore, do not be anxious about tomorrow, for
tomorrow will be anxious for itself. Let the day's own trouble
be sufficient for the day." (Matthew 6:27, 34)

Jesus' message is clear: Live in the here and now. Yesterday
is no more. Tomorrow is yet to come. Live today. We are given
the power and great glory of Jesus to live each day as it comes.

As surely as Christ died, Christ rose; and as surely as Christ
rose, Christ will come again in a cloud with power and great
glory. But this power and great glory is ours to embrace today
as we focus on the presence of Christ among us here and now
and carry the message of love to our brothers and sisters
throughout the world.

Jesus, teach me to live with you in the present
moment, so that I may receive the eternal life you offer,
both now and when you come again to call me home.

† † †

It was gently raining as I walked from the parking lot to the Apex Plumbing store, and there he was, standing beneath a tree, his red, swollen hands outstretched, asking for money. We talked briefly and I learned that he had fallen upon hard times. I could see he was addicted to alcohol.

His very presence communicated his pain and I felt a bond with him, for I, too, am an addicted person. I am addicted to worrying and guilt, to chocolate and coffee, and to money — to name a few of my addictions. These things consume my thoughts, my energy, my time, and just as surely as alcohol debilitates the man I met, my addictions prevent me from loving God wholeheartedly and from loving my neighbor as I love myself.

How do we get beyond these attachments that consume our days and keep us from the love we yearn for? By ourselves this is impossible, but with God all things are possible.

Take time now to get in touch with your deepest longing for God — the desire that gives meaning to your life. If you can't find that longing within you, simply pray that you may find it today. Then consider your own addictions, whatever they may be: relationships, money, food, sex, guilt — those things that are not your deepest desire, but are the things to which you devote an inordinate amount of energy. Focus on a troublesome one and pray for the willingness and grace to leave it behind.

Let us pray this prayer for each other today, knowing deep in our hearts that with God all things are possible.

† † †

To prevent the trumpet vine from devouring the garage, we cut it out in April. But by June the vine had sprouted anew and climbed nine feet to entwine itself under the eaves of the garage roof, its beautiful orange flowers soon to bloom again.

To keep the grass from growing over the sidewalk, I edged the walk this spring, leaving almost an inch of bare earth on each side. After the last rain I noticed that the bare space had disappeared and the fresh green was on its way again.

Pruned and uprooted, growing and changing as our life journeys take shape, we find ourselves filled with the pain of loss. We lose our youth, our health, our illusions, our dreams. We lose friends and loved ones. But loss is not a choice we make, and we seek distractions to avoid the hurt.

Yet one who loves us always can be heard in the still of our hearts, reminding us to stay present even in the depths of our pain. "Now!" the voice whispers insistently. "Be present with me now! Be with me in your hurt, your anger, and your grief. Just be with me as you are, and pray for the strength to pass safely through the ordeals you find before you."

Hear the voice of life within your heart and resolve to live fully this day that God has given you. Like the vine that gets cut back and the grass that is uprooted, you cannot control your journey. But even in your darkest hour, you can grow as God would have you grow.

† † †

This week I learned that I was physically abused as a child, a secret too painful to bear that lay hidden deep inside me all these years. Recently it began to seek the light, and with this revelation came a holy message: "Now it is time to uncover the truth. Go and prepare for your healing."

The same day that I understood this message, a person I had never met came up to me — like the one whom the disciples encountered carrying a jar of water. She told me of her own childhood abuse and invited me to join a group for the healing of memories. I said I wasn't ready for such a group, and though I didn't mention it, I felt afraid. As she gave me her phone number, I recalled those words, "Go and prepare."

There's risk in going; I'd rather stay and prepare, I say to myself. But to do God's will is to go, to make some change in our lives, however small it may seem at the time. The going is part of preparing, making way for transformation. When we know not where to go nor what to do, we set out in faith, one step at a time. The one who cherishes us from the depths of our being will show us where and when to make the next footprint.

So let us meditate this day on the words of Jesus a few hours before that Last Supper: "Go and prepare . . . ." Specifically, what do they mean for you today? In what direction is God calling you? Let us pray that we may each hear and be faithful to the call in our lives, wherever it may lead us. And let us rest in the assurance that we will meet each other along the way, carrying jars of water.

† † †

Two friends invited me to dinner last week. Nine of us assembled, the table elegant with stemware and silver on a rose-colored cloth. Cucumber and mint soup and other delicacies carefully prepared and served by the hosts created a special occasion for the guests.

We laughed and told stories, on the surface enjoying the evening; yet there was no communion with one another, and around midnight we went our separate ways feeling somewhat tired. We had played well the parts that our culture teaches us: we were the self-sufficient, confident, amusing and successful people we want to be, keeping our deeper thoughts and feelings to ourselves, for to expose them would have been awkward and unpredictable.

And so we find ourselves a superficial and lonely people. We long for meaning in our lives, for the closeness and community that we do not find as we move from one social occasion to another. How do we connect with our deeper selves when our culture constantly bombards us with the importance of appearance?

"Take this, and divide it among yourselves," said Jesus as he passed the cup to those gathered together for the Passover meal. Sharing himself with them and with all believers through the ages, Jesus showed us the way.

Meditate today on communion, this sharing of self that invites others to participate. Pray for the courage to be true to your deeper self, without regard for appearances or what others may think. Be alert for opportunities to commune with the people you meet and with the one who loves and sustains you.

† † †

When I graduated from law school, I began receiving mail with the title "Esquire" printed after my name. Eventually I had business cards which stated "Attorney at Law." A pastor writes "The Rev." and "M.Div." by her name, and our elected officials are usually "The Honorable." We like to advertise our titles and our credentials. They surely give us status in this world.

Recently I took a sewing course at the neighborhood community center, and as we introduced ourselves the first day, one woman said: "My name is Cathy. I'm just a housewife." Cathy's remark was painful to hear because it suggested low self-esteem. The teacher replied: "Please don't say *just* a housewife." At that point we left the conversation and began to learn about sewing machines. Yet Cathy stays with me in spirit as I ponder her self-introduction.

We need our titles for our self-esteem, we say. "But not so with you," Jesus responds, standing our thinking on its head: "Rather let the greatest among you become as the youngest, and the leader as one who serves."

In meditation today, ask yourself who you are. When a worldly person asks this of you, the information usually sought is what you do, what degrees and other possessions you have, where you live, who your parents, spouse, or children are. But what about the person that God is calling you to be? Not the one with status and titles, but the one called to serve. Who are you?

How will you introduce yourself?

† † †

Peter did not suffer from the low self-esteem that many of us do. He believed he could do all sorts of things, and when he tried them he would often fail. He told Jesus he was ready to go with him to prison and to death, but when Jesus was arrested, Peter lied to save himself. Satan had control of him then and was sifting him like wheat.

I tend to come from the other direction, believing that I can't do something I haven't done before. The power of this negative thinking then prevents me from experiencing life fully, and I, too, am "sifted."

The good news is that Jesus, who is able to see all our possibilities, prays for us whether we are exuberant or cautious, fearful or bold. Jesus knew that Peter would deny him, but he could see beyond this mistake to a time when Peter would turn away from fear and self-protection. "When you have turned again," Jesus said to him, "there will be work for you to do strengthening your sisters and brothers." Note that Jesus did not say, "*If* you turn again." Jesus prayed and had faith that Peter would change.

Jesus prays for us, too, all the time, and we, too, are transformed by the power of prayer. Do you understand what this means for you?

Take time now to quiet yourself and to know in your heart that, while negative forces are trying to sift you as wheat, just as they did Peter, so Jesus is praying for you that your faith may not fail. Let this prayer embrace you and give you hope.

Receive the embrace, drink deeply of the hope, and know that wherever your journey takes you, Jesus is holding you in prayer.

† † †

JULY

For Jesus, prayer was an integral part of life. Through prayer he maintained a continuing relationship with God that gave him God's own perspective on himself and his mission in life and prepared him for the important acts and events of his ministry.

During his earliest sojourn in the wilderness, he found the limits of his ministry defined by the temptations he experienced in prayerful solitude. (Luke 4:1-13) Before choosing his disciples, he prepared himself by spending time in quiet reflection with God, seeking divine guidance for the important choices he was about to make. (Luke 6:12-16) At the mount of Transfiguration, Jesus entered into prayer at the turning point of his ministry, seeking and finding strength for the sacrifice that lay ahead. (Luke 9:28-36)

Gethsemane was therefore not an isolated experience of prayer for Jesus, a sudden turning toward God in a moment of crisis, but one of many times when Jesus turned to God to review the conflicting claims on his life and to reconcile his own will with God's. In Gethsemane, Jesus' ongoing relationship with God therefore strengthened his already existing unwillingness to save himself at the expense of God's perfect will and solidified his refusal to acquiesce to violence against his attackers. So firm was this refusal that when one of his disciples impulsively resorted to the use of a sword, Jesus healed his attacker.

Without such a deep relationship with God, cultivated by regular prayer, we become like disciples who sleep, unaware of the struggle between good and evil raging around us all the time and unable to cope with its intensity. To us Jesus comes today and says: "Why do you sleep? Rise and pray that you may not enter into temptation."

† † †

"By what authority are you doing these things?" is an inquiry often posed from a defensive posture. The question arises from people who believe they have authority over those whom they doubt or with whom they differ. The chief priest and the elders were annoyed by the crowds Jesus attracted. The attention he was receiving because of his teaching and healing made him a threat to the status quo. The question concerning John's authority which Jesus placed before them simply angered them further.

Perhaps if the elders and priests had listened calmly to John and to Jesus and observed their acts of healing compassion, they might have discerned that their authority came from the God of their ancestors. Certainly their works displayed a power and authority beyond what was merely human. Yet the fear felt by the elders and priests drove them relentlessly to resist those works, to call them evil, and to try to drive out the ones who performed those works. In the end, they found themselves driving out God.

In our own lives, circumstances and events which we could not have predicted or desired sometimes develop. Our world, with all our neat classifications and clear controls then begins to crumble. At such times we are tempted to think that evil has attacked us, and, like the chief priests and elders, we want to challenge such threats to our control. Often, however, what we fear so greatly is in fact God breaking into our lives, discarding the old and bringing in the new. At such times the call on our lives is to bring the tax collector, the harlot, and even the chief priest within us to Christ, where they can "repent and believe" and enter the new age in which "All authority in heaven and on earth has been given to [Christ]." (Matthew 28:18)

Dear God, you gave all authority to Christ.
Help the chief priest and elder within me today to accept
Christ's authority over every aspect of my life.

† † †

Personal and social recognition have become an obsession in Western society. Our world places great value on holding "the proper credentials," graduating from "the best schools," and being a member of the "correct" social and professional organizations. In addition to these pressures to achieve social and personal recognition, we are incessantly urged by TV commercials, highway billboards, and magazine advertisements to seek recognition by following the latest style craze or buying the trendiest fashion designer label. Recognition is for many the be-all and end-all in our culture.

And yet, do any of us envy Peter as he is repeatedly recognized in the high priest's courtyard on the night of Jesus' arrest? So recently Peter had been sure of his unshakeable loyalty! Now, each time he opens his mouth he exposes his inner weakness and paranoia with words of condemnation and cowardice. The recognition which he received was not what he had anticipated! He makes swift and repeated denials. And at the third denial, when Jesus "turned and looked at Peter," he remembers Jesus' earlier prediction and recognizes himself for who he really is. In this full self-recognition, Peter "went out and wept bitterly."

We are not so very different from Peter. We often attempt to hide behind labels and disguises and brave words that deny who we are, where we have been, and what we have done. And often, when these masks are torn from us and we stand exposed, we weep bitter tears of shame.

The pain and suffering we experience at such moments cannot easily be relieved or dismissed. Like Peter, we must wait in our newly found nakedness for the healing grace of the risen Christ.

> *God, you know our denials and our fears. Be*
> *merciful to us in our weakness and strengthen*
> *us in your love and grace. Amen.*

† † †

One of the enduring paradoxes of life is our constant need for answers to our questions and our equally constant rejection of any response which does not fit our preconceptions. Jesus encountered this phenomenon before the council of elders, chief priests, and scribes. "If you are the Christ, tell us," they asked. His response: "If I tell you, you will not believe." Not only would they not accept his answer, but Jesus affirms that if he had put the question to them, they themselves would have been unwilling to respond.

Such experiences are by no means confined to our Scriptural ancestors. We encounter such denial and deliberate confusion in our own social, political, and religious life continuously. The problems that apartheid has engendered in South Africa are blamed on tribalism. Gay men are blamed for the tragedy of AIDS. The plight of the homeless is explained away as the result of the supposed laziness of the poor. Responses which require an adjustment of our attitude or behavior are difficult for most of us. In the life of Jesus, such intransigency on the part of his accusers led to his crucifixion.

So we are left with the continuing struggle to determine whether or not we really want to know the truth with regard to our life, our faith, and our world. Perhaps only as we adopt a stance of confession, humility, and prayer can we open ourselves sufficiently to receive or give honest answers to our questions. Only through such honesty can we free ourselves from the victimization, prejudice, and blame with which so much of human history has been shrouded.

Jesus knew the truth about his life. His confession is: ". . . from now on the Human One shall be seated at the right hand of the power of God." This was a direct and unambiguous declaration of truth in the face of hostility. Perhaps it is even more an affirmation of trust in the dependability of God in a seemingly hopeless situation. "What further testimony do we need?"

† † †

Pilate and Herod were unanimous in their decision. They found no crime committed by Jesus. Perhaps Jesus had been a little too zealous in his claims and preaching, but his two judges found that he had done nothing deserving death.

His accusers, however, were adamant. They needed no proof or adequate reason. Irrational fear was sufficient then — as it has been through the ages — to unravel and destroy the civility needed for a human community to survive.

Pilate and Herod were not villains at heart, nor were they bloodthirsty powermongers. As rather ordinary middlemen, with limited power and courage to match, they were simply desperate to find a way out of the dilemma without causing their little world to come toppling down around them. Little did Herod, Pilate, or the Jewish political and religious leaders comprehend the real consequences of their vacillation — that in their lack of courage and conviction, they were condemning the Messiah to death.

Ironically, the cowardice of the leaders in this scenario and the mocking accusations of the crowds stand mocked by history. While they seemed to have won the day in the short term, Jesus in his silence commands faith and respect which continue to grow and find new expressions in human history. Today, Bishop Desmond Tutu, Rev. Troy Perry, and homeless activist Mitch Snyder still stand, in spite of the judgments against them by political and religious establishment figures. Even so, these leaders continue to be met with persecution and rejection. Is it too much to ask that such unnecessary rejection be replaced with dignity and respect for the prophet? Will we ever learn to give a hearing to the dreamers?

Jesus, help me today to recognize you in those
who give their lives every day in the struggle for truth.
Bear up with your strength these prophets of today,
whose names I now raise to you . . . .

† † †

One of the ironies of history is that the release of Barabbas at the crowd's demand neither accomplished the goals of Pilate and Herod nor satisfied the crowd's anger and hysteria. Before that weekend and the ugly deed of the crucifixion were over, rumors of the Resurrection had spread with such persistence that their decision must have tormented both of them. Now they and their successors had to contend not only with Barabbas, the insurrectionist and murderer, but also with Jesus, who was being proclaimed as the risen Christ. As Christ's followers multiplied and became legion, Christ's fame burst through Palestine's borders and spread across the known world. Torture in prisons, persecution in dungeons and in arenas filled with lions, conflagrations and immmolations served only to spread the exact opposite of the message that Pilate and Herod had intended to spread.

The ironical consequences of short-sighted choices persist for all of us when we seek quick solutions to complex, turbulent situations. We want to rid ourselves of our most immediate pain and confusion and preserve as much of our power and prestige as possible. But difficult choices seldom afford us the luxury of easy decisions. Truth and justice have their own terms that recognize neither expediency nor popularity.

Difficult and unresolved situations, then, may call us simply to bear the painful tensions of the moment, watching and waiting for a shift in the landscape of reality that opens a pathway to the truth. Such, at least, is the stance that Jesus displayed in the midst of the turbulent circumstances pressing in on him in today's Gospel. In the end his patient endurance, which was simply an expression of his deep trust in God, brought him through the difficulty to a resurrected life.

Jesus, when turmoil and confusion swirl about me, teach me to be still as you were, trusting that, no matter how hopeless things may appear, God is in control.

† † †

Jesus had choices on the road to Calvary. He could have spoken up at his trials and defended himself. He could have promised to cease his activities and gone back home to his family and the local carpentry shop. But his commitment led him on.

On the other hand, Simon of Cyrene had no choice. The Roman officers seized him as he traveled on his own private journey, laid the cross on him, and demanded that he carry it behind Jesus to Calvary. There is no room for Simon's reaction to his forced servitude, nor is any description of his future to be found in the Gospels, even though three of the Gospels record this event in exact detail.

Simon of Cyrene's crossing of the stage of history in this way reminds us of all those others whose fate is sealed through no choice or conscious decision of their own. Their life journeys from one experience to another are suddenly interrupted by some circumstance which compels their immediate involvement and changes the course of their lives, perhaps even their ultimate fate. Black women and men, especially, have, identified with Simon in bearing their own unchosen burdens and oppression. Indeed, Simon continues to live in all those who bear indignities and trials through no choice or fault of their own.

Simon of Cyrene and all his brothers and sisters, his heirs of every generation, of every race, of every nation, of every sexual orientation, want to understand the "why" of the burdens of their lives. Perhaps some intimate word or gesture or glance between Jesus and Simon, his cross-bearer, unknown and unrecorded for history, may have redeemed this passer-by's burden and endowed it with meaning. If not, he too waits with the many.

† † †

"Give us a break! Turn the mighty trick, get yourself down from here and save us, too! Nothing special for a Messiah; just use the power for which you are known. There's nothing to lose in trying. All we'll do here is die. Give us a break!" Words of bargaining and "realism" from one side of the cross. From the other, quiet resignation to the justice of his own fate and an acknowledgement of the injustice of Jesus'. The second thief displays himself in honesty and humility.

I suspect, however, that most of us would side with the first thief in pleading for one more chance. After all, what is wrong with trying to strike a bargain? Such behavior is common in the face of crisis, certainly in the face of death.

The good news from the cross is that it is in accepting death that we find life. When we stop our bargaining and simply accept the inevitable suffering that is part of life, then, paradoxically, the gates of paradise open up to us. By embracing rather than fleeing the reality of death, Christ offers us, as part of the mystery of life and death, the same experience of resurrection of which Christ was assured.

In much of the Western world we strenuously deny the reality of pain, suffering, and death. We pretend we can bargain our way out of the inevitable. We search for ways to escape via drugs or food, sex or power, possessions or prestige — all because we are not listening to the good news of peace given to one who was suffering and about to die: "Today you will be with me in paradise."

Perhaps our most powerful prayer in the face of pain, suffering, and death is, therefore, not to try to strike a bargain, but simply to pray, "Jesus, remember me."

† † †

A disturbing image of God seems to emerge from today's Gospel. God is compared to a ruler who, upon learning that the invitation to his son's marriage feast had been rejected and that some of his messengers had been killed, became angry and "sent his troops and destroyed those murderers and burned their city." This image becomes even more unsettling later in the story when that same ruler, upon encountering a wedding guest who was not wearing the proper wedding garment, commanded his servants, "Let the guest be bound, hand and foot, and cast into the night . . . ."

Since this image is very different from the patient and forgiving God that Jesus reveals elsewhere in the Scriptures, Jesus must have been using it in order to make a different point. That point may be this: God is unalterably determined to remove every obstacle that would prevent union between Jesus and us. By comparing God to someone who would destroy murderers and cities and have improperly dressed guests removed from the marriage feast of his son, Jesus seems to be saying that the ultimate goal of all of life is union with God through Christ, and that nothing must be allowed to displace or diminish that priority.

Today's Gospel therefore invites us to consider what is most important in our lives. Do we today accept the invitation to come to the marriage feast (i.e., to take the time to draw near to God), or do we make light of it, giving our work, business affairs, or even church ministry a higher priority?

What if a servant of God came to you today and called you to leave your affairs for a time and come to the marriage feast? Are you prepared to say yes?

> *O God, come and remove today all obstacles*
> *between us so that I may know the sweet joy of*
> *union with you through Christ. Amen.*

† † †

Throughout the ages, art, drama, and music have depicted with poignancy and pathos the mystery of death. *Aida*, *Madame Butterfly*, and *Othello* present but a few of art's unforgettable portrayals of death. And artists since the time of Christ have painted the crucifixion scene, reminding people of every generation of the power of this unforgettable event.

The directness and simplicity of Luke's account also capture the mystical drama of the crucifixion. The eclipsed sun, the piercing last cry of Jesus, the centurion's confession of faith, and the mourning crowd all convey the idea that this death is more than ordinary.

The cruelty of the event is softened, however, by the compassion of Joseph of Arimathea. Opposed to the council's decision, Joseph is one "who was looking for the reign of God." And so he requests of Pilate the opportunity to bury Jesus' body. Through the Gospel account, we watch with the women as he compassionately takes the lifeless body from the cross, carefully wraps it in a linen shroud, and gently places it in a new rock-hewn tomb.

This cruel death and compassionate burial remind us that both human cruelty and hatred and a resolute expression of love and sensitivity exist side by side in much of life. The civil rights struggle in America cannot be comprehended apart from the cruel force of Bull Connor on the one hand and the compassionate leadership of Martin Luther King, Jr., on the other. Similarly, the struggle for lesbian and gay rights cannot be understood apart from the attacks of Anita Bryant and Jerry Falwell on the one hand, and the sacrifices of Leonard Matlovich and Troy Perry on the other. In history, in addition to the villains, there are also the heroes and heroines.

Luke's portrayal of the crucifixion spares nothing of these realities of life. The destructiveness and the redemptive meaning of the cross live side by side. The cross is real, embracing both pain and sorrow, compassion and redemption. And the question it leaves us with is this: In the events of history with which my life intersects each day, which side am I on?

† † †

In his hymn, "Easter People, Raise Your Voices," William James wrote these words for his Harlem congregation:

> Easter people, raise your voices
> Sounds of heav'n in earth should ring.
> Christ has brought us heaven's choices
> Heav'nly music, let it sing.
>
> Fear of death can no more stop us,
> From our pressing here below.
> For our Lord has now empow'red us
> To triumph over ev'ry foe.
>
> Ev'ry day to us is Easter,
> With its Resurrection song.
> When in trouble move the faster
> To our God who rights the wrong.[1]

Although the Easter account begins with the disbelief of those to whom the women told their story, the fact remains that the disciples did, in the end, become "Easter people." Not only did they become convinced that Christ had risen from the dead, but they also recognized their call to live new lives as followers of Christ and to be witnesses of the resurrection story for the whole world. Easter people they were, not only startled by the resurrection event, but transformed by it.

Often we greet the experience of newness of life with the same disbelief as the disciples. Often we are slow to accept the complete redemption of our failures, mistakes, and sins. Often we linger at the tombs of our past, sure that we will find the evidence that we have been defeated and that our hope is dead.

The good news is that the Easter is still there for us to discover in our own time and life. We, too, are invited to walk into even the bleakest of situations and to discern there the same power of God that raised Christ from the dead once again at work to restore, heal, and transform life. "Ev'ry day to us is Easter" whenever we remember the good news that Christ lives and "has now empow'red us to triumph over ev'ry foe."

[1]Copyright © 1979 by William M. James. Used by permission.

† † †

There is always a certain ambiguity about a stranger. Will the stranger be friend or foe? Can this unknown person be trusted? Is it safe to open up to this stranger?

In the Scriptures, the stranger, with his/her ambiguity, often represents the future — life as it emerges on our horizon. Further, because all of life comes from God, the stranger comes to represent God, and the way one welcomes the stranger reveals one's basic stance toward the future, life, and ultimately, God.

Today's Gospel about welcoming the stranger is therefore a story about trust. The disciples were returning home after the death of Jesus, and as they walked away from their defeated dreams, a stranger began to walk with them. The critical moment in the story came when the two disciples reached the city gates and had to decide whether or not to invite into their home this stranger who had been walking beside them. In other words, in spite of their pain, would the disciples still trust that life, the future, and ultimately, God, were good?

At that critical moment, the disciples turned to the stranger and said, "Stay with us." As a result of their trust, even after the painful loss of their most precious hope, they received the promise of God for a future beyond their wildest dreams.

And what of us today? What is our response to the stranger? To painful losses that God allows to happen? Today's good news challenges us to keep our faith even when we have lost our hope. It assures us that no matter what road we are on, Christ is walking beside us. It instructs us that if we will trust life as God offers it to us, then we will discover Christ present to us in wondrous ways that we have yet to recognize.

Risen Saviour, teach us to see you in all the ways that you seek to reveal yourself. With the disciples of Emmaus we say to you, "Stay with us."

† † †

Luke's report in today's Gospel passage is not just one more retelling of the resurrection story, for he recounts here the commissioning of the disciples: "You are witnesses of these things." They are to preach repentance and the forgiveness of sins "to all nations, beginning from Jerusalem." Such early universality immediately established a world stage for the spread of the Gospel.

Are we able to comprehend our purpose as Christians in such broad dimensions? Are we in fact witnesses to Christ, or mere appendages of a respectable institution called "the church"? Do we accept a world mission, or are we comfortable with casual conformity to familiar ideas and ordinary surroundings? Do we who call ourselves Christian perceive ourselves as a joyous company sent by Jesus to proclaim to every person on earth, without exception, the good news of God's unconditional acceptance and love?

It will take prayerful time and thought to evaluate our relationship and responsibility to the world as followers of Christ. Yet it is a necessity in a culture as comfortable as ours, where God and country, church and country club, Christian and socialite are often almost indistinguishable.

As living witnesses of Jesus' death and Resurrection, we are challenged today to discover what the divine encounter with the risen Christ means for us. If it does not at some point issue in sharing the Gospel with our world, then we have not heard all of the good news.

Jesus, come in your risen power.
Let this time of worship be a hallowed hour
in which your presence calms, instructs, and empowers
my spirit to serve and proclaim you
in our world.

✝ ✝ ✝

Like a great landscape painter, Mark with broad strokes intro-duces us to the good news of Jesus Christ. Setting the scene squarely in Judaic prophetic history, he first brings John into focus, highlighting his ministry of calling attention to the com-ing Messiah. Then in a few compact sentences he tells of the baptism of Jesus, the descent of the Spirit on Jesus, and the temptation in the wilderness. Mark expects his readers to recognize, in this brief account of the earliest events of Jesus' public life, that Jesus is the fulfillment of the prophecies of the Jewish Scriptures.

The Gospel's challenge to us as it announces the coming of Christ into our world is equally brief and succinct: "Prepare the way of the Lord." There is no room here for lengthy discourse or second thoughts. When Christ appears on the horizon, some response is required of us. The politician in us will try to evade the issue to no avail. The religious authority in us will resist the changing of the status quo. The child in us will seek to draw near to Christ. The leper in us will cry out for Christ's mercy. The intellectual in us will meet Christ by night to ask for instruction. No part of us will escape Christ's powerful presence.

How then shall I prepare to encounter Christ appearing on the horizon of my life today? I will go out into the wilderness for a time, to the edge of my life, away from the frenzy of my daily routine, and there I will listen for the voice announ-cing Christ's arrival. I will confess my sins and immerse myself in the waters of God's mercy, which cleanse and purify my soul. I will simplify the paths of my inner life so that Christ may enter easily and find the way to my heart open and clear. In this way there shall be a new "beginning of the Gospel of Jesus Christ" in my life today.

† † †

In today's Gospel, the urgency of Jesus' ministry cannot be missed. Following the arrest of John, Jesus moves center-stage, preaching, teaching, and healing. His recorded sayings are nearly all imperatives, and the word "immediately" is used repeatedly to describe the events that unfold around him. Jesus appears to hurry along, avoiding distractions and focusing on the essential.

Along with this sense of urgency, Jesus communicates an authority that impresses all whom he encounters. When he calls the disciples to leave their occupations and follow him, they respond without hesitation. When he teaches in the synagogue, people are astonished, "for he taught them as one who had authority." In confronting an unclean spirit, his command brings immediate obedience.

Such urgency and authority are often sadly lacking in our own ministry. Even though we may manage at times to rise above our spiritual lethargy to take a few steps in the service of others, our commitments are too often short-lived and self-serving. All too quickly we revert to the comfort and security of the status quo. It is no wonder that much of what we preach goes unheeded.

One reason why Jesus' ministry was filled with energy and authority was that he gave himself wholeheartedly to God's call on his life. And although his commitment to the life God had called him to was tested in many ways and at many times, he remained faithful, even in the face of the cross. Because of his faithfulness in life and in death, even the unbelieving centurion proclaimed, "Truly this man was the Child of God!" (Mark 15:39)

If our message and ministry are ever to have the power and authority of Jesus' message and ministry, then one thing is clear: we will have to put ourselves on the line as single-mindedly as Jesus did. Today's Gospel accordingly invites us to examine the level of our commitment to God's unique call on our lives. Divided loyalties bring diluted results. Complete commitment brings authenticity, authority, and urgency to our message.

† † †

Forty years ago the congregation of the Chicago Temple, under the inspiration of Dr. Charles A. Goff, commissioned the carving of a scene to be placed over the altar of the Chapel in the Sky. In this sculpture, Christ looks over the skyline of the city of Chicago. There is a companion piece similar to this one over the altar of the main sanctuary, in which Christ sits above the city of Jerusalem, brooding over its life and people. These twin pieces of art and history capture unmistakably today's Gospel message concerning Israel's past and our present.

In today's Gospel Jesus denounces the false piety of the religious leaders. These were people who, while praising and honoring their ancestors, tried piously to separate themselves from the latter's misdeeds and cruelty. Jesus confronts them with the duplicity of their ancestors and the hypocrisy with which they themselves presently live — killing, persecuting, and beating new prophets that God has sent to them.

After this denunciation, Jesus goes to sit and brood over the city. "O Jerusalem, Jerusalem," he laments. He weeps because the whole society is in danger. He weeps for the way true spiritual leaders have been silenced in the past. He weeps for the way he himself is being silenced. And no doubt he weeps for the ways that true spiritual leaders will be silenced again and again in the future.

Before we look to the past to ease our own consciences, however, let us consider the message of the altar pieces in Chicago. Their message is appropriate to almost any city or town today. The existence of racism, poverty, homelessness, homophobia, crime, and substance abuse places all of us squarely in the company of our ancestors. We too must seek repentance, must move our will and behavior until the confession of our lips is that of our heart. Our new creed will then be: "Blessed is the one who comes in the name of the Lord."

† † †

Jesus did not enter into his ministry to become a spectacular healer. Healing was included in his ministry because it demonstrated God's loving and faithful response to human need. Similarly, Jesus' preaching was not intended to draw attention to his powers of insight or declamation, but to point to God's presence in the world as the fulfillment of the promises of ancient prophets. In short, Jesus wanted those who heard his words and saw his works to recognize their deeper meaning: "The realm of God is in the midst of you." (Luke 17:21)

In delivering this good news, Jesus went out of his way to keep the focus on the message and off himself. When a man with an unclean spirit shouted out Jesus' true identity, Jesus commanded him to be silent. (Mark 1:25) When "the whole city" came in pursuit of him, he withdrew, first from the house in which he was staying, then from the entire town. When, "moved with pity," he healed a leper who had come to him for help, he sternly charged him to tell only the priest what had happened.

Jesus adopted this posture because from the very beginning his primary desire was to extol the loving and faithful presence of God among the people. He therefore never sought to make something of himself. In fact, he always sought to diminish himself. And even though he himself was God, he "did not count equality with God a thing to be grasped, but emptied himself, taking the form of a servant." (Phil. 2:6-7) And he continued to humble himself, day after day, until finally he lowered himself to the level of a criminal worthy of the cross. In the strangeness of the mystery of salvation, this humble death of Jesus on the cross became the ultimate fulfillment of Jesus' ministry, for it was the quintessential revelation of God's love for all people.

Today's Gospel challenges us to repent of the subtle and gross ways that we turn our proclamation of the Gospel into a vehicle for self-glorification. It invites us to put on the humility of Christ in order to magnify the glory of God. Are we willing to diminish ourselves to that extent?

† † †

A young clergyperson, returning to his pulpit in Chicago after having undergone heart by-pass surgery, recounted his experiences of anxiety, fear, doubt, and pain. He wished, he told his congregation, that he could report some story of personal heroic faith, some uncommon valor in his struggle. But there had been no such story. He told, rather, of very special "litter-bearers" — persons who, seeing his condition and expressing their kindness in words, deeds, and prayers, had carried his fragile body in faith from his place of need into the loving, healing presence of God.

The Gospel likewise pays tribute to litter-bearers in today's passage. It was when Jesus saw *their* faith that he healed the paralytic. Black saints used to speak of "making a way out of no way." These four, climbing to the roof and actually removing the tiles (!), made a way out of no way to place their friend before Christ.

The onlookers were more concerned with the form than the substance of what happened. They were concerned with flash; Jesus was concerned with faith. They were concerned with authority and right order; Jesus was committed to love and the relieving of human suffering. Here before all to see, Jesus demonstrated the power of divine love to forgive sins, heal broken bodies, and honor human faith and trust. In the face of such great love, the people's disbelief turned to amazement and praise: "We never saw anything like this!" they exclaimed. It is as if we are all constantly amazed at Christ's power to transform life.

There are times in our lives when we, like the paralytic and like the young clergyperson, have no great faith, no uncommon valor, no more strength, and no way to get to Christ. At such times God has a way of sending "litter-bearers" into our lives, people whose faith, valor, and strength "make a way out of no way" so that Christ may heal us. Then, if we listen, we will hear the voice of Christ saying to us not only "Your sins are forgiven," but also "Rise, take up your pallet and walk."

† † †

How many mornings have you awakened wishing for something new? A new job, or home, or car, or clothing? We sometimes find we just have a yearning for some change. On the other hand, many of us are totally dependent on the constancy of the old and familiar. We see anything new or different as a violation of the established order of the world.

Today Jesus comes with something new. He proclaims that he and his ministry represent the inauguration of a new era. He eats with tax collectors and other sinners, and he announces that they are the people to whom he comes as "physician." His detractors point to the fasting of John's disciples: Is this not the tried and true way of devotion and purification? Not so. Jesus is the special guest, the bridegroom among them whose message and behavior represent new wine worthy of new wineskins.

Jesus makes no apology for his behavior, message, or associations, which are neither careless nor accidental. They are intended to express news of new life, new freedom, and new acceptance. It is a new morning, filled with new light on the meaning of salvation and redemption. Acceptance is opened to all, especially to those who need it most. Jesus knows the past, but his Gospel is for the creation of a new age and for the empowerment of a new people.

It has always been too easy to cautiously comfort and isolate ourselves with the traditions and rites of the past. This is not the path Jesus offers us. Instead, when Jesus enters our lives, it is with something transforming and new. Perhaps today it would be good to listen to his invitation to hear the "news."

† † †

The need for Jesus and the disciples to gather food and eat as they traveled from place to place was essential. Neither a luxury nor a disrespect for tradition, it was merely a necessity of life for a traveling band that had no permanent home. The Pharisees, however, were so preoccupied with religious restrictions that they accused Jesus' disciples of sin when they plucked grain on the Sabbath. Similarly, they sat in stony silence in the synagogue when Jesus healed the man with the withered hand on the Sabbath. No amount of persuasion or explanation seemed to free them from their servitude to law and tradition. Such enslavement enables people to avoid responsible decisions for themselves and compassionate service to others.

We are still not far from our religious ancestors in Israel. Social prejudice and irrational fear of those who hold opinions different from our own still exist in our churches and communities. And when it comes to justifying such prejudice and fear, we are all too likely to hear a favorite verse from the Book of Leviticus or the letters of Paul.

According to Jesus, religion, the Sabbath, and life itself are gifts of God given for the benefit of humankind. When we become willing slaves of legalism, we not only lose our freedom, but we lose the power of shared kindness and respect as well. Instead of being instruments for good, we become rigidly separated from the companions with whom we are called to live in fellowship, and ultimately even from God.

In a world where we still struggle to feed multitudes and to heal persons of life-threatening disease, today's Gospel calls us to examine our attitudes and behaviors in order to shed legalistic positions and discover how we can gain greater freedom. By ending our prejudices, by abandoning our fears, and by surrendering our often vicious tools of control, we can make of the Sabbath and every other day new days of freedom for humankind. Only then will we learn to live, to be fed, and to be healed.

† † †

Jesus' power to preach and heal brought huge crowds to him. His own human limitations in coping with such large crowds led him to make the most significant selection in history. The twelve whom he called to himself, and whom he sent out to preach, heal, and cast out demons, found their lives irrevocably changed. Thrust to the center of this impromptu stage of Jewish and world history, the twelve were never again to be private citizens or idle bystanders. With Christ, through Christ, and in Christ; in preaching, teaching, healing; in betrayal, denial, and even in death, they were never to escape having been selected by Jesus. They were his, and he was theirs. And even after the death and Resurrection of Jesus, they devoted themselves to a ministry of witness that consumed them to the end of their lives.

They were, nonetheless, very ordinary people with very ordinary ways of sinning: jealousy, doubt, denial, betrayal, and all manner of selfish pursuits. Yet it was to this band of twelve very ordinary persons that Christ entrusted the good news of the reign of God.

As Christians, we today are challenged with the same trust that Christ placed in the first unlikely group of disciples. Still called, sent, and commissioned by Christ through the church and God's particular call on our lives, we struggle to love, minister to, and care for the people of our world. Still oppressed with disease, hunger, poverty, with demons and unbelief, the crowds come in search of healing and hope.

The challenging question to us from today's Gospel is this: As Christians called by Christ to preach, teach, heal, and cast out demons, what do we offer the crowds when they come?

Jesus, you have called me to serve you in the people I encounter today. Strengthen and empower me to fulfill the ministry with which you entrust me.

† † †

For as many years as I can remember my mother returned to her home in the South each summer. Her sisters, who, like herself, had left the South in young womanhood, made the same pilgrimage, bringing their families and, of course, never failing to boast of their new positions and achievements in far-away cities. Discussing these annual visits with my mother years later, I was surprised to hear her interpretation of them: "Each year we all returned, and soon after greeting each other, we always seemed to fall back into our traditional roles." The rivalry, the dependency, the behaviors of childhood always reasserted themselves.

When Jesus came home, the crowds who had heard of his preaching and healing elsewhere pressed around him. His family was concerned about the scene he was creating. The rumors were that he was beside himself. He was accused of being possessed by demons. In the face of this criticism, Jesus continued his prophetic message. It is the work of the Holy Spirit, he responded, and he continued his ministry, almost defiantly.

Of course the family of Jesus knew him. Or did they? His mother, hearing the reports and the rumors, came with his relatives to get him and bring him home. Certainly, she wanted to protect her son from danger and to place him in the familiar, familial safety that was his by right as a member of her family. For Jesus, however, the decision was clear: he had moved beyond the roles defined for him by his family. Now his mother and brothers were those who followed his word and did the will of God. Now, having moved beyond the family of Nazareth, he was in the midst of the family of God whose home is in the heart of God. There he remains for us all.

† † †

Risk-taking is one of the most confusing and complex realities that humans confront. Some people thrive on risk and adventure. Others, aptly depicted by Jesus as the servant with one talent, are prisoners of fear who constantly protect the little they have. We have all met persons who, while fiercely protecting their meager possessions, lose them in that very process.

Jesus gives no honor to the fearful who refuse to take risks with the talents given them. Instead, he drives home the point that what we have should be used and extended to the greatest possible extent. We are encouraged to trust that the gifts we possess are for our multiplyling and sharing with others. There is no encouragement for selfishness; rather, sharing and giving are described as an integral part of receiving.

These principles are exemplified in the life of Stephen Hawking, the renowned English physicist. While still a young man, he faced a diagnosis of Lou Gehrig's disease. His future seemed hopeless. He abandoned his doctoral studies and resigned himself to living out his life and then dying. Then he met someone who loved him. Buoyed by this love, he made a decision to risk living even in the face of the odds against him. Today, having learned to deal with incredible handicaps, he is a great educator and scientist, known and honored the world over. Through the power of unselfish love, he overcame his fear, risked investing his talents, and won a worthwhile and rewarding life.

All that we are, all that we know, all that we possess, however great or small, are the gifts of God, talents entrusted to us to trade with as we walk through the journey of life. Each day offers us the choice: Take a chance and invest these talents, or avoid all risk and isolate ourselves from the experience of life generating more life.

What will your choice be today?

† † †

A parable is an allegorical story which seeks to make one particular point. Jesus knew that only those who were concerned with his message and goals would fully comprehend the meaning of his teachings. Yet the disciples themselves, who should certainly have understood his message, failed to see his point, making it necessary for Jesus to explain even to them the meaning of his parable.

Jesus is himself the sower of the word. He uses the common experience of their agrarian life in trying to describe the spreading of his word and the anticipated yield of the effort. He had no illusions concerning the loyalty of the crowds. He knew well the shortness of the average human's attention span, and he rightly understood a crowd's momentary fascination with the spectacular and the miraculous. He also clearly understood that no moment of excitement or grand miracle would establish and sustain the divine purpose in the sowing of the word. Hence the disciples were chosen both to learn this word directly from him and to disseminate it through preaching, teaching, and healing as they traveled among the people. Their task, begun while Jesus was still among them, was to continue after the Resurrection and throughout the remainder of their lives.

Jesus was the sower who went forth to sow upon the soil of human need and experience the good news of God's love for all people. His disciples were not far behind in spreading this same good news. Today as we listen, the singular point of the parable to us is that we, too, are sowers sent forth to sow.

Jesus, give me the opportunities and the
words today to sow the seeds of the Gospel
in the earth of human need.

† † †

In today's Gospel Mark gathers a number of parables and sayings remembered from the preaching and teaching of Jesus. The several images they offer us — a lamp, a measure, seeds of grain, a mustard seed — all have one central purpose: to affirm the reality, the dynamics, and the effects of God's presence among us.

Jesus teaches us first that, although God's presence among us initially seems hidden, secret, and obscure, it is nevertheless very real, very like the mustard seed, "the smallest of all seeds on earth." Jesus' teaching therefore invites us to look at the world with eyes of faith, and to trust that God is present with us, however imperceptible or unobtrusive that presence may be.

Jesus also teaches here that the Spirit of God grows of itself in our world and in our hearts, in much the same way that "The earth produces of itself, first the blade, then the ear, then the full grain in the ear." This does not imply, however, that we ought to adopt an attitude of passivity with regard to our spiritual growth. Rather, like the farmer who removes stones from the soil, waters the earth, and removes weeds from among the grain, so we can work in the world to create the best conditions for the growth of the life of the Spirit by involvement in social action, dedication to a life of prayer, and working to change those habits and attitudes that keep the life of the Spirit from growing in our lives.

Finally, Jesus teaches us here that when God's reign is given a chance to grow and mature, it will become the one haven that the whole world can call home. This good news invites us to come to the single place of refuge that can offer us true rest and peace: the heart of God.

Jesus, your Gospel tells us that privately, to your disciples, you explained everything. As I pause now to consider your parables about the reign of God, quiet my spirit and open my heart so that I may hear the words of truth you would speak to me through them.

† † †

"Who then is this, that even the sea and wind obey?"

It is easy to be so impressed by the extraordinary nature of Jesus' miracles that we do not see them as signs of God's presence with us in every circumstance and at every moment. Yet God's abiding presence with us is the true miracle to which all others point. The miracle in today's Gospel is a case in point.

Storms are as inevitable in our lives as they are in the world of nature. Sometimes they are as life threatening as the one described in today's Gospel, in which there is "a great storm of wind," "waves" that beat against our lives, and a boat that is "already filling" and close to sinking. The storm may be financial, brought about by the loss of a job, a sudden change of circumstances in our life, or even theft or robbery. The storm may be emotional, as waves of anger, pain, fear, or guilt rise and wash over us uncontrollably. The storm may be spiritual, as dark forces from within and without attack and threaten to overwhelm our little faith.

In such storms there is something we can do: cry out to Christ with all our might, "Teacher, do you not care if we perish?" Such a cry is good! A storm is not the time for the prayer of quiet! It is the time for a prayer that is an outcry so loud that not even God could sleep through it! Such a prayer awakens the Christ asleep within us who has the power to rebuke and calm the storm swirling around and within us.

So the next time you are caught in one of life's storms, cry out to God with all your strength, "Teacher, do you not care if I perish?" You will awaken Christ within you and hear the words: "Peace, be still!" And the wind will cease, and there will be a great calm. And you will learn once again that God in Christ is with you in every circumstance and in every moment, and therefore in every storm.

† † †

Often our response to the experience of grace is to declare our willingness to leave everything to follow wherever Christ leads, even to the ends of the earth. Such is the case in today's Gospel, when the healed demoniac begged Jesus to take him along with him on his journey.

For his part, Jesus responded with clear, simple advice: "Go home to your friends, and tell them how much the Lord has done for you, and how God has had mercy on you." The simplicity of Jesus' command is significant. He did not encourage theological debate and speculation or a new pattern of worship and adoration. He simply told the man to go home and tell others about the gift of God's mercy in his life. In addition to these words, his changed behavior and attitude would show the world the tremendous power of God's grace to transform lives.

Like the Gerasene demoniac, we too are sometimes confused and tormented by the circumstances and events of our lives. At such times, Christ enters our lives to teach us our true identities and to release us from the legion of conflicting desires that keep us repeating self-destructive patterns of behavior. A few among us are then called to leave everything to follow Christ. For most of us, though, faithfulness to Christ means returning to the place where we were before and proclaiming there with simple words and changed lives what God has done for us and what God can do for others. This is the good news of salvation, the message of healing and wholeness which we are sent to live and share today.

Jesus, sometimes I think that I must speak
eloquent words, do dramatic deeds, or travel to
faraway places in order to proclaim your mercy. Today
you bid me share the good news of what you have done
for me right here at home. Thank you for teaching
me once again that your presence abides always
in the ordinary persons, circumstances,
and events of my life.

† † †

Today's Gospel invites us to reflect on two healing events. Jairus, a ruler in a synagogue, has come to tell Jesus that his daughter is near death. He makes an anguished plea for Jesus to come to his home and heal his beloved child.

En route to Jairus' house, they encounter a humble woman who is sick and hemorrhaging. Her greatest hope is to touch even his garments. Indeed, while pressing through the crowd, she is able to reach Jesus and touch his robe. Jesus insists on knowing who has touched him: he is determined to reassure the woman that her faith has been well placed. That day she is not only physically healed, but she receives the inner peace that only Christ can impart.

But what about Jairus? He had pleaded with Jesus to come and help his daughter. And Jesus had indicated that he would come; but on the way, he had begun to take care of someone else! Jairus' frustration must have turned to despair as messengers brought to him the news that his daughter had died.

Have you ever had a similar experience? A time when it seemed that Jesus had forgotten about you, when even though others were receiving Christ's gifts of healing and peace, your own life was falling apart? What are we to do in such circumstances?

The response of Jesus to Jairus and to us is very simple: "Do not fear, only believe." And sometimes Jesus asks us to believe even the impossible. After all, from a rational point of view, who would have expected Jesus to raise Jairus' daughter from the dead? Certainly nothing in the Gospel text indicates that Jairus had asked for such a miracle. And yet he did trust Jesus enough to turn complete control of the situation over to him.

In the end Jairus was not disappointed when he put his trust in Jesus. Nor will we be disappointed when we put our faith in Jesus. If Christ does delay to answer our prayer, it may well be only to do a greater work than we had thought to ask. When bad things happen in our lives, that is the time more than ever to heed the words, "Do not fear, only believe," and to turn the situation over to Christ; and then, of course, to expect a miracle.

† † †

What are things like when you return home to your family? You have changed in the months and years since you were there last, but are the homefolks still locked in your yesterday? This is exactly what happened to Jesus. The local boy, now the man of Galilee, was not taken seriously by those who had known him as a child. It does not appear that they failed to recognize his wisdom or to marvel at his ministry of healing; it seems rather that they could not reconcile this new Jesus with the carpenter's son whom they had known. In their minds they had control over the carpenter's son, but this new Jesus was another matter.

Some people would brood and become distraught at such a situation. Jesus simply turned to the new family of God emerging around him. He did not dwell on the unbelief of his townspeople, but at once "he went about among the villages teaching." And he "called the twelve, and began to send them out two by two." In other words, he forged ahead with God's call on his energies and his life, for he had not returned home to surrender his ministry. He used the callous reception to expand his vision to a broader outreach to the world.

What are things like when you return home to your family? Sometimes the homefolks will not accept our growing and changing into our true identities. When that is the case, we have two choices: we can revert to our childhood selves and be accepted as children, or we can continue the process of becoming all that God intended us to be, even at the risk of losing family and community support.

The reward for a decision to be true to ourselves is a new family of God, an expanded vision of ourselves and our world, and a deeper peace. In time it becomes clear that sacrificing our childhood identity is a price worth paying in order to have lives in which we are truly at home with God, with ourselves, and with others.

Jesus, help me to be true to God's call on my life as you were true to God's call on your life, even if it means the loss of my family's or my community's support.

† † †

The invitation to eternal life, "Come, O blessed of God," is based upon the most concrete expression of love and human kindness imaginable: the simple bonding of ourselves in compassion and service with those who are in need. However complicated we tend to make the definition of loving service, the essential element given by Jesus is this: "As you did it to one of the least of these my sisters and brothers, you did it to me."

In our cities there is an increasing number of homeless men and women. Who of us will minister to the needs of "the least of these my sisters and brothers"? Increasing numbers of gay men are living and dying with AIDS. Who of us will minister to the needs of "the least of these my brothers and sisters"? More and more black families are falling into poverty. Who of us will minister to the needs of "the least of these my sisters and brothers"? Only as we discover not only Christ's call to serve the least of those around us, but also that we ourselves are in their company, do we really comprehend Jesus' teaching in today's Gospel.

For Jesus' teaching today is not about class or status. It is more a description of a community bound together by need and by sharing. In the communion of loving service we become one with each other and with the purposes of God. Jesus himself lived this kind of loving community life and demonstrated its implications in his own sacrificial service to others. He served one person after another in our world, teaching, feeding, always providing for the need of each from his own resources. This was God's way that Jesus followed and, by following, revealed. He commends it to us as the gateway to God's everlasting presence.

† † †

John died an innocent man whose death served only the ironic whims of court intrigue. A weak king, a shrewd and conniving woman, and a daughter whose use as a pawn eluded her youthful understanding, each played a part in the tragedy. Still, John died, untried and innocent. Such was the world's justice, and so much for its mercy. Strangely, the Gospel records no public outcry, rage, or mourning. We are simply told that John's disciples heard about his death and requested his body for burial.

It is possible even today to live in a society where murder, violence, and hatred exist and thrive in a matter-of-fact fashion. In many of our cities, especially in the poverty-stricken ghettos, riddled with illicit drugs and gang wars, Herod's little court play would be mild entertainment. Day after day we retrieve bodies, both the innocent and the guilty, and quietly bury them, only to hear news of the next victim.

God's reign among us, which John foretold and Jesus embodied, is still our best hope for breaking the cycle of rage and death in which we live. Christ still brings direction for the lost, healing for the afflicted, and release for those possessed by all manner of demons. Perhaps, instead of acquiescence to injustice, we can find the inner resources, the social clarity, and the moral commitment to counter oppression, whatever its form, with the good news of God's reign — a reign in which life is good, love is real, peace is viable, justice is universal, and mercy flows like a river.

Jesus, sometimes the social problems in our
world seem so enormous that we feel immobilized.
Help us to find ways to end the senseless
slaughter of innocents in our cities.

† † †

AUGUST

Although the word "love" is not mentioned in today's reading, love is the central message of the passage. Jesus seeks for his disciples and himself a quiet place apart to rest and eat. But, pursued by a hungering crowd, Jesus foregoes his own needs to attend to and satisfy theirs, both spiritually and physically. He feeds their souls and nourishes their bodies.

We tend to think of love as something abstract or dramatic. Yet today's reading illustrates the way that love often expresses itself in simple, ordinary actions. The few words of Jesus connected with this event that are passed on to us concern concrete, almost mundane instructions to the disciples: at Christ's command, they organize a hungry community, take an inventory of resources, and share the bread they have. The result is a miracle.

Every day God invites us to assist one another in equally ordinary ways. Someone is in a hospital and we can visit him or her; someone is in financial need and we are in a position to help; there is a meeting and someone can help by setting up the chairs. Such ordinary acts, performed at Christ's request, almost always issue in a miracle: people are brought together, nourished, and satisfied. In the process, we, too, are nourished and satisfied as faithfulness to Christ becomes participation in the miraculous transformation of life.

Today's Gospel therefore invites us to give concrete expression to our love for those who enter our lives by serving them. The outcome will surely be a renewed sense of joy and well-being. In the words of Mother Teresa of Calcutta:

> "The fruit of love is service.
> The fruit of service is peace.
> And peace begins
> with a smile."[1]

---

[1]Mother Teresa, Commencement Address, Gonzala High School, Washington, D.C., June, 1988.

† † †

In today's passage, Jesus goes off alone to pray. Like him, we, too, need to go into our own desert place of solitude to pray, to center ourselves, to learn, to listen, to grow. When was the last time I took a day apart to center and attune myself to God?

In today's passage, Jesus also comes out of a time of prayer in order to serve his community. Christ shows us that the Christian life is not a mere "God and me" phenomenon. As members of the body of Christ, we are given our gifts so that we may serve others and work for the establishment of God's reign. The community needs us, calls us, and, in fact, is incomplete without us — as are we without it. What gifts do I bring to my community?

Jesus demonstrated power in his ministry because his ministry was rooted in prayer. Conversely, Jesus demonstrated a great need for prayer because his was an active ministry. The goal of the Christian life is not either prayer or action alone, but a balance of the two. As with Jesus, we go into the desert at least in part for the sake of the community. What we find in the desert place is to be brought back for and shared with the community. But if we have not fed on the Spirit, we have nothing to share. How is the balance between prayer and action in my life?

Lord God, alone and in quiet I seek you.
Feed me and nourish me so that in community I may
share, serve, know, and manifest you. Amen.

† † †

The innermost part of each of us, the heart, is pure love, the very essence of God. Ideally, we reveal God to the world by words and deeds which flow from this divine center. However, when our hearts become overgrown with impurities — "evil thoughts, fornication, theft, murder, adultery, coveting, wickedness, deceit, licentiousness, envy, slander, pride, foolishness" — we end up reflecting those impurities rather than the love of God to the world.

In order to purify and recenter us as a people and as individuals, God sent Jesus, the Christ, to dwell in our hearts. Christ begins by cleansing our hearts of the impurities so that the love of God can shine through us to the world. With Christ in our hearts we can grow to love with the love of Christ.

As Jesus loved the tax collector, the thief, the prostitute, the disciple who denied him, the disciple who betrayed him, the leper, the children, the poor, and all others, so he showed me how to love the co-worker who wronged me, the friend who was false, the lover who rejected me, the one who hurt me, the one who needs me, the one who used me, the street person who confronts me. It isn't always easy to love, but Christ in my heart makes it always possible.

*Come, O Lord, into my heart and cleanse it of
all impurities. Empower me to see you in others and
to love and serve God by loving and serving them. Let
me be a true manifestation and reflection of your
love to all those whom I encounter today
and every day. Amen.*

† † †

The story of the Canaanite woman graphically illustrates that the good news is for all and that no one is outside of God's grace. The story is also a portrayal of the recognition and healing by Jesus of very human constraints within himself. It shows that he did not find his identity in himself alone, but also in and through others. The Canaanite woman was the instrument through which Jesus recognized and confronted his own cultural bias and prejudice against a people whom he as a Jew felt were less worthy in the sight of God. In challenging Jesus, she was the means through which he recognized and threw off the cultural bonds of hatred, pride, and prejudice. Through her own faith and presence, she liberated him and thereby empowered him to broaden the scope of the good news.

Prejudices, mind-sets, pride — these also keep me from loving completely and from fulfilling my God-given powers. Who are the ones whom I feel are expendable, whom I look down upon, whom I think are my inferiors, whom I dislike, whose needs I don't want to bother with, who have hurt me and whom I haven't forgiven? The ones whom I disdain the most are often Christ in Christ's most distressing disguise. Yet these very souls may well be the means of our own empowerment and liberating self-discovery — the discovery of ourselves in God, of God in ourselves, and of all other persons in God with ourselves. And this self-discovery then becomes the discovery not only of ourselves, but also of Christ, the center of all creation.

O Lord, send the Canaanite of my prejudices to
confront me. Open my mind and heart to discover you
in all whom I encounter. Teach me to love fully.
Amen.

† † †

My strongest memory of James, a friend who died of AIDS, is of a postcard he once sent, a picture of a young man on roller skates dressed as a fairy godmother, waving a wand, and holding a sign which read: "It takes guts to be a butterfly!" How true. Even the caterpillar must die to its old self, must trust that in becoming a vulnerable chrysalis, it will emerge as a new being, a butterfly.

I remember, too, another gay man, lying on the sofa at his sister's house in the middle of an afternoon, dehydrated, unable to keep food down, with a high temperature, a headache, and the sweats; not even diagnosed yet, he had already stopped caring and was ready to die. Suddenly, his three-year-old niece, playing quietly in the same room, silently got up from her play, walked over to the sofa, studied him a moment, then bent over, lightly kissed his forehead, and without saying a word returned to her quiet play. As he later said, that simple expression of love gave him both the motivation and strength to fight the illness. She had, he said, burst open the walls of his cocoon.

Death, suffering, and the pain of breaking open are all integral parts of the human experience; but so, too, are joy, love, and hope. Think of Jesus' willingness to trust God enough to be broken and put to death. In the end, he rose, not as a resuscitated corpse, but as a new being. The human heart, in dying to itself, can also become a new creation.

Although often cited as an example of Christ's miraculous powers, the miracle most meaningful to us in today's reading may not be the multiplication of the loaves and fishes, but rather the miracle that new life can be engendered by dying to self and serving others. Just as the physical limits of this world's time and space were transcended by the breaking again and again of the loaves and fishes into a meal for four thousand, so the passage also contains an invitation to us to love and serve others, and so to break out of our shells and experience the miracle of transformation.

Jesus, I place myself and my life in your hands today.
Give me the trust, faith, and just plain guts to break out
of myself in the service of others. Amen

 † † †

The Feast of the Transfiguration

Today I walked a farmer's fields, preferring the spaciousness of a fallow one to all the others. Like Peter at the Transfiguration, I thought.

Now is a time to be, not do. Simply be in the presence of the Saviour. ''But I want action,'' cries Peter. ''Let's put up three shelters. It is good for us to be here.'' And then we are told that he did not know what he was saying.

Not now, Peter. The time for you to act comes later — after the cock has crowed, after the terrible death, the burial, and the Resurrection. Then it will be your time, and you will spread the Gospel far and wide, telling the story of Jesus, the Christ.

For Peter this is fallow time, a time of preparation. But for Jesus the same moments bring a mountaintop experience, a prayer so intense, so focused, so deep that God's presence changed his very appearance.

And so it is with us. You and I may share this day together, and yet our paths will differ. For one it may bring heightened awareness, for another dullness and lack of comprehension. The fallow field lies beside the burgeoning cornfield.

Take time now to still your activity and quiet your mind. Open your heart to the one who created you. Let Peter show you that your own experience, whatever it is this day, has the power to shape you in the image of God, whether you are in the dark or in full bloom.

† † †

"Take heed, beware of the leaven of the Pharisees."

Although the disciples concluded that Jesus had made this statement because they had no bread, Jesus was in fact referring to a symbolic meaning of yeast. The leavening work of yeast occurs as it dissolves and becomes part of the essence of the dough; then it cannot be separated from the other ingredients. Moreover, a tablespoon of yeast added to several cups of flour markedly changes the texture of the dough itself, so that it can be made into leavened bread.

In like manner, the metaphorical yeast of the Pharisees dramatically changes the texture and quality of an individual's life. One major aspect of a Pharisaic way of living is a skepticism which seeks for a sign or looks for clear proof for those things best known by faith or intuition. While Jesus is emphatic in telling the Pharisees that no sign will be given, he is just as emphatic in reminding the disciples of the miracles they have witnessed. The disciples are reminded that, rather than seeking another sign, they should be looking for the graciousness of God already surrounding them in their daily lives. It is as if Jesus were asking, "What more do you need in order to see?"

It is much the same for us. During times of doubt, times when we wonder if God is present or really cares for us, or when we find it difficult to accept our own goodness or the goodness of life around us, we are called as people of faith to the remembrance of the graciousness of God that permeates our lives. If we are willing to look for these gifts of God around us, what need have we for further signs?

† † †

The story of the healing of a blind man at Bethsaida contains two important themes relevant for our lives as modern people of faith.

First, we find that Jesus identifies with the man by taking him by the hand and leading him outside the city. In other words, Jesus respects the man's need for and right to privacy. Unlike other instances in which Jesus heals others, this healing takes place away from the crowd.

In like manner, in providing care and support for another, we need to maintain an awareness of the other's need for the security of privacy. Our society easily stigmatizes individuals, especially in their time of need, in the time when they are most vulnerable. Part of our commitment to support life necessitates that we take care not to jeopardize the security of others who may be facing the loss of home, employment, friendship, or respect. We are called, rather, to provide supportive care in ways which respect their dignity and privacy.

Secondly, this is the only healing story which happens in stages. The man first sees shadows and only later sees clearly.

More often than not, this is the way we experience healing. There may be an easing of the raw pain of a tragic experience followed later, perhaps much later, by a visitation that somehow brings further resolution and healing integration. The Gospel example is clear. Sometimes healing takes time, and we must learn to be patient with the process of being brought to wholeness.

Gracious God, teach me to be patient when the process of healing and recovery seems slow. Help me to trust that your presence will sustain me, especially in those times when I see only shadows. Amen.

† † †

As followers of Jesus, we sometimes believe that our call has been to a life of joy, peace, and happiness. Indeed, there are times when these things are in the forefront of our experience as Christians. Yet the fundamental call to follow Jesus comes with the assurance that there will also be times in our lives which could hardly be described as either peaceful or joyful.

In today's reading from Mark's Gospel, we hear Jesus calling us to something unsettling and disquieting: "Take up your cross and follow me." Surely the original hearers of these words must have been shocked at this summons. For us, these words have lost their startling impact because of the familiarity born of repetition, but the meaning of Jesus' words is clear: The call of Jesus is an invitation to us to live our lives with such faithfulness to Christ's vision of life that we are willing, if called, to be seen as criminals sentenced to the death penalty.

This was, in fact, the appalling reality of Jesus' own death. Jesus' commitment to follow the truth of God was embodied in a life of compassionate empowering of others which so threatened the status quo of that society that he was accused of treason.

In a similar way, our call to faith is a mandate to resist the acceptance of cultural values which minimize and dehumanize our own lives and the lives of others. Our call requires that we ourselves, by taking unequivocal stands in support of justice and compassion, work actively toward empowering ourselves and others. Ours is a revolutionary call to transform human society so that it becomes the realm of God, a transformation for which Jesus taught us to pray.

This call to pick up our crosses and follow Jesus has far-reaching implications. Let us pray for the strength and courage to follow the path of Christ in justice and integrity.

† † †

Six days after Jesus first announces that he will suffer and die, a strange event occurs. Taking his intimate companions, Peter, James, and John, up to the mountaintop, Jesus is transfigured before them.

This Transfiguration is not simply a change in Jesus' appearance. Jesus stands, in a sense, outside of himself, entering a new state of awareness. For him, life after this experience is markedly different, changed, and new. Through this experience of Transfiguration, Jesus is affirmed in his ministry, an affirmation which will require that he suffer many things.

As Jesus embraces this frightening turn of events in his life, a profound and personal affirmation of him is given in the words from the cloud: "This is my beloved Child." The affirmation empowers Jesus to bear the suffering and death to which he is called and endows him with a heightened authority. Therefore the voice from the cloud commands the disciples and us: "To this one you shall listen."

For Jesus, the Transfiguration is a celebration of life — life in the very face of the pain which often results from being true to God, to oneself, and to one's call. Jesus now directs his ministry to Jerusalem, the place of his ultimate sacrifice.

The story of the Transfiguration of Jesus encourages us to expect God's direct affirmation of our own lives as we embrace the pain and suffering which come as a result of our faithfulness. Jesus' Transfiguration is an invitation to move through and beyond these hard times to a newness of life that empowers us in personal and unexpected ways.

*Jesus, as I listen to your gentle voice, empower
me to move through the painful parts of my life to find
the newness of life which you promise. Amen.*

† † †

Raphael, in his painting of the Transfiguration, depicts two scenes: Jesus on the mountaintop and the casting out of the demon from the possessed boy. The artist clearly has grasped the vital connection between these two events.

On the mountain of the Transfiguration, in a place of solitude, Jesus refocuses on his special mission and unique identity. In turn, Jesus is affirmed in the deepest fullness of his being, symbolized by the radiating light and the voice from the cloud.

While these events are occurring on the mountain, the disciples apparently fail to cast out the demon from the boy. They are perplexed, while the boy's father becomes ever more frustrated by his son's plight.

Upon returning from the mountain experience, Jesus encounters the boy, his father, and the disciples. Jesus almost nonchalantly assesses the situation, expresses his own frustration concerning their lack of faith, and heals the boy.

Later, when the disciples ask why they had failed in this seemingly simple task, Jesus tells them that this type of healing can only come about through prayer.

What is this prayer of which Jesus speaks? It is the experience of transfiguration where, in solitude, one comes to the knowledge of the unique giftedness of one's own being. It is the experience, in prayer, of discovering that one is indeed created in God's image and likeness, and is called in a special way to reflect that image to the world in accordance with the gifts that one has been given. It is this prayer that empowers the believer to use those gifts and overcome evil.

Creator God, as I sit in the stillness of prayer,
may your empowering presence be with me. Call to my
remembrance the goodness with which you created me
and the purpose of my life.

† † †

The disciples, keenly aware that Jesus has come to establish a new reign, naturally assume that this reign will include a new form of government in which the disciples will hold positions as major leaders.

In his role as teacher Jesus attempts, by word and example, to reshape the disciples' expectations of the coming era, and to this end he contrasts the timeless human yearning for upward mobility with the need for a certain amount of self-effacement.

From Jesus' perspective, using power and position for the purpose of getting ahead of others limits one's opportunities for experiencing life in its fullness, that is, for encountering life situations and other people in their fullest potential.

In contrast, by opening oneself to such encounters and seeking to meet the needs of others, one makes oneself vulnerable enough to allow the life experiences which the world has to offer to touch one's very being. Only thus can a person experience the wonder of living as a child does, and so become enriched and refreshed through the mystery of life itself. Upward mobility must be foresworn, but in compensation one gains the grace-filled experience of finding new meaning in life.

God of simplicity, keep me from being swept
into the currents of upward mobility. Allow me to
rest gently in your presence, savoring the beauty of
creation, and to be as content as a child
on its mother's knee. Amen.

† † †

Today's passage places us in the middle of a significant contro-versy concerning the role of the purification rite of baptism in the life of the first-century Jewish community. The role of the purification rite of baptism. In this passage, the controversy between the disciples of John the Baptist and an unnamed Jew arises because of confusion concerning the relationship bet-ween the baptism of John and the baptism of Jesus' disciples.

John responds to the confusion and controversy deliberately and insightfully, saying that although he has been called to play a unique and special role, he has not been called to do everything.

John is able to see clearly the place of both his own ministry and that of Jesus within the cosmic order: Jesus' ministry must increase, while John's must decrease. John has plumbed the depths and dimensions of his call and knows that it is enough for him to be where he is. He is content, and he sees no need to take on those things which he is really not called to do.

In the same way, we are reminded that each of us has been called to do something unique and special, and that we are called and gifted in different ways. This does not diminish the worth of any of us, it simply makes each of us special. John is an example for each of us to emulate in recognizing and fulfilling his or her own call while remaining free of anxiety or jealousy about the gifts and missions of others.

Spirit of God, you have called me and gifted me in special and unique ways. Teach me how precious is the mission you have given me. Enable me to be faithful and content through your leading. Amen.

† † †

In this passage, Mark presents us with a collection of the sayings of Jesus, beginning with a harsh challenge about sin and concluding with three seemingly unrelated sayings about salt. Taken together, however, this passage forms a natural parable about two alternative life options for the believer.

While salt was used in ancient times as a seasoning much as it is today, its primary use was as a preservative. Without salt, meats and prepared foods spoiled within hours. By analogy, Jesus calls his listeners to preserve their lives in a zesty, flavorful way just as food is preserved by salt.

What is this salt of which Jesus speaks? It is described in these sayings as possessing an inherent preserving quality which purifies our lives and draws us closer to God and others. Clearly, this is not merely an additive to our lives, but something that should be inherent in our way of life. The salty, zestful life is the life lived in the awareness of the Spirit of God dwelling within and around us, an awareness built on our personal relationship with God and nurtured through prayer and self-sacrifice.

The alternative to this preserved life is likened to the smoldering fire of Gehenna. While we often equate Gehenna with Hell, Gehenna is actually another name for the Valley of Hinnom, a smoldering garbage dump outside of Jerusalem which had been the place of idolatry and infanticide during prophetic times. The smoldering fire of Gehenna, with its worms that never die, is clearly the epitome of decay.

The mandate of Jesus is therefore clear: do those things necessary to preserve a zesty and godly life and remove from your life those things that are the roots of dissipation and decay. In sum, season your life with that which enables you to live in communion with God and at peace with others.

† † †

In ancient Hebrew society, women and children held few legal rights. Instead, they found their social status through being related to a man, such as a husband or father. Legally, women and children were considered to be the property of this man.

From this legal perspective, it was lawful for a husband to divorce his wife for any of a host of reasons, including allowing food to spoil, speaking too loudly, or being no longer attractive to him. On the other hand, it was practically impossible for a wife to divorce her husband. Moreover, women and children were defenseless after divorce since there was no social institution that would support them and no man to give them legal identity.

In this passage we encounter Jesus establishing a new aspect of the social order: he clearly rejects his culture's unfair divorce practices and focuses attention on the sanctity of commitment between two mutually consenting adults. Moreover, in blessing the children and using them as examples of the coming reign of God, Jesus also rejects the social view which equated children with property.

In breaking the boundaries of the social divisions of his day, Jesus underscores the sanctity of each person. As followers of Jesus, we are called to respond to our own social structures in a similar way, moving beyond the many forms of prejudice and social division so as to create a community that includes all people.

† † †

The question is posed to Jesus: "What must I do to inherit eternal life?" One interpretation of this question is, "How do I make it to heaven?" Jesus' response makes it clear, however, that he interprets the question to mean, "How do I really live? Not just make it through life, not just get by, but how do I live meaningfully now?"

Jesus' response therefore focuses on life in the here and now. He summarizes the major commandments, which are rooted in an ultimate reverence for everyday life. In recounting the commandments, Jesus calls the inquirer to find fullness of life by respecting the lives of others, by honoring the life-giving relationship between two people, by not taking from others those things needful to their lives or good names, and by honoring and respecting the source of one's own life.

Clearly the man asking the question does not understand the underlying meaning of what Jesus is saying to him, for he responds that he has kept these commandments since his youth. Jesus then makes the message clearer: ". . . sell what you have and give to the poor." In other words, take whatever is important in your life and give it to others. In giving away what is important in your life, you will find fullness of life for yourself.

It is significant that Jesus directs the man to give what is important in his own life to those who can use what he is giving: there is a matching of the man's resources to the needs of others. Jesus does not call us to give away indiscriminately all things that are needful or important to us, but to give whatever we give in a way that supports and empowers the lives of others. The promise to the young man, and to us, is that this kind of sharing will result in the experience of eternal life even now.

† † †

"And they were on the road, going up to Jerusalem,
and Jesus was walking ahead of them."

Jerusalem, the Holy City, is the center of Jewish life. This city holds such a prominent place in Hebrew life because it is here that one finds the Temple, the central place of worship and sacrifice. It is therefore to Jerusalem that Jesus goes, leading the way for all who would follow him.

On the way to Jerusalem, Jesus explains to the disciples what will happen there, disclosing his mission, his sense of purpose, and surely, his fear. Jesus will be mocked, spat upon, flogged, and killed. How painful it must have been to speak these words!

And the disciples respond — or do they? Could they really have heard what Jesus said? Two of them ask Jesus for places of honor! They are concerned with who among them is the most important. Their insecurity and self-concern deafen them to the intimate self-disclosure made by Jesus. How painful it must have been for Jesus to hear this "response."

Each of us, whether Black, White, Asian, or Hispanic, homosexual or heterosexual, male or female, knows the experience of trying to share some important part of ourself only to find that the sharing falls on deaf ears. The response of Jesus to this experience of not being understood is a gentle firmness which reasserts the truth of his life: for the Messiah "came not to be served but to serve, and to give his life as a ransom for many." Jesus is aware that he will be misunderstood, even killed, for sharing the truth of his life, yet he is faithful to God and to himself.

Following the example of Jesus, let us not grow tired of journeying on this road which calls each of us to speak the truth of our lives.

† † †

As Jesus arrives in Jericho, he hears the call of the beggar Bartimaeus: "Have mercy on me!" The call of Bartimaeus is often a difficult one for us to hear. Perhaps our difficulty lies in not quite understanding the Biblical sense of mercy. For us, mercy is most often associated with forgiveness, but for the ancients, mercy was synonymous with compassion, whose literal meaning is "to suffer with." The cry of Bartimaeus is therefore a plea to Jesus to suffer with him, to feel his pain.

The townspeople, resisting the experiencing of another's pain, attempt to silence Bartimaeus. Jesus, however, calls Bartimaeus, inviting him into his life and asking him what he wants. Bartimaeus answers: "Let me receive my sight." The response of Jesus is simple: "Your faith has made you well." This statement which accompanies the restoration of Bartimaeus' sight is full of insight for us.

First of all, faith gives birth to insight. It is faith which enables us to perceive the graciousness of God despite apparent evidence to the contrary in our lives. In the midst of the limitations on our lives, faith challenges us to see the presence of God providing for us in our deepest need.

Secondly, Jesus affirms that Bartimaeus has the resources for his own healing, resources that enable Bartimaeus to transform his blindness into vision, his weakness into strength. It is not that Jesus heals Bartimaeus, but that Bartimaeus' faith in Jesus gives him new sight.

Let us take, then, the example of Bartimaeus, allowing Jesus to be present in our pain so that we, too, may be empowered for our own healing, finding God's loving care around us in places where we least expect it.

† † †

Jerusalem is the center of Jewish life and worship, the home of the Temple, the center of sacrifice. It is in Jerusalem that the paschal lamb is slaughtered, that blood is shed, that religious fervor is surrounded by the pain and anguish associated with these oblations.

Jesus enters into this city in a most deliberate way, quite unlike the way he entered into Jericho, where he called on Zacchaeus to host a dinner party for the crowd that had met him. Here in Jerusalem, Jesus rides through the midst of the crowd and goes directly to the Temple, the center of the pain of the people, looking closely at this place and gathering in the heartfelt concerns of the people. Temple worship, with its daily ritual of blood sacrifices poured out day after day, symbolizes the living sacrifice of the people.

Today we are also aware of other forms of pain. There is the pain and sacrifice experienced in racism, sexism, and homophobia. There is the pain experienced in our families through addiction, abuse, and separation. There is the personal pain of rejection, loneliness, and broken relationships. The ministry of Christ moves directly to the points of our pain and is present in them. It is this presence of Christ which empowers us to move through the pain of our lives so that we are able to enter into the new life, the full life, the integrated life of the resurrection.

† † †

Today's discourse by Jesus is his response to being questioned about his healing of a crippled man on the Sabbath. Asserting his own integrity, Jesus employs the legalistic tactics of his day to demonstrate both his own Messiahship and the hard-heartedness of his listeners.

In juridical fashion, Jesus cites four sources that bear witness on his behalf: John the Baptist, our Mother-Father God, the works Jesus performs, and Scripture. Jesus remonstrates his hearers for refusing to accept the honesty of his claim to Messiahship, which is testified to by these sources, while willingly giving credence to self-proclaimed Messiahs.

Important for us is the reason Jesus gives for his listeners' behavior. Jesus states that the religious Jews of his day lack the willingness to enter into the glory of God because of their eagerness to have their egos affirmed and their accomplishments noticed and because of their drive to get ahead.

We live in a highly competitive and commercial society where the reward of upward mobility is also offered on the basis of our accomplishments and our acquisition of worldly goods, rather than upon the affirmation of our integrity, honesty, and genuine character. Striving for this reward almost always means the dishonesty of actually denying or repressing our deepest and most loving compassionate self, the self that fundamentally cares for the well-being of others rather than seeking to use others for its own advancement. Failing to live with integrity and honesty means that we fail to live in faithfulness to God, the one who made us who and what we are and affirmed that we are radically good.

Faithfulness to God calls us to live with integrity and honesty so that we may mirror the integrity and honesty of Jesus and see life around us in all its richness.

† † †

In this passage, Mark presents us with a face of Jesus with which we are often neither familiar nor comfortable. This unfamiliar face is that of an angry Jesus.

This passage begins with Jesus' cursing of the fig tree for not bearing fruit. Mark takes special care to note that Jesus vents his anger at this tree when figs are not in season. Even though there can be no reasonable expectation for the tree to have figs, Jesus is frustrated and angered and shows his feelings by cursing the tree, which is later found to be withered.

Next, Jesus enters the Temple, discovering merchants and money changers conducting their normal business. From these merchants the worshippers bought the animal offerings prescribed by law for sacrifice, and through these money changers they exchanged their Roman coins, considered ritually unclean, for Temple currency to be used in the offering. Jesus, angered by these practices, lashes out, overturning tables and clearing the Temple of the buyers and sellers.

Within this passage, Jesus also says that if one has faith in God one can do anything. The placing of this statement next to these two stories about Jesus' anger suggests that the quality of faith of which Jesus speaks is comparable to the experience of anger: that when one is angry one sees distinctly that something must be done immediately and that the conviction of faith gives the believer a clear vision of what it is that must be done. Such faith-filled conviction possesses the astonishing power to move mountains in much the same way that the astonishing power of Jesus' anger withered the fig tree.

The vitality of faith, then, should empower us with the same urgent potency as does the emotional release we experience in a flash of anger.

† † †

Are you afraid of emotions like jealousy and fear? Do you sometimes try to conceal or avoid them by "people-pleasing," by doing and saying whatever will make you look good in the eyes of others instead of truly acknowledging the feelings you have? Those of us who have had such experiences can see ourselves reflected in today's Scripture.

"What shall we say?" "How can we get out of this one?" The chief priest, teachers, and elders argued together about how they could answer Jesus' question without exposing themselves to criticism or appearing foolish. "How will we look if we say this?" "What will people think if we say that?" In the end, they were so fearful of the way they would look to others that they never thought of simply trying to see and say the truth about the question or about themselves.

Take a few minutes to recall a recent instance in which you acted like the chief priest and elders, tailoring your response to the way you thought others would see you, concealing from them, and perhaps from yourself, what was in your heart. Now reflect on yourself as God knows and loves you. Imagine the way that you would have responded to the same situation had you been true to yourself and true to your Creator. Pray for trust in your Saviour, the kind of trust that will set you free to be, without pretense or subterfuge, just who you are — the beautiful and mysterious one whom God created, knows, and loves.

† † †

Under ancient Jewish law, if a married man died childless, it was his brother's duty to marry the widow and produce offspring. Here the Sadducees construct a scenario in which each of seven brothers dies childless after marrying the widow. Then the Sadducees ask the key question: "In the resurrection whose wife will she be?"

The Sadducees did not, in fact, believe in resurrection, and their question is framed to prove that the notion of a resurrection is ridiculous. Jesus replied that they were badly mistaken, inasmuch as they knew neither the Scriptures nor the power of God.

While a debate about a widow's marital status seems somewhat quaint to us today, the question of how we arrive at spiritual truth is as significant now as it was in the days of Jesus. Do we read the Bible to confirm and prove our own theological, political, or social ideas, or do we approach Scripture with hearts and minds open to the guidance of God's Holy Spirit? To be open to the Holy Spirit involves a willingness to give up the comfort of what we think we know and to let God change us.

Take a few minutes now to pray for a sincere willingness to learn and to be changed, for the ability to set aside your preconceived notions, for openness to hearing and understanding the special truth God's Word has for you this day.

† † †

"Tell me of your wants and desires and I'll tell you what kind of person you are," the radio evangelist boomed forth as I was driving to the supermarket. "I don't want to know anything about your possessions, what you have, or what you do — just tell me your desires."

I don't recall the rest of the program, but these words came back to me as I read today's Scripture. A new car, a lover, a Caribbean cruise, to be the best trial lawyer or the most creative hairdresser — these are typical of the desires our culture encourages, and most of us are motivated to strive for them.

Jesus offers a striking alternative — to love God with our whole being. Think for a minute what it might mean to love with all your heart, all your soul, all your mind and all your strength. Most of us live fragmented lives, hurrying from one obligation to another, our minds often scattered, jumping from this to that. We are divided within ourselves. This great commandment is not something we can do on our own, for only God can teach us to love wholeheartedly. But we can make it the central, conscious desire of our lives to love God with our whole selves, to be at one with our Creator.

Pay attention to your inner self . . . . Deep within find your own desire to be united with God . . . . Remember that the greatest commandment is available for you . . . . Jesus asks that you make it the central aspiration of your life.

† † †

Today we find Jesus teaching in the Temple courts. We know he is speaking to a large crowd, but we are not told who the people are. Imagine yourself there in the crowd, listening to the teacher. You are among first century Jews, taught from your earliest days to expect a Messiah of Davidic descent, and Jesus raises a question about your belief! He also challenges the authority of those who taught you.

In questioning this teaching, Jesus does not say whether it is right or wrong. He leaves no doubt, however, that the belief of the most important people in church or society does not necessarily make that belief true. Jesus simply examines the teaching in question in the light of Scripture and opens it to the power of God for resolution.

In seeking spiritual truth, we must learn to open our questions, open our very selves, to the light of God's power, and then wait for the answer, however long the wait may be. In this case, the answer to Jesus's question did not come until after his death and Resurrection when his own Davidic descent was claimed and reconciled with Scripture. (See, for example, Matthew 1:1-17, Luke 3:23-38, Romans 1:3, and 2 Timothy 2:8.)

Has one of your beliefs come under question recently? If so, recall the circumstances and how you felt on that occasion. Offer your questions to God now, along with all the feelings your uncertainty stimulates. As you wait for God's answer, let God bring life to your questions.

† † †

Throughout the ages people have loved to construct places of worship, from great cathedrals and temples to simple one-room chapels. To this day, we find that raising funds for new buildings captures the imagination and loyalty of churchgoers in countless congregations.

In today's passage we read of an unidentified disciple who calls to Jesus' attention the magnificence of the Temple in Jerusalem. Jesus, though, is emphatic in his response that buildings are not important. His teaching here is forceful, a message of urgency, hard for many of us to hear. Like the disciple, many of us prefer to focus on the beautiful sanctuary.

You must be on guard, Jesus says, lest you misunderstand the dangers of the world. Not only will wars and earthquakes, sickness and famine occur, but also deceit and betrayal, hypocrisy and murder. The magnificent stones of the Temple will not help you to navigate the shoals your life will encounter. As a disciple, this is what you must do: you must spread the good news and take the consequences when powerful people try to silence you. You must stand firm in your faith, no matter what your life brings.

We may say that Jesus' words reflect first century expectations of the apocalypse and thus distance ourselves somewhat from the teaching. But try to stay with the concept of discipleship that Jesus had in mind. Ask God to strengthen your faith, and then ask God to use you to bring the Gospel to one who needs it. Let the Holy Spirit guide and give you words.

† † †

I feel the darkness within. I can, of course, pretend it doesn't exist. Yet I feel a restlessness within, a desire for something more, and along with it, a realization that I can, if I choose, live out my days in habitual security, somehow disengaged from the wellspring of life. Still, I find myself just staying where I am, doing reasonably well in the eyes of the world. I don't know how to change.

"Be bold," I hear a voice saying as my attention is directed to the actions of Jesus. He defied the social conventions of his time. He went right into the Temple and challenged the Pharisees, the very ones who had been charged with interpreting and explaining God's commandments to the people. Jesus did not think and act by worldly standards. He must have seemed crazy to people of the world. Yet he knew and was faithful to God's plan for his life, even though it involved confronting powerful leaders who riddled him with scorn and hate, and being eventually nailed onto a cross.

Afraid to risk change, I hear Jesus calling. "I am the light of the world," Christ says. "The one who follows me will not walk in darkness, but will have the light of life."

Do you know where you come from? Do you know where you are going? Meditate on God's will for your life . . . . Pray for the boldness to step out in that will. Let us pray the same prayer for each other.

† † †

Jesus foretells that one day the world will fall apart and that when that happens, you will find yourself in deep distress.

What can you do about it? You yourself will not be able to deal with the situation, and you may well be tempted to follow those in your midst who claim power and authority even though you know that they may be "false Christs and false prophets." Jesus warns you to watch out for them and to pay attention instead to Jesus, who promises that at that terrible time Christ will return "in clouds with great power and glory," and angels will gather you and all God's people "from the four winds, from the ends of the earth to the ends of heaven."

As you meditate today, allow yourself to feel for a few minutes the unsettling certainty that the world as you know it will come to an end. Open yourself to the knowledge that your sense of control over life is an illusion.

And now, focus on the poetry of the biblical verses and let them come alive for you. Can you see Christ coming on the clouds? Do you hear the sound of angels, feel their gentle touch? Know deep in your heart that when your world is coming to an end and you are in deep distress, God is there with you, gathering you in gentle, loving, almighty arms.

† † †

The heat wave broke in the night and we needed a blanket to finish our sleep. The cool of the morning refreshed my spirit as I hung wash on a line between trees in the yard. The birds sang and the yellow wildflowers stood bright in the morning sun — but a feeling of change permeated the air, and we all knew that summer would soon turn to fall.

Yesterday I visited a friend in the hospital. The sickness has touched her central nervous system now, and it causes her to tremble. The simplest manual task, like putting on slippers, becomes a lengthy labor requiring patience, determination, and the concentration of prayer. Although she says the shaking is "a bummer," I see that she has accepted the challenge of learning a new way to put on her slippers, a new way of experiencing her life. Her sickness ministers to her friends, her daily struggle illuminating the truth that we cannot control our lives, that change is inevitable, that our choice lies in how we respond to it.

Take some time now to consider the way you receive change in your life. If there is fear, resistance, and the need to control, see if you can let go, remembering the image that Jesus gives us of the household servants, each with an assigned task in the owner's house. The word Jesus says to you he says to everyone: *"Watch!"* Whatever your circumstances may be, whether in sickness of health, in creating or simply sustaining, you are called to be alert and watchful, fully conscious of God's presence in your life.

† † †

Feelings ran high that day in Simon the Leper's house. Everyone knew the teaching of Jesus that the rich should sell their possessions and give to the poor. Yet here was a woman of wealth who squandered much of it in one extravagant act. We who have our own confusions about money and extravagance and pleasure are invited to come into the house and join the party.

Where are you to be found? Are you hoping that you, too, will be anointed luxuriously? How wonderful that must have felt when she began to pour the exquisite perfumed oil on his tired body! Does the woman's boldness in coming forward so unexpectedly put you off? Who is she, after all, to take such liberties with Jesus? We don't even know her name. And what about the poor? Do you feel discomfort at the fact that there are homeless women, men, and children on the streets all the while that a jar of perfumed oil costing enough to pay three hundred days' worth of a laborer's wages is being poured out in one extravagant gesture?

The words that Jesus spoke that day, as emotions overflowed in Simon the Leper's house, have healing power for us all. "Let her alone . . . She has done a beautiful thing to me . . . She has anointed my body beforehand for burying."

Whatever you face as you look ahead, ask Jesus for help in leaving alone what is not right for you, for the ability to see beauty in what you and others do, for the courage to do what you can, and for the grace to hold in reverence the mystery you cannot understand.

† † †

"Where will you have us go?"

Lord, we seek your direction now just as the disciples did on that long-ago Passover. When they asked, you spared no detail. You told them where they were to go, the person they were to meet and follow, the house they would eventually enter, and what to say and do when they arrived.

Our hearts cry out for direction as we restlessly pace the plateau of our lives. Where are we going and what are we doing? We feel inadequate and tired from the struggles of our days and years. Yet as we seek your guidance, you do not respond with such specifics. Why will you not tell us as you told them?

"I do," Jesus replies, and we begin to read about the Lord's Supper. "And as they were eating, Jesus took bread, and blessed, and broke it, and gave it to them and said, 'Take; this is my body.' "

"Take." The word begins to sink in. Lord, you have given your life for us. And your surpassing love is offered for us to take. Out of the fullness of this love, your call for our lives takes form, keeping time with the rhythm of all creation.

Let us pause this day, allowing our hearts to feel the love we are invited just to take. And let us experience, too, the wondrous mystery of the love that embraces not only us, but all of God's creation. *"Take,"* our Saviour says. You seek direction for your life? *"Take."*

† † †

SEPTEMBER

"You will fall away; for it is written, 'I will strike the shepherd, and the sheep will be scattered.' But after I am raised up, I will go before you to Galilee."

Jesus' love for the disciples never faltered. Even while prophesying that the disciples would desert and deny him, Jesus promised to return to them. Jesus kept the promise, returning and bringing the Holy Spirit to be a comfort and a counselor.

As Christ loved the disciples, so Christ loves us, and that love is alive today. We can say with assurance, "Christ has died, Christ has risen, Christ will come again." Christ keeps promises to us, too.

In the hustle and bustle of each day, it is easy to become flustered and unfocused. We can become unfocused by big things: a close friend's illness, conflicts with one's spouse, turmoil within ourselves. We can be flustered by small things: a forgotten grocery list, a chore left undone, a work project thrust on us suddenly.

On another level, we can be shaken when we read and hear each day of death, destruction, and violence — evidence of a broken world that seems beyond hope. Yet God, our source of light, is present in the midst of all darkness. Focusing on God's redeeming love helps us to deal with the ups and downs of our lives. Remembering that God keeps promises gives us something to anchor ourselves to in a world gone topsy-turvy.

Draw strength from the depth of God's love for you. In a world that is often unfaithful, God is always faithful. In a world that is always changing, God never changes. God's love for each of us is everlasting.

† † †

"Have you come out as against a robber, with swords and clubs, to capture me? Day after day I was with you in the temple teaching, and you did not seize me."

Why did the crowd come with swords and clubs when they could have seized Jesus without them? Jesus was a teacher, not a robber or a thief. Throughout his ministry, Jesus had demonstrated his commitment to change through nonviolent means.

The crowd had all the advantages in the Garden of Gethsemane. They outnumbered the disciples; they had one of Jesus' own followers, Judas, among them; they had the prestige of the high priests and the scribes and the elders behind them. Why were they so afraid that they came with swords and clubs?

Perhaps they were afraid because a small, inner voice told them they were doing something wrong.

Jesus had not done anything to deserve death. Even Pilate, who would play a part in crucifying Jesus, sensed this — "For he perceived that it was out of envy that the chief priests had delivered up Jesus." (Mark 15:10) Surely the crowd in the garden knew it, too.

During those moments in life when we must choose between one path and another, we can learn something from the crowd at Gethsemane. When we consider one path, do we find ourselves trying to justify it? Can the path we are choosing stand on its own merits, or are we arming ourselves with "weapons" to defend it?

Each day, as we draw closer to God through our ministries, through prayer, and through study of the Scriptures, we can trust God to help us discern what is best for us; all we need do is open ourselves to God's presence. Like the crowd at Gethsemane, we need to listen to that small, inner voice.

† † †

"Truly, truly, I say to you, before Abraham was, I am."

To the Jews, Abraham was the parent from whom they had all descended. Ancestors were considered sacred, for they represented the beginnings of the tribe. In the Hebraic culture, to name a child after an ancestor was a high honor, laden with significance; it was hoped that the child would emulate his or her namesake. Some scholars have suggested that ancient Hebrews sometimes even bore children primarily because there was a name that they wished to pass on. Thus the Jews perpetuated a never-ending renewal: as ancestors died, they lived on in the children named for them. Life was a constant ebb and flow of beginnings and endings. No one now living was present when God first made a covenant with the Jews, yet the chosen people survived; the covenant lived on in the lives of those who kept it.

For Jesus to say, "Your father Abraham rejoiced that he was to see my day" was therefore quite radical, even blasphemous. This was because Jesus was claiming to have existed even before Abraham, which confused and upset the Jews. How could this young man have lived before Abraham? And if Jesus had lived before Abraham, that meant he was claiming to be greater than Abraham, claiming to be the focal point of their faith. In their minds, Jesus was dishonoring Abraham, a sin worthy of stoning.

Yet Christ *is* the eternal one, the alpha and the omega, the beginning and the end. Christ *is* is the focal point of our faith. Christ *is* the way to which we return again and again in our lives, a way that works, a way that lives on today in Christians all over the world. Jesus in human form is gone from this world, but the church, the body of Christ, lives on in us.

Make Christ the focal point of your life today. Bring Christ closer to you and to those you meet by making Christ the center of your being. Make the way of Christ your journey, which begins and ends with God's love for you.

† † †

*"Again, the high priest asked Jesus, 'Are you the Christ,
the Child of the Blessed?' And Jesus said, 'I am.' And they
all condemned Jesus as deserving death."*

The chief priests and elders gathered in the temple to condemn
Jesus to death. However, there were a few obstacles: Jesus had
done nothing wrong, and Jesus wouldn't answer any of the
false charges. He didn't attempt to justify anything. Jesus didn't
try to counter the lies witnesses told. He didn't hit back when
struck by the guards. When the chief priests finally managed
to pronounce a death sentence, they condemned Jesus merely
for telling the truth. When asked if he were the Christ, the
Child of the Blessed, he said, "I am."

Many of us were raised to believe that a believer could not
be both homosexual and Christian. As gay and lesbian Christians, some of us have been accepted in a faith community
only by staying silent about the deepest part of ourselves. Some
of us have been ostracized from a faith community for speaking
out about this important part of our identity. Even if we are
not gay or lesbian, we may still hide, afraid to be who we are
in our community. We may keep parts of ourselves secret,
fearful of what others may say or do.

Jesus' strength in today's Gospel seems to come from the fact
that he knew who he was and he was not afraid to stand in
the truth of his identity. We, too, can gather strength from
knowing who we are and being unafraid to stand in the truth
of our identity. Whether gay and lesbian or heterosexual, we
know we are children of the Blessed and that God will never
desert us. And in the face of oppression, we know that we
are free to be who we really are and to tell the truth about it.

"I am the light of the world," Jesus said. (John 8:12) Seek out
the hidden parts of your life this day and warm them in the
light of Christ's care for you. Bring those hidden places to
Christ today and say, "I am."

† † †

". . . the bystanders said to Peter, 'Certainly you are one of them; for you are a Galilean.' But he began to invoke a curse on himself and to answer, 'I do not know this Jesus of whom you speak.' "

If asked the question, "Do you know Jesus Christ?" most of us would not deny it. Of course, most of us aren't asked the question directly. Indirectly, however, the question is asked of us many times. We are asked the question whenever we see someone hungry and homeless. We are asked the question whenever we are called upon to recognize each person's worth as a child of God. We are asked the question whenever we are confronted with hatred and oppression. Whatever the situation, if we respond with violence, or with contempt, we are denying Christ. If we choose to do what is Christ-like, we are saying, "Yes, I do know Jesus Christ."

We come to know Jesus Christ by acknowledging God's presence within ourselves and within each other. We come to know Christ through prayer, meditation, and the study of Scripture. We come to know Christ through worship and the sharing of the good news of the Gospel.

As we come to know Christ more fully within ourselves and within our community, Christ moves to the center of our relationships and they are transformed. As we claim Christ's love and forgiveness for ourselves, we are able to extend that same love and forgiveness to our other relationships.

Whenever we follow the path of Christ, we are saying "yes" to God's working in our life. Like Peter, we may deny Christ at times. Like Peter, we will be forgiven if we do. God works through weakness, as Peter's life testifies: From denying Christ, he went on to become the leader of the early Christian church. Knowing Jesus Christ does not require us to be flawless persons. God asks only that we begin to say "yes" more than we say "no."

† † †

*"And Pilate again asked Jesus, 'Have you no
answer to make? See how many charges they bring
against you.' But Jesus made no further answer,
so that Pilate wondered."*

In catechism class I used to read a book of children's stories
called *What Would Jesus Do?* In each story, the children
decided how they would act by asking themselves, "What
would Jesus do?" The other kids in my class and I often made
fun of that book; we thought it was sappy and silly. But now,
again and again, I turn to the actions of Christ's life for inspiration and answers. I learn as much from what Christ did as from
what Christ said.

In today's passage, we learn much from what Christ did *not*
say. Pilate must have been puzzled by Jesus. Here was a person
facing an ugly, painful death, yet Jesus said nothing in answer
to the charges brought by the chief priests. Pilate said, "See
how much power these people have over you? How much
power I have over you? If you do not answer, you will surely
die." By not answering, Christ said, without words, "You have
no power over me at all." Christ silent before accusers is a
moving example of the power in powerlessness.

It is often difficult to let power rest where it belongs — with
God. When we are faced with a dilemma, it can be hard to
turn the problem over to God, for to do so requires relinquish-
ing control. However, we will find the best solutions to our
problems only if we surrender control over them to God. After
all, that is what Jesus' whole life was about. He gave ultimate
control of his life and his ministry to God.

"What would Jesus do?" is not such a silly question after all.
If you are faced with a dilemma today, remember that God
stands ready to receive burdens — all we have to do is let them
go. That's what Jesus would do.

† † †

*"Then what shall I do with the one whom
you call King of the Jews?"*

Pilate was not the kindest man in the Roman empire. By modern standards, he would be considered a despot. Still, Pilate did not want to condemn an innocent person to death. He was aware that the chief priest and elders resented Jesus, and that many of the charges against Jesus were probably false. Pilate asked Jesus to answer the charges, perhaps hoping that Jesus would say something that would allow him to set Jesus free. But Jesus kept silent.

When it became clear to Pilate that he could not escape condemning Jesus, he wanted at least to escape responsibility for Jesus' death. The Gospel according to Matthew even depicts Pilate washing his hands before the people, saying, "I am innocent of this man's blood; see to it yourselves." (Matthew 27:24) He left the final decision up to the crowd, and it was the crowd who said, "Crucify him." Perhaps this salved Pilate's conscience as he watched Jesus being led away to be crucified. Like Hitler's officers at Nuremberg, he could say to himself, "I was only following orders."

Pilate did not want to acknowledge the consequences of his decision; however, he did have a hand in Jesus' death. By not making a choice, he in fact made a decision that had crucial implications.

Our lives are the result, at least in part, of various decisions we've made. Each time we decide to wash our hands of Christ and the consequences of Christ's presence, we take a step away from wholeness. Each time we decide to take a step toward Christ, our lives become richer and fuller.

Pilate's words in today's Scripture call us to respond to his question: "What shall I do with the one whom you call King of the Jews?" What *are* we doing with Jesus? Are we striving toward union with God, or are we growing further away? Are we holding ourselves accountable for what we do, or are we, like Pilate, refusing to take responsibility for our actions? Today, make a decision to draw closer to this Jesus whom they called King of the Jews.

† † †

Christ Crucified Today

He lies in bed.
His eyes open wide to greet me.
He extends his hand.
His face is ash white.
His cheek bones protrude
    from a face too tired to hold its shape
    from a body too sick to eat.
His lips are cracked and broken.
Sores cover his mouth.
His hands tremble as they stroke mine.
He reaches for the basin and begins to retch.
I gently stroke his back
As spasms subside, tears stream down his face.

The I.V. drips slowly
    into overused, collapsing veins.
Purple lesions violate his body.
The marks stand stark on his bare arms and face.
The spasms return.
He clutches my arm.
Pleading eyes reach out —
    pulling tears from my own.

Anxiety pounds through my chest.
I'm dizzy, breathless.
I want to run — can't bear to look — to see him suffer.
    "How are you?" he asks from eyes burning with pain.
    "Are *you* taking care of yourself?"
    "I hurt too much to hurt with you any more," I finally admit.
His eyes release me.
His eyes forgive me — and everyone.
His eyes say good-bye, fill with tears, and close.

Above his head
    on the wall
    the inscription,
    the charge against him:
"AIDS"

† † †

*"And the curtain of the temple was torn in two
from top to bottom."*

The religious Jews of Jesus' day were afraid to look on God directly. The curtain of the Temple separated the people from the holy of holies. Year after year, the people of God strove to make themselves perfect by following the laws as closely as possible. Year after year, the high priests offered sacrifices for the people's sins. Year after year, the curtain between God and the people remained.

Jesus' death changed all that. Jesus broke down the barriers between God and us. The crucifixion speaks of the ultimate sacrifice, the laying down of life for the forgiveness of all our sins.

We're still not the perfect people of God, but we are a *forgiven* people. Jesus' death on the cross united us with God forever. Now, therefore, ". . . we have confidence to enter the sanctuary by the blood of Jesus, by the new and living way which Jesus opened for us through the curtain . . . for the one who promised is faithful." (Hebrews 10:19,23)

Sometimes the hardest thing to accept is the fact that God loves us just as we are. Sometimes we twist ourselves into knots trying to be perfect, thinking that if we could just achieve perfection, then we would become God's children. Our effort to follow the laws never justifies us; only Christ does. Through Christ, we are all God's children. Through Christ, we are all forgiven.

Reflect today on what is separating you from God. Do you feel you must be perfect before you can receive God's forgiveness? Are you convinced God will never forgive you because you cannot forgive yourself? The good news Christ brings is that no mistake, no fault, no sin can separate you from the love of God. Draw near. Tear down that curtain.

† † †

". . . understand that God is in me, and I am in God."

When Jesus said, "I and God are one," the crowd around him became so angry that they picked up stones to stone him. Jews of Jesus' day were able to accept themselves as God's chosen people, but to say that God is in you, and you are in God? Radical, impossible, blasphemous . . . so they thought.

Without realizing it, some of us may echo the same sentiments of that same crowd. We say, "God couldn't possibly be in me because I am so flawed." We forget that God created us and loves us. Some of us can believe that God is in us but we have trouble living as if it were true. We abuse ourselves in various ways — through self-hatred, overwork, homophobia, alcohol, compulsive sex — instead of treating ourselves with the dignity we deserve as God's loved ones.

If we begin to comprehend that God *is* in us, then we can begin the process of stopping self-destructive behavior. By discovering that God loves us, we can begin to love ourselves.

Think today about the ways that God has shown love for you. Have your actions toward yourself reflected that love? Know today that God loves you, and that you are in God, as God is in you.

† † †

"There were also women looking on from afar . . . who
. . . followed Jesus, and ministered to Jesus."

It is painful to watch someone die. Sometimes it seems harder
than the dying itself. The women who followed Jesus from
Galilee and Jerusalem watched Jesus' agonizing death. At times
during the crucifixion, it must have seemed impossible to
watch any more. Something inside must have said, *"Enough!*
I can't stand it! I can't watch any more!" Yet they stayed.
They watched. And when it was over, they took care to notice
where Jesus' body had been laid. After the Sabbath they would
return and perform one last gift of love — the anointing of
the body for burial.

When faced with dying all around us, we too are afraid. We
try to avoid suffering and death; we want to look away. We
don't know what to do or say. It's hard to watch someone
struggling with pain. We want to be able to make it stop.
Something in us, too, says, *"I can't stand it. I can't watch*
any more!" Deathbeds make us uncomfortable; they remind
us of our powerlessness.

It helps to know that God is present even in pain and death.
We can be servants of Christ to the dying, like the women who
watched and served Jesus. When some of the brutal realities
of dying overwhelm us, even while we say, *"Enough, no*
more," we remember that suffering, death, and burial are not
the end, but the gateway to a promised resurrection. While
we mourn the loss of those we love, we can still hold fast to
the comfort of Christ, pick up, and go on.

† † †

"They were saying to one another, 'Who will roll away the stone for us from the door of the tomb?' And looking up, they saw that the stone was rolled back . . . ."

The women set out in the early morning to anoint Jesus' body with oils. They went even though there was a crucial obstacle: the stone that closed the entrance of the tomb was much too heavy for any of them to move. Even several of them working together could not move that stone. How would they get to Jesus?

How often do we shrink away because of an obstacle that we feel is separating us from Christ? The obstacle could be our sexuality, the anger we've kept bottled up inside, or the feeling that we're not good enough. Often we're convinced that the obstacle can't be removed, and we never start on the journey toward Christ at all. Yet no wall can keep us from Christ, unless *we* let it get in the way.

Learn from the women who started out on that resurrection morning. They began the journey, even though they had no idea how the stone would be removed. When they reached Christ's tomb, the stone was already rolled back and the news of the risen Christ greeted them. Begin the journey toward living in union with God *today* and never mind about the huge stones. God will find a way to remove them when the time is right.

Is there anything keeping you from accepting Christ fully into your life? Offer it today to the love of the Redeemer, the love which knows no bounds and removes all obstacles.

† † †

*"For we have seen his star in the East,
and have come to worship him."*

For many of us, the three wise men are the most colorful
figures in the manger scene. They intrigue us, and yet we know
little about them. Other than their encounter with Herod, the
Bible doesn't describe much of their journey. It tells us only
that they found the child with Mary, and that they rejoiced.

The journey from their homeland was probably long, arduous,
and full of adventures. The Gospel author makes no mention
of what they had to endure to get to Jerusalem. Like an editor
crossing out a clumsy phrase, the author skips over the
travelogue and brings us to the essential point: after much
searching, they found the child.

The way to a closer walk with Christ can be long, arduous,
and filled with adventures for us, too. We can't see ahead to
what God is planning for us, and we don't want to return to
the place we've come from. All we know is that we must keep
walking forward, step by step. There is often pain and
discouragement in the pathway, but most important, at the
end of the journey, and often along the road, we find the child.
Isn't that what makes it worthwhile?

Take some time today to evaluate where you are going. Are
you moving toward union with God? Are you growing closer
to the spiritual goals you have set for yourself? Today, make
your life journey a faith journey. Take a step toward Christ.

† † †

"And Joseph rose and took the child and his mother by night, and departed to Egypt . . . ."

Picture yourself as Joseph. In a dream an angel tells you to get up and escape to Egypt. You wake up. The bed is comfortable. The last thing you want to do is wake up your spouse, pack all your belongings, and head for the Nile. Wouldn't you want to roll over and go back to sleep, saying "It can wait until tomorrow"?

Sometimes we pray for God's call in our lives, and when it comes we say, "Not now, maybe later." Or we say, "Not now, wait until I'm perfect."

Joseph got up *by night* and took Mary and the child Jesus to Egypt. He didn't wait until morning to see if the weather would be good for travel; he didn't wait to see if what the angel told him was actually true; he didn't waste time analyzing and re-analyzing the message. He went, and the child's life was saved.

The call of God can be exhilirating — and frightening. Sometimes when God leads us in new directions, we become confused, uncertain, even angry. At such times, we may be tempted to ignore the messages God sends us. The example Jesus teaches is that the only way we can save our lives is by discovering what God wants for us.

Take time today to discern where God may be calling you. Make sure to listen during your prayer time today.

† † †

*"Even now the ax is laid to the root of the trees;
every tree therefore that does not bear good fruit
is cut down and thrown into the fire."*

John the Baptist must have made people uncomfortable. He
said and did things no one else would have dared; he made
the Pharisees squirm on many occasions; he challenged people
to change.

John the Baptist confronts us with the waste in our own lives,
too. All of us have "trees" in our lives that don't produce good
fruit. Our trees take many forms: harmful relationships, abusive
behavior, addiction to drugs, alcohol, sex, or work. Our trees
can be lives overburdened with anger and self-hatred. Our trees
can be so choked with memories of the past that they can't
produce good fruit in the present. Often these trees have been
our means of survival for years. They've become so deeply
rooted in our lives that we don't see how we or anyone else
could uproot them.

Today's Gospel invites us to take the ax to the roots of these
old and unproductive trees in our lives. It can be scary and
it is never easy, but it is the only way to stimulate new growth.
Be patient with yourself when it seems as though you will
never clear your way out of the underbrush. After all, some
of those trees have been there for a long time. The important
thing is to learn to respect yourself as a child of God, to keep
cutting, and to throw the dead wood into the fire of God's
consuming love.

† † †

How many times have you felt that Christ was making a request of you, and you've said, "I can't do that,"or "I'm not good enough," or "I'm not spiritual enough," or "I'm not smart enough," or "I don't know enough"? John the Baptist is an example of an instrument of God who was reluctant to fulfill his ministry because he felt too unworthy. When Jesus came to him to be baptized, his response was to ask, ". . . do *you* come to *me?*"

Like John, we too are sometimes called on to perform works that we may not have imagined for ourselves. It may be praying for someone's special needs; it may be visiting an AIDS patient in the hospital; it may be receiving a phone call from a troubled sister or brother in the middle of the night; it may be serving in some simple way in our church. Surely Christ comes to each one of us and asks us to serve others in some concrete way.

What is it that Christ is asking you to do for God today? The good news is that when we accept Christ's invitation to perform an act of service, the heavens are opened and the Spirit of God descends to fulfill God's purpose in what we do.

How many times have you said no because you felt unworthy? Look to John the Baptist today and see how the heavens open when you say "no" to your fears and "yes" to Christ!

Jesus, be with me today. Guide me, teach me,
and through faith give me strength to say yes when
I am called upon to minister to your people. I know that
through faith I can do all things that you of me.
Amen.

† † †

*". . . being high priest that year [Caiaphas]
requested that Jesus should die for the nation, and
not for the nation only, but to gather into one the
children of God who are scattered abroad."*

Through Christ's death on the cross, all of us, as children of God, were forgiven, set free, and made whole. Once a people separated from each other, we became a community united by Christ's love. Once scattered, we were gathered together in Christ.

Christ set before us a new way. No longer would God's people offer burnt sacrifices to expiate sin; Christ's Resurrection and death paid for all time the debt of our sin. No longer would the people of God exchange ". . . eye for eye, tooth for tooth, hand for hand, foot for foot, burn for burn, wound for wound, stripe for stripe . . . ." (Exodus 21:24-25) Christ's example showed that love is the only answer to hate. No longer would God's salvation be available to only one nation; the "chosen people" of God became *all* people.

Once we have received this good news of new life, we too must declare a different way from the path the world offers. We are then called to work for the equality of all and to proclaim the good news of God's love for all people.

The transformative power of Christ's Resurrection and death is available for us today. We can claim that transformation and redemption for ourselves and put it to work in our lives. Today, if we accept the gift given us through the death of God's own Child, we can give of ourselves to others.

Take some time today to consider that Christ died "to gather into one the children of God." Are you separated from a brother or sister? If so, bring that separation to Christ, who will open the way to reconciliation.

† † †

*"... the devil took Jesus to a very high
mountain, and showed him all the nations of the
world and the glory of them; and the devil said to Jesus,
'All these I will give you, if you will fall down and
worship me.' Then Jesus said, 'Be gone, Satan! For
it is written, you shall worship the Lord your
God, and God only shall you serve.' "*

Day after day, we are bombarded with messages about how
to improve our lives by using the "right" clothing or hairstyle,
a certain perfume or aftershave lotion, a different brand of
cigarette, a new kind of toothpaste. If we only buy this
product, the advertisements suggest, then we will land a better
job, make more money, get the love we want. We are told
to place more importance on possessions than on people. We
are, in a sense, told to worship *things* rather than God.

Often, too, we are told that what we do is more important
than what we are. A person's worth is sometimes judged
entirely by the accomplishments listed on his or her resume.
As a result, we sometimes try to "earn" the love and respect
of others by our work alone. We may even try to earn God's
grace.

Christ's words to the devil in today's Gospel are enlightening.
On another level, perhaps, Christ is even saying to us that the
power and glory that the devil offers are illusions, that majesty
belongs only to God. Just as a different perfume won't
transform us magically into attractive, desirable creatures, so
having realms and riches won't ultimately give us power or
glory. Our glory comes from fulfilling God's will for us.

If today there are things that prevent you from worshipping
God and God alone in your life, seek to remove them. Seek
fulfillment in growing closer to God rather than in achievements, power, or possessions. Just for today, seek God's reign,
and rediscover peace.

† † †

"From that time, Jesus began to preach, saying, 'Repent, for the realm of heaven is at hand.' "

Jesus' message to us today is to repent. But how do we repent? What does repentance mean for us today?

Repentance means acknowledging the ways in which we have separated ourselves from God. Some of us may find peace in sharing these acknowledgements with a trusted friend or spiritual counselor. For some of us, admitting harm to others and making reparation is an important step in our recovery and healing process. For all of us, acknowledging what we have done is the first step in accepting God's forgiveness so that we may also forgive ourselves.

Repentance also means that, having accepted God's forgiveness, we are willing to change. It means that we are sorry for the ways in which we have not allowed God to fulfill God's promises in our lives. It means that we are committed to growing closer to God, that we are ready for God to transform us, and that we expect this transformation.

Finally, repentance means that we actively turn away from that which has kept us from becoming one with our Creator, that we release the wrongs we have done in the past, and that we focus on what we can do today. Knowing that we are forgiven, we resolve to begin again, and we renew this promise to ourselves and to our God as many times as needed.

Today, take some time to examine the ways in which you have grown away from God. Keep in mind the fact that, as you repent, God's realm is at hand and available to you. Forgiveness is yours; all you have to do is turn to God and receive it.

† † †

*"And Jesus went about all Galilee, teaching in
their synagogues, preaching the Gospel of the realm
of heaven, and healing every disease and every infirmity
among the people . . . and they brought Jesus
all the sick . . . and he healed them."*

Reflect for a moment on this phrase from today's Gospel: "He
healed them."

Today's Gospel does not say, "Jesus healed the ones who
earned it." It doesn't say, "Jesus healed those who were the
right gender, age, race, sexual orientation, and creed." It says
that Jesus healed them all.

Today's Gospel also says that Jesus healed every infirmity and
disease. It does not say, "Jesus healed all the diseases of all
the people who deserved it." Jesus knew the truth, that no
one deserves to be ill. All of us deserve to be well and whole
simply because we are children of God.

It is not only those of us who are living with serious diseases
who desire healing. All of us crave the healing power of Jesus
in our lives, for to be healed is also to be freed. We may want
healing from our addictions. We may wish healing for broken
relationships. We may want to be released from painful
memories in our past. We may wish to be freed from rejection
and despair. Jesus' healing is available to us for all these
wounds.

"When nothing else could help, love lifted me," says an old
hymn. Let yourself be lifted by Jesus' love today. Ask Jesus
to soothe the pain and hurt in your life, in the calm assurance
that your prayer will be answered. Finally, even in the midst
of sickness and death, know that Jesus has won the victory.
We shall all be well.

† † †

At the time Jesus walked this earth, people believed that human affliction, sorrow, and disease were signs of God's punishment for sin. But Jesus had a different theology. Instead of referring to the afflicted and sorrowful as sinners, Jesus, in the Beatitudes, called them "blessed." By using such a word, Jesus broke thousands of years of religious tradition that linked sin and disease.

"Sickness and sorrow are not signs of my punishment," Jesus might say. "I don't send disease and suffering. People attribute characteristics to me they don't even give the devil. I've never heard anyone claim that disease was a consequence of the devil's wrath. I always get blamed for it. Would a mother give her child a stone if the child asked for bread? Would a father give his child cancer, tuberculosis, or AIDS? If only the world would stop bearing me false witness.

> "To the poor in spirit, I send my Spirit, because I am love, not disease.

> "To the sorrowful, I send my comfort, because I am comfort, not affliction.

> "To the lowly, I give the whole earth, for only those who have the least can receive the most.

> "To those who hunger and thirst for a relationship with me, I give them my heart, my spirit, and my body.

> "To the merciful, I also give my blessing. Their mercy for others stems from my mercy to them.

> "To all peacemakers, I offer a piece of my heart.

> "And to all those who are persecuted for seeing and proclaiming me as a God of love, I give my unquenchable joy.

> "Blessed are you all, in all circumstances, but especially blessed are you when you call me in affliction, in sorrow, and in disease, for there I am in your midst."

† † †

"You are the salt of the earth . . .
You are the light of the world."

Being the salt of the earth and the light of the world does not always mean serving God in a dramatic, starring role. Sometimes we find our most meaningful service in the most humble tasks, far from the attention of crowds, and without anyone to applaud or acknowledge us.

Being the salt of the earth and the light of the world may simply mean a gentle gesture, a caring glance, or a kind word at the right moment. It may mean saying a quiet prayer that no one but God hears, but which provides a little extra light for someone to see their path. God invites us to be a gift to others in hundreds of minor, quiet ways.

There is a group of friends who gather three times a week to prepare food and go into the community to feed hundreds of homeless people out of an old van that is parked in a poor section of the city.

There is a man who visits an AIDS patient every day and occasionally takes him out for a haircut or a movie or dinner in his home.

There is a woman who cooks dinner once a week for men living in an AIDS hospice. She shares their meal with them and spends the evening visiting them.

God invites each of us to flavor our world and let our light shine in similar ways. That is why Jesus says to us today, "Let your light so shine before others, that they may see your good works and give glory to your God who is in heaven."

Jesus, I am your salt and your light. Give me
opportunities today to love, serve, and witness to those
with whom you bring me into contact. I am grateful to
be able to serve you in even the smallest,
humblest task. Amen.

† † †

*"Think not that I have come to abolish the law
and the prophets; I have come not to abolish them
but to fulfill them."*

Christ is the fulfillment of God's covenant with us. Christ's life was itself an expression of God's love for us — God's own Child sacrificed for our sins. Jesus tells us that he will not abolish the law, but fulfill it. What does this mean for us today?

When something is "fulfilled," it becomes complete, and the next step in the process can occur. Fulfillment also implies transformation. Thus the law that God's people had followed before Christ appeared had served its purpose and was finished, but it was not thrown away totally. Instead, it became fulfilled and transformed into a law of freedom. It is in this new law of freedom that grace saves us.

By Christ's life and death, we too, like the law, have been fulfilled and transformed. We are fulfilled in Christ because Christ's death on the cross paid the penalty for our sins. We are transformed because Christ's death and Resurrection established a way for us to receive a new nature, the very nature of God. That is why Paul wrote, "Though our outer nature is wasting away, our inner nature is being renewed every day." (II Corinthians 4:16) Once we acknowledge and accept this transformation in Christ, we begin to see ourselves as whole and complete.

Sometimes it can be hard to really accept fulfillment in God's grace. We may feel unworthy and unlovable. But all aspects of ourselves are worthy in Christ's eyes. We do not need to earn God's grace or God's love; all we need to do is open ourselves to receive it. We are worthy not because of our accomplishments or our possessions, but merely because we are children of God. God's grace is enough for us.

If there are parts of you that are hurting or ashamed, let the peace and fulfillment of the Holy One comfort and heal you today. Know that you are loved by God today and always, loved fully in every part of your being. Allow this love to flow into your life, transforming all it touches.

† † †

In today's Gospel we see John the Baptist ministering to the people and announcing salvation. Why were so many people willing to listen to John? Perhaps it was because he offered them new hope. Giving specific examples, he encouraged them to make changes in their lives that would make salvation possible. Above all, however, in everything that John did, he pointed the way to the one who was mightier than himself. The central focus of his ministry was showing people the way to God.

John the Baptist was not all that different from you and me. We, too, are called to lead people to repentance, to assist them in making the changes in their lives that will make this salvation possible, and to lead them to Christ, the source of salvation.

In order to fulfill this call, we do not need to go out to a desert wilderness; we can fulfill this ministry by bearing witness to Christ in our everyday lives. Whether at home, at work, or at play, we can, by the quality of our presence, be as available and ready today as John was two thousand years ago to tell others the good news.

Today, allow God to guide you to the ones who need to hear the good news, just as people were guided by the Spirit to John the Baptist. Never be overbearing or boastful. Simply and gently allow the Holy Spirit to work through you to touch others in need and point the way to Christ.

Dear Lord, allow me to be the instrument
that you use today.

† † †

Although we generally think of murder as a physical act, today's Scripture reading invites us to look at the way we often commit murder in the spiritual sense.

I'm sure you've heard the phrase, "If looks could kill . . . ." Well, they can kill the spiritual self, if they convey the message that the other person is inferior or worthless. They can do this because the spiritual self is the central part of our identity: when that central part is attacked, our sense of self-worth, of simple value as a human being, can be seriously damaged or destroyed. Looks or words that convey such destructive messages are surely a kind of murder of the soul.

Destructive words or actions aimed at another indicate that something is wrong, not only with our attitude toward ourselves, but with our attitude toward others and God. If personal insecurity about ourselves leads us to put others down so that we can feel better about our own lives, we need to develop a caring and loving attitude toward ourselves. If fear of others leads us to isolate ourselves so as to protect ourselves from hurt and avoid vulnerability, we need to develop a more trusting attitude toward others. If fear that God does not care about us leads us to seek control over every aspect of our life rather than risk disappointment, we need to develop an attitude of receptivity to the voice of the Holy Spirit.

Changing attitudes is never easy; it takes time, prayer, and constancy. If, however, we can acknowledge our real attitudes and turn the matter over to God, the Scriptures tell us that it will be done, because "with God nothing will be impossible." (Luke 1:37)

> *Dear Lord, help me today to recognize and*
> *surrender those attitudes that have a negative*
> *impact on myself and on my relationship with*
> *you and with others. Amen.*

✝ ✝ ✝

"Do not swear by your head, for you cannot make one hair white or black. Let what you say be simply 'yes' or 'no' . . . ."

Jesus' advice seems wise: simply say what you mean and mean what you say. After all, persons commit their entire lives to each other with a few simple words. For example, several years ago, I witnessed the marriage of two friends before a judge. The ceremony took fifteen minutes. Coming out of the courthouse, the bride turned to me, laughing, and said, "It took longer to buy this dress than it did to get married!"

But if it is so simple to say what we mean and mean what we say, why do we sometimes find it hard to do? Sometimes the truth is not so simple, nor is it always easy to say. We may think, "I'm angry with you," yet we say, "Oh, I'm fine." We may think, "I'm worried about John's drinking," but we never mention this to John. We may avoid telling the truth because we fear the conflicts that may arise from truth-telling. In the end, though, the truth *is* the easiest and best thing to say. The more we do not acknowledge what we really think and feel toward ourselves or toward each other, the further we have gone from the Holy One.

Perhaps the secret of saying what we mean is to say to ourselves, "How would Jesus say this? How can I say it with love?" Each day we are confronted with choices about what we say and do. If we focus on the Christ within, then our words and actions will reflect God to others. Saying what we mean and meaning what we say can require an enormous amount of will power at times, especially if we are not accustomed to it. Some of us may have lied all our lives about how we feel, what we think, who we are. Yet if we are patient with ourselves and open ourselves to the loving Creator, then saying what we mean becomes easier, for we begin to realize ourselves fully as the whole persons God meant us to be.

Today, let your words be an expression of the godliness within you. Tell the truth to yourself and those around you. Let your day be an overwhelming "yes" to yourself, to God, and to God's will for your life.

† † †

*"Love your enemies . . . so that you may be
children of God who is in heaven; for God makes
the sun to rise on the evil and on the good, and
sends rain on the just and on the unjust."*

How can we love our enemies? Is it possible to love someone
who has hurt us? Yes, Jesus says in today's Gospel, not only
is it possible, but we must do it. As Christians, we are asked
to love our enemies and pray even for those who persecute
us. God loves us, and so we must learn to love each other.
We are to love each other even when we disappoint each other.
But how can we do this?

Love is not just a feeling, it is an action. To truly love someone,
we must be willing to *act* with love, even when we don't *feel*
particularly loving. We must become willing to love someone
just because he or she is also a child of God. Once we have
opened ourselves to this kind of loving, our love and respect
for our fellow humans is not easily shaken by external circumstances. We begin to love people because of who they are,
not what they do.

We can love a person even while saying that we will not accept
certain behavior. Ghandi showed both his love and his protest
by using nonviolent means. Loving someone also means being
willing to speak out when we do not agree with the person's
actions. If we allow people to abuse themselves or others in
the name of love, we are not following the way of Christ. We
are choosing to live in fear or denial instead.

Take time to reflect today on those whom you love. If there
is hatred within you toward any of God's children,
acknowledge it, then let it go. Offer it up to God and do not
take it back. Experience the healing love of Christ, and be set
free. This is the way we learn to love one another.

† † †

*"Beware of practicing your piety before others
in order to be seen by them."*

Aristotle wrote that there are several kinds of good persons.
There are those who will to do good because they are afraid
of what might happen to them if they do not. There are those
who will to do good because they want to be praised. Then
there are those Aristotle called the "truly good." They will
to do good, purely because it *is* good. In other words, they
perform good deeds because it is right and just that they do so.

Jesus' words in the Gospel today invite us to join the ranks
of the "truly good." Jesus tells us to give to the needy, not
to be praised by others, but simply because there is a need to
be filled. Jesus asks us to pray, not because we want others
to think we are holy persons, but because we wish to
communicate with God. Jesus invites us to fast and make
sacrifices with joy, not asking to be pitied. We are to do good
because it *is* good, and because our Heavenly Parent desires it.

In many ways, Jesus' words about good deeds are specific
guidelines for a ministry of service. To be a servant of God
is to relinquish control over our lives and offer them to God
for God's glory. Because we know who we are, we do not
crave our own glory. We testify to others about the wonderful ways that God works in all our lives; we seek to reveal
the Christ to all whom we meet.

True servanthood can be challenging in a world where we are
taught much more about selfishness than we are about
selflessness. We are taught that we must toot our own horn,
for no one else is likely to toot it for us. But if we are seeking
only God's grace and God's reign, we seek only to become
one with God, to live in union with the divine. Only through
giving up our ego, our desire to control, letting go of the part
of ourself that seeks to be praised, can we truly become one
with God and with all creation.

As you read today's Gospel, reflect on the attitude with which
you serve.

† † †

*"Your Heavenly Parent knows what
you need before you ask."*

God knew us before we were formed in our mother's womb.
It is therefore no surprise that God knows what we need before
we even form the words.

Once during a worship service in our church, a man sitting
near the choir began to sob during the opening hymn. A choir
member reached out and placed her hand on his shoulder. She
didn't say anything or stop singing, she just placed her hand
there. She sensed the man's need to be touched and loved;
he didn't have to say a word. She didn't need to say anything,
either; her hand on his shoulder said, "I care."

When we pray, God senses our prayers without our saying
a word; all we have to do is open ourselves and allow God
to be present for us. We can have simple and yet complete
communion with God, like lifelong lovers who have become
so attuned to each other that they communicate without
words. Prayer is placing ourselves in the presence of a loving
Creator. Like a visit with a trusted friend, prayer also includes
time to *listen* as well as to speak.

Jesus teaches us a basic and well-known prayer in today's
Gospel. It covers every human need. It is not an appeal to an
indifferent deity. It is a comfortable chat between old friends.

Today, seek a gentle and loving conversation with your God.
Ask that your prayers be answered in the sure knowledge that
they have already been heard.

† † †

"Do not lay up for yourselves treasures on earth . . . lay up for yourselves treasures in heaven . . . for where your treasure is, there will your heart be also."

Material things, though they can provide ease and comfort, can also rule us if we are not careful. We find ourselves wanting a "new and improved" microwave, even though the old one is perfectly fine. We buy gadgets to help us care for our other gadgets. Last year's computer system, which was state-of-the-art, is already outdated this year. Short skirts, which were in last year, are out this year. The merry-go-round never stops, for there is always a new fashion, a more deluxe model, a better brand — we can never have enough.

"Instead of impressing people with your possessions, impress them with your life," says an old Quaker maxim. Each time we choose to concentrate on seeking God's reign, we are choosing to let go of material things, and grow closer to God. When our lives are filled with the search for God and the fulfillment of God's will, material things begin to lose their importance. We find letting go easier.

My friend Tony taught me a lot about both giving and giving up. He was an actor whose room was as plain as a bomb shelter, yet his parties were well attended, for he had more friends than anyone I've ever known. If you gave him a gift, he thanked you and enjoyed it to the full, but he often didn't keep it for long — eventually he gave it away if he didn't absolutely need it. If you admired something of his, he often offered it to you, whether it was a bicycle or book. People who tended to hoard things usually had less love in their lives than Tony, who never hoarded.

Today, seek to let go of things in your life that you are clutching. Eliminate those things that may be keeping you from a deeper union with God. Take a step toward freedom. Give up something you don't really need, and focus on Christ, whose yoke is easy and whose burden is light.

† † †

OCTOBER

"God is my co-pilot," a popular bumper sticker declared to passing motorists a few years back. Judging from the actions of some of those drivers, God should have taken the wheel.

Sometimes, it's not easy to let God take control. But when we do, we find that the blessings are abundant.

For years, a man named Tommy professed to be a Christian. Tommy willingly turned over to his Saviour the control of his home life and of his family. He sought God's leadership in personal matters, praying frequently and sincerely about issues of health, friendships and church life.

Tommy drew a line, though, when it came to his job. He was a newsman, and a good one, as his co-workers and editors agreed. Here, Tommy believed he knew what was best. With four years of college training and twelve years of on-the-job experience, he knew what it took to succeed.

Only Tommy didn't succeed. Time after time, he was skipped over for promotion. People he trained got the jobs he applied for. Gradually, he grew more and more dissatisfied with the career he had once loved.

Just as Peter knew how to catch fish, Tommy knew how to report the news. But Tommy's "nets" were coming up empty. In anguish, he turned to the friend who had helped in so many other areas of his life. Tommy gave control of his workplace to Christ.

The blessings were abundant. Just as Christ had a special job for Peter, Tommy was also called. Peter became a "fisher of people." Tommy was called to spread the good news as a minister.

Whether it be in a professional ministry or not, our God has a special job for each of us. We may not even have to change careers to find it. But we do have to turn over the controls. We have to let God be our pilot.

† † †

Outside my patio window, wine-colored impatiens and pink begonias peek out for sunshine from a mass of ferns, Swedish ivy and assorted other greenery.

In central Florida, gardens left as unattended as mine is become lush from the summer rains and by autumn develop a mind of their own. Still, the flowers in my garden hold special memories. Most began as cuttings from friends' gardens or as castoffs from neighbors who were moving back north.

Amid the tangled garden, I see the vine that began as a leaf snipped off by my friend J.T. from a plant at Cypress Gardens. I see Jeff's bromeliad and Henry's ivy. And I smile, remembering their laughter and their hugs.

The three friends are gone now. AIDS claimed J.T. and Jeff. Unable to bear his grief, Henry took his own life. They were three men who lived, labored, and loved; three human beings who touched the lives of others before giving up their own lives.

While they lived, they struggled as all people struggle. J.T. fussed about his appearance and mothered a hopelessly neurotic collie. Jeff worried about Henry. Henry worried about Jeff. And together, Henry and Jeff built a beautiful home.

Their struggles are over. I thank God for that. And I smile, knowing my friends are with Christ. But still, I can't help but marvel at how fragile life is. How futile it is to worry about tomorrow when our lives can end even before winter's cold destroys our gardens.

"Seek first the realm of God," Christ says. The message is clear. The needs of our short lives will be met by a gracious and loving Heavenly Parent. Our concern should lie with our souls. For unlike our present life, our souls are eternal.

† † †

Many of us daydream about what wonders we could perform if only we were to win the state lottery. With millions of dollars at our disposal, we could ease our own daily burdens and do so much good for others.

Just imagine. We could help our families, our churches, and our charities while we cruised the Caribbean. After all, we're Christians.

"Ask and it will be given you; seek and you will find," today's Scripture tells us. So what do we do? Do we simply jot down our lottery guesses, say a prayer, and wait patiently while thumbing through travel brochures? Do we quit our jobs and pencil in several extra zeros on our tithe check?

No. From past experience, we know it doesn't work that way. Our God is a wise and loving Parent who answers our requests in a wise and loving manner.

Imagine the chaos that would follow if everyone who prayed to win millions did so. Our government would go bankrupt, inflation would soar, non-winners would fall into extreme poverty, and our winnings would melt away as we tried to correct the havoc caused by sudden mass wealth. We'd be worse off than before.

A wise pastor advises us that if our prayers seem to be going unanswered, we should question the prayers, not our God.

And she's right. We should pray with our hearts that God's will be done in our lives. We should ask not just for deliverance from troubles, but for the wisdom and strength to live through them. Instead of praying to win the lottery, we should pray to be empowered to do wonders without winning.

When our prayers truly come out of love for God, the door will be opened to us. We won't need a million bucks to be winners.

† † †

As children we are quick to learn that if something tastes bad we should spit it out. Once we've bitten into a rotten apple, we're slow to try fruit again. Perhaps that's why false prophets seem so despicable: because of their bad fruits, too many of us have chosen to go hungry.

But we mustn't let one bad apple keep us from enjoying Christ's abundance. Pardon the mixed fruit, but if we'd never tasted lemons, could we really appreciate the sweetness of oranges?

Bible commentator William Barclay provides a few good pointers for successful fruit picking. Good fruit comes from church leaders whose interest lies in those they're leading, bad fruit from leaders whose main concern is self. If the leader teaches in order to gain money and prestige or to espouse personal views, the fruit will be foul.

Barclay advises us to "go to another tree" if the teachings exclude certain groups of people from Christ, if the teachings separate religion from life, or if they seem too easy. We also are told to be wary of teachings that dwell on outward appearances and those that offer only prohibitions.[1]

Sounds like the guy knows his fruit. After all, it's the fruit, not the trees, that we're interested in. A final note about religious produce: the fruit is always there, and it doesn't take a degree in agriculture to know if it tastes good.

Dear God, help us to be wise enough to recognize the wolves among our religious leaders. Help us to know who would lead us astray to gain power and money for themselves. Help us to be brave enough to continue our search for your good fruit even when the dangers seem so great. Amen.

[1]Adapted from THE GOSPEL OF MATTHEW, Volume I (Revised Edition). Translated with an Introduction and Interpretation by William Barclay. Copyright © 1975 William Barclay. Adapted and used by permission of Westminster/John Knox Press. (pp. 286-288)

† † †

As a young boy ignorant of the ways of nature, I snipped off dozens of blooms from my grandmother's rosebushes in order to create my own garden.

My grandmother's flowers amazed me with their bright colors and sweet fragrance. None were more special than her roses, and I wanted to put that magic in my own backyard. Carefully, I lined up the fragile blossoms, sticking them side by side in the dirt my mother had tilled for a vegetable patch. Sweat dripped from my brow. Gardening was hard work, I decided.

The next morning I hurried outdoors, expecting to see flourishing rosebushes. Imagine my disappointment when I found dried twigs.

The memory of that morning stayed with me. The lesson, traumatic at the time, proved to be valuable. In order to survive, roses must have roots firmly planted in the soil. That's where the real magic occurs. As Christians, we learn a similar lesson. In order to endure, our faith must be firmly planted in Christ. Well-established roots give plants power to stand when the wind blows and the rain falls. Through the roots, plants draw water and nutrients for new growth.

How often we see new Christians quickly blossom and fade. We wonder what we could have done differently. Perhaps they simply lack roots. Their faith is washed away in the first storm, or their tender new growth withers from too little nourishment.

Gardening helps us grasp the lesson in today's Gospel: if our faith is firmly rooted in Christ, we stand sturdy. Watered by the Holy Spirit, we grow into beautiful creations of God. For with the Trinity, true magic occurs.

Dear Saviour,
teach us to be gardeners, preparing
new Christians so their roots will sustain them.
Help us to take them to heavenly places before
we expect heavenly blooms. Amen.

† † †

Sunlight dances on gentle waves. Salty sea breezes tangle my hair. My mate's brown arm brushes against mine. I am alive. I am excited. I believe in miracles.

God's magic still happens. It happens so often that our senses — miracles in themselves — aren't able to keep up. Try as we may we can't experience all the wonder around us. We grow numb to our precious world.

Waking on the beach at sunset, it's easy to believe in miracles, easy to praise God for the glory of living. The trouble is, most of our moments aren't spent in such idyllic settings. We rush through our daily lives being jostled and pushed by others who are also in a hurry. We struggle with bothersome inconveniences, striving to meet human deadlines. And we do it all in surroundings that bore us with their familiarity.

Not only do we long for miracles, but we want them to be so dramatic that they can't be ignored. We want them to be quick, big, and complete. Bang. The miracle has occurred.

But our Saviour fills our daily lives with quiet miracles. We flip a switch, we have light. We put on glasses, we see. We dial a phone, and we hear a friend. The fact that the medical world took centuries to defeat polio doesn't make the victory any less of a miracle.

"A miracle does not come by lazily waiting for God to do it all," a Bible scholar says. "It comes from cooperation of faith-filled effort with the illimitable grace of God."[1]

Some miracles, though, require nothing more of us than that we open our senses to what God is doing around us. If the leper hadn't looked at his body, how would he have known Jesus had cleansed him?

[1]Altered from THE GOSPEL OF MATTHEW, Volume I (Revised Edition). Translated with an introduction and interpretation by William Barclay. Copyright © 1975 William Barclay. Altered and used by permission of Westminster/John Knox Press. (p. 300)

† † †

Floridians are fascinated — possibly terrified, perhaps even petrified — but definitely fascinated by hurricanes. As a newcomer to the state a few years ago, I was amazed at the amount of effort that goes into preparation for storms that seldom come.

Beginning shortly after Easter and continuing well into fall, strategies for surviving the big wind are broadcast, published, and televised repeatedly for eager audiences. Phone books include tracking maps so that residents need not be surprised if the storm does come.

When hurricane Elena parked off the Tampa coast a few years ago, the world, or at least our part of it, stopped for three days.

At the risk of sounding jaded, I must confess that I couldn't understand what all the fuss was about. I don't mean to belittle the mighty force of hurricanes — the wind did blow and the rain did fall. But I'd seen worse, much worse, a year earlier when a string of deadly spring tornadoes ripped through my native North Carolina. And those folks had no warning. I'll take my chances in a hurricane over a tornado any day.

Unfortunately, we don't often have a choice. Like the people in Florida and in North Carolina, we must take whatever storms come our way. And sometimes our lives are filled with quick and nasty tornadoes that sneak up without warning.

Like the "great storm" that frightened the disciples, the storms that we meet with most often come suddenly. We may not have the benefit of tracking maps or televised warnings, but we can still plan our survival strategy.

During those rough times, it's reassuring to know that we've already invited Jesus Christ aboard our "boat." Christ can control not only the sea and the wind, but everything else, too.

† † †

Twenty-nine white balloons, one for each year of Jeff's life, rose into the azure sky over Florida. As mourners watched below, a gentle autumn breeze tossed the balloons, and they clustered, forming what appeared to be a solo cloud in the clear sky.

Those who loved Jeff, and they were many, stared upward until the soaring balloons became specks and finally disappeared altogether. The balloons, lifted into the heavens beyond the grasp of mortals, served to remind those who grieved that Jeff's soul, too, had risen.

A gentle man reared in the rolling hills of Tennessee, Jeff stood more than six feet tall, but he possessed a boyish innocence that made him seem younger than twenty-nine. Even during his last days, when AIDS had ravaged his body, he retained his tender charm. The lesions that disfigured Jeff's face couldn't touch the beauty of his soul. And it was his soul that rose.

In today's passage, Jesus tells the widow's dead son to rise, and the youth does, claiming a new life. We marvel at this beautiful and miraculous story of Christ's power and mercy. We long for the same merciful power to retrieve our loved ones from pending death.

Yet, that power does retrieve them. The story is no less beautiful nor miraculous when our loved ones answer Christ's command to rise to a new life in glory.

We can assume that the young man in today's Scripture eventually died again. Perhaps he lived a good many years and did a good many wonderful things, but eventually his mortal life came to an end.

How good it is to know that our loved ones, like Jeff, only have to die once. As Christians, their new lives are eternal.

Blessed Saviour, show mercy to us when we mourn.
Remind us that while bodies are fragile,
souls endure forever. Amen.

† † †

Imagine the peace the men in today's Scripture must have felt as the demons left them. What a sweet burst of freedom that must have been. No longer forced to live in the darkness of the tomb. No longer tormented by evil. No longer out of control, but touched by Christ, free to be just as God had made them.

What a marvelous cure Jesus wrought simply by using the instruments near at hand: a herd of wild pigs. In the hands of Christ, these ancestors of our farm animals became mighty tools that Christ used to destroy demons and drive evil out of our world.

Jesus could have called for a flock of eagles. With a snap of his fingers, he could have commanded a pride of lions to take away the demons. Actually, no snap would have been needed. If God had wanted them, the lions and eagles would have been there. Instead, Jesus used simply what God had provided to do what was needed. Pigs were sufficient.

Jesus' example teaches us to use the means available to us to perform God's work. When yoked to the power of God, even the most ordinary instruments can become a part of the healing and transformation of the world. We do not, therefore, need to look for the extraordinary in order to fulfill our call to proclaim the Gospel. With Christ at our side, we are more than equipped to heal, teach, and drive out evil.

And if a few "wild pigs" come our way, that's okay, too. Christ works wonders with unruly livestock.

Precious Jesus,
show us the means to drive out evil
from our world today and to restore the peace and
harmony you intended for us. Amen.

† † †

You might say I inherited Terry's friendship. He was introduced to me a few years back by a dying man, a mutual friend, someone who loved Terry as much as I would grow to love him.

And I do love Terry, for he has proven so easy to love. As if his strawberry blond hair and charming green eyes weren't enough, he also possesses a kind heart, a quick wit, and a bright mind. A professional man in cowboy boots. A body builder in a men's chorus. A collector of antiques. A dancer.

Our friendship has stood the test of time and distance. Terry moved to the Midwest two years ago. Yet we remain close through letters, phone calls and shared memories. I don't see Christmas lights, hear disco music, or pump iron without thinking of him.

Together, we have giggled like children and cried like babies. We have shared our deepest joys and fears. When Terry's AIDS virus test proved negative, I sent him a two-page letter. One page said "PRAISE," the other, "GOD."

Although we've never been spouses, our friendship has made us as close as lots of long-time mates. But despite our closeness, one thing we cannot share. Terry doesn't know God loves him. No matter how many times and in how many ways I have told him, he has not accepted it — at least not yet.

Most of us know people like Terry, friends with whom we long to share God's glory. But like the friends who brought the paralyzed man to Christ, we can only do so much. We can only love them and pray for them. We can only make sure that they are brought into the healing presence of Jesus Christ. It is their choice to accept or reject that healing. It is their choice to walk or not to walk.

Still, our experience and our faith tell us that, like the paralyzed man in the story, our friends will eventually experience Christ's love and walk in a new life, if we will continually bring them into the powerful presence of Christ in prayer. For God wants our friends not only to walk, but to run.

† † †

My friend's problem: only five hundred copies of the church newsletter to be circulated among patrons at fifteen lounges, bookstores, and restaurants.

The politician's solution: divide the number of outlets into the number of copies and distribute them equally.

The socialite's solution: the biggest share of the copies go to the newest, most trendy discos and dining spots because those people add class to the church.

The accountant's solution: the largest outlay should be invested in establishments that will bring the biggest return of people with monetary assets.

My friend heeded Christ's words in developing his own distribution formula. The more skittish he was about entering a particular business, the more newsletters he left behind. Bars with the darkest corners and cheapest neon got fifty copies. He threw in five more copies at clubs known for attracting underage hustlers.

Discos whispered to have fights in the parking lot and drug deals in the restroom got a full sixty.

My friend loved the newsletter, seeing it as a major outreach of God's love from the church into the community. Delivering it to the right people meant a lot to him. He also loved the people of the community and knew that the newsletter could be there for them when no one else was.

Christ's solution: put God's word in the hands of the people who most need to read it, the sisters and brothers who are in the greatest immediate need.

"Those who are well have no need of a physician," Christ says. "For I came not to call the righteous, but sinners."

† † †

An illustration in my mother's Bible shows a pale, fleshy lady draped in pinks and whites. The woman's face is distorted, her body cramped by the mob around her. Into this mob, she reaches. Her arms strain to touch the Saviour whom she can barely see, the Saviour whose power she knows will make her whole. With her outstretched hand, she grasps the hem of Christ's garment.

Like the woman, we still reach for our Saviour. How often we see outstretched arms in our churches. What a beautiful picture these arms and hands make as they symbolically grasp for heaven and a closer communion with Christ. Big arms, small ones. Dark ones, pale ones. Strong ones, weak ones. The picture glows with as much intensity and emotion as the illustration in my mother's Bible.

Like the woman, we long to be made whole in our daily lives. We long to feel Christ's healing power. And perhaps, most of all, we long for assurance that our faith is enough.

If only we could make it through the mob, then we'd know. If only we were lucky enough to touch our Saviour's clothes, and if only Christ were to turn to us and say, ''Your faith has made you whole,'' then we'd be sure.

We're indeed lucky that we don't have to fight our way through a mob or even stretch our arms in order to find the assurance that comes from closeness with Christ.

All we have to do is fold our hands and pray. And if our hands are busy, the folding is optional.

† † †

The tall thin man propped himself up, leaning his frail frame against the back of a church pew, and made a statement that initially sounded strange.

"I'm so happy . . ." Randy said, pausing to gasp for air and to wipe tears from his darkly circled eyes. Smiling weakly, he finished, ". . . to be here."

The words were spoken with too much effort for them to be doubted. Randy was sincere about his happiness. A few days earlier it had looked as if this gentle twenty-six-year-old human being, this child of God, this new Christian, wouldn't make it to church. He had been hospitalized, barely able to breathe, suffering from AIDS-related pneumonia.

But Randy was determined. Like the blind men in today's passage, he struggled, crying out to God and refusing to be denied a closer union with Christ. This Sunday was special for Randy. It was his Sunday to be officially baptised into the family of God. He left his hospital bed to be in God's house with his brothers and sisters in Christ.

Sometimes, it's too easy for us to think of reasons to stay away from church. After all, God is everywhere. We needn't track Christ down to be healed. We simply have to call Christ's name.

Perhaps that's the problem. Perhaps if Christ were a little more difficult to find we would be less likely to forget to look for our Saviour. How often we suffer simply because we fail to call on Christ.

Randy and the blind men knew the value of being close to God. Most surely, God was with Randy in his hospital room. But he wanted more. He wanted to feel the healing presence of Christ that comes from being with other Christians.

And most surely, he did. As he put it, "I'm so happy . . . ."

† † †

God doesn't call extraordinary people to do ordinary works, but ordinary people to do extraordinary ones.

A student pastor had prayed for someone who could take snap-shots for the church scrapbook and was thrilled when a newcomer to the congregation said she was a shutterbug.

Kathy balked, though, when he offered her the assignment. "I'm not a professional," she said. "I had hoped to work with someone who was, someone who could help me improve."

The student pastor thought for a minute. He had no one else.

"Kathy, you have a camera and you're willing," he said. "You're the closest thing to a professional that we have. Ask God to help you improve. God will make you into a pro."

Ever so slowly, a smile crept across Kathy's face. "Okay," she said. "I'll do it." Still smiling, Kathy started to walk away, then turned back to the student pastor.

"Me, a professional? Imagine that," she said.

The pastor-to-be nodded. "Imagine that."

God calls each of us, just as the disciples were called. And just as the disciples were ordinary people with ordinary skills and ordinary shortcomings, so are we. The student pastor knew that well from the recent calling in his own life.

He also knew that through Christ's life we are given a wonder-ful job description of what our tasks will be. All we have to do is be willing. God will supply everything else that is needed to make us pros.

Dear Saviour, give us the wisdom to follow the course that you have set for our lives and our ministry. Be with us as we follow your call for us. Amen.

† † †

I liked my spouse when he baked chocolate chip cookies for a church social. I liked my spouse when he created colorful costumes for Halloween. I liked my spouse when he hung shelves in the pantry.

But when, in tears, he put tap water on the parched lips of a hospitalized friend, I loved my spouse.

When we make commitments to one another, we never know how far we will be asked to go or what thirsts we'll be called upon to satisfy.

Friendship among Christians requires the willingness to be servants to one another, going the second mile, doing more than what is simply socially correct. We must be willing to love one another deeply and completely, for that is how we show our love for Christ.

No, we'll never have the opportunity that the prostitute had. We'll never, at least not in this lifetime, be able to wash the feet of Christ with our tears, or to dry them with our hair. But we can show how much we love Christ.

We show that love every day by the way we treat our friends, the guests in our homes and, indeed, the strangers on the streets. If we are rude, spiteful, and inconsiderate of them, we have mistreated Jesus, for Jesus' spirit lives in all of us.

Christ expects us to be gracious in our show of hospitality to those around us. But even more is expected of us. We have to be willing to humble ourselves to meet their needs. And those needs can be great, requiring a lot of foot washing. People need someone to listen when they're troubled, someone to care for them when they're sick, and someone to love them when they seem unlovable.

The task isn't easy. But the next time the needs of a friend, or even a stranger, seem particularly disagreeable, we should remember that the task is actually done for Jesus.

How else will we show that, given a chance, we, too, would gladly wash Christ's feet?

† † †

Bright red, yellow, and orange snapdragons create a three foot wide rainbow on Mark's lawn. Each flower's spike is abloom, packing the garden with a mass of color so thick that the ground, and indeed the leaves, are hidden. But, when complimented on the snapdragons, Mark simply shakes his head. "They're getting there," he says.

In Florida, autumn's milder days create beautiful gardens of "spring" flowers. But try as I might, I can't imagine how Mark's garden can improve. Although they're only snapdragons, flowers don't get any better than his.

But I can't see the garden through Mark's eyes. Only he, as its creator, knows what it is capable of. Only he knows what he expects of his garden and its simple snapdragons.

Perhaps when Jesus looked over the twelve disciples, he, too, would have said, "They're getting there." Surely, the disciples must have felt that they had gone through much already. They had left their homes, families, and jobs to risk death by following the Saviour. They had been led through much, seen much, and heard much. How could they possibly improve? What more remained for them?

But when Jesus gave them their marching orders, he made it clear that their journeys had just begun. They would experience much more as they continued Christ's work. Their ministry would grow and blossom, but not without toil.

Christ wanted them to prosper, fulfilling God's plan for their lives. Their Creator knew what they were capable of becoming as well as the obstacles that lay in their way.

The situation is no different for us. We can only hope that Christ believes "we're getting there."

† † †

A young pastor arrested at a nuclear arms protest arrived for her day in court with only a Bible.

Staring down at her from behind the bench, the judge asked, "Where's your lawyer?"

"Jesus Christ will defend me," the pastor responded calmly.

The judge scoffed. "I've not seen any paperwork on that," he said with sarcasm. The pastor opened her Bible and began to read. It contained all the counsel she needed.

Now, don't get me wrong. I wouldn't suggest that we wage our legal battles without a lawyer, any more than I would advise mending broken bones without a physician. God has created great minds which, when touched by our Saviour's grace, can perform wonderful deeds on our behalf.

But sometimes, we must face our trials without the help of others. Sometimes all we need to know is that God is with us.

In today's passage, Christ gives the disciples fair warning that they will face trials, tribulations, and even death for their beliefs. Governments, religious bodies, and even their own families will persecute them. But Christ follows the warning with a beautiful promise. As Christians, they need face no hardship alone.

The protesting pastor knew the warning and the promise well. She knew that they applied to modern-day disciples, too.

Through Christ, we receive courage to face persecution, knowing that God has promised our trials will one day end in victory. We receive wisdom, knowing the Holy Spirit will speak through us. Most importantly, we simply feel our Saviour's presence, bringing peace amid chaos, warmth amid coldness, and hope amid despair.

The world's best lawyer couldn't offer as much.

† † †

The creature's twisted body lay sprawled among the marigolds. Brown stripes ran down its sides. Its battered head pointed toward the sidewalk. I stood frozen, terrified, but unable to look away.

That was weeks ago. And yet the very thought of the dead snake still makes me cringe.

On the day I first noticed it, I had been on my way to the bank in the small town where I work. As usual, I had turned to look at the bright yellow flowers at the corner of Main and Central Streets. There it lay — a garden snake, about two feet long, very obviously dead.

The fact that it was dead didn't make a whole lot of difference to me. When it comes to snakes, no amount of reasoning can calm me.

At first the mere idea of going to the bank made me shudder. I knew the dead snake lay in my path. But I'm an adult, and a busy one at that, so a few days after my initial discovery I vowed that no dead snake would slow me from my errand.

The next morning, I got close enough to glimpse the decaying corpse before I lost my nerve and darted into oncoming traffic. From then on, I walked blocks out of my way to avoid the horror in the flower bed.

Most of the fears that affect our lives seem a lot less silly than a dead snake. And some concern is good. We aren't being foolish when we give up cigarettes or check for body lumps out of concern about cancer.

Fear becomes bad, though, when it controls us, blinds us, and leads us from the path God has called us to take. With our Heavenly Parent at our side, we can walk the straight route, knowing that the snakes that await can do no harm.

† † †

A sign over the door at my neighborhood weight room pro-claims in bold letters, "NO PAIN, NO GAIN." Anyone who has ever pumped iron knows the message to be true.

Those guys who stop by the spa for thirty minutes once or twice a week and spend their time talking about football get nowhere. Nor do those women who work diligently for a few days and then backslide, skipping weeks at a time. Bellies still bounce and skin still sags on the bodies of half-hearted weight lifters.

Physical strength and muscle tone don't come without some struggle and discomfort. In today's Scripture, Jesus tells us the same is true for our Christian faith.

Our faith doesn't stop with peace of mind and a rosy outlook on life. True Christian commitment often leads to tension and conflict. Christians don't always feel happy. They face troubles and plenty of them, some even coming from their own family members.

My pastor calls today's Gospel message one of the things she wishes Jesus hadn't said. And it's true that being a Christian would be so much simpler without the pain.

But Christ isn't saying that joy doesn't come, nor that we won't find peace in Christ. Christ is simply saying that hardships may stand in the way of our reaching those goals.

We can take heart, though, knowing that just as the crucifix-ion was followed by the resurrection, so conflict is followed by joy. Just as muscle aches result in stronger muscles, life's toils result in stronger Christians.

A country and western ballad title puts it still another way. *"I Never Promised You A Rose Garden,"* it says. Neither did Jesus. Just, in the end, roses.

† † †

Deacon Helen leaned against her crutches and gazed at the dust and disarray of our partially remodeled sanctuary. "Things always look worse before they get better," she said, smiling.

Helen can smile because she knows that when the remodeling is complete, our sanctuary will shine again, better and brighter than ever. Her assurance comes from years of experience — Helen has endured far worse times. She has survived times when the dust and disarray of her own life seemed to separate her from Christ.

Years ago, a motorcycle accident cost her a leg. This year, while helping with the remodeling, she bore the pain of recent knee surgery on her remaining leg.

John the Baptist must have felt a lot like Helen as he spent his final days in prison. He had labored long and hard in the wilderness, sacrificing his own comfort in order to minister to the souls of others. He had devoted his life to preparing the way for Christ.

Yet now he faced his mortality, locked away from both the ministry and the people he loved. Worst of all, John was physically separated from Christ, the Saviour whose coming he had foretold.

How bad things must have seemed to John. And how his heart must have leaped for joy when he received Jesus' message. As Helen might say, things were truly getting better. John's wait was over. Miracles were happening. The Saviour had come.

Sometimes we, like John and Helen, must endure hard times. But we, too, can rest assured that Christ has better days in store for us. And when the dust clears, we, the true sanctuaries of the Holy Spirit, will shine again.

† † †

A gray-haired couple well into their senior years caused a stir among the lunch-time crowd at a fast-food restaurant. As the pair munched hamburgers, the husband began barking questions at his wife.

"Can't you hear me?" he demanded in a voice loud enough to be heard throughout the McDonald's. "Have you heard anything that I've said?" he continued, his voice gruff with age and agitation.

His timid wife nodded.

"Well then, why don't you let me know?" the man asked. "If you don't respond, how am I supposed to know you hear me?"

How indeed? The man's questions, though spoken harshly, were valid. Whether it be a simple nod or a lengthy spoken response, we expect some sort of reaction when we speak to others. That's how we know that our message is being received.

The same is true with Christ. Repeatedly in the Gospels, we find Jesus advising, "Those who have ears, let them hear." The advice follows profound words of wisdom, messages that Christ doesn't want us to miss. In today's passage, Jesus has just acknowledged John as "Elijah who is to come," the one who would herald the coming Christ. And if the listeners accept John as the prophet, they accept Christ as the Saviour.

How do we let Christ know that we have heard the message? By simply responding to its content.

But not just any response will do. If the elderly husband had asked his wife about her health and she had responded by telling him the time of day, he would have known that his message hadn't gotten through.

In responding to Christ, we need to acknowledge that we accept Christ as our Saviour. And to do that, we must live our lives in the loving manner Jesus taught us. Then Christ will know that the message has been not just heard, but understood as well.

† † †

The bullet, no larger than a fingertip, cut a sinister path through my church.

Fired from a distance from a high-powered weapon, it pierced, but didn't shatter, an office window. It continued through a thin wall and traveled the length of the sanctuary, gliding over the backs of the pews, skimming the top of the pulpit and slamming into the concrete behind the piano.

The marks left by the bullet will soon be erased by a remodeling project. My spouse looks at me with surprise when I say I'll miss them.

But I have often stared at the crisp holes left in the window and wall and marveled at how destructive the bullet could have been. Often, I have shuddered at the sight of the cracked concrete near where my spouse plays music for our services.

The marks are a stark reminder of how God has blessed our congregation. The bullet sped through the sanctuary on a Sunday afternoon between services. A few hours either way would have meant disaster.

The bullet marks also remind me of the persecution that all Christians face as "lambs in the midst of wolves." Our lives aren't easy, especially as Christians who are part of a hated minority.

No one knows who fired the bullet, nor why. But we can be certain that our lives wouldn't have been endangered in this way if we had not chosen to gather as the body of Christ. Our church wouldn't have stood as a target for a person with a gun if our people hadn't stepped out in faith years ago.

Perhaps the marks give to me their sweetest reminder when I recall they were left there three years ago, and that our church continues to prosper. Jesus has given us power "to tread upon serpents and scorpions, and over all the power of the enemy." And bullets can't harm our spirits.

† † †

Four late-comers to Julie's pool party gathered in a corner of the patio, sipping beer and whispering to one another as they looked over the crowd. Party guests included a mixture of Julie's friends from the local church and her friends from elsewhere in the community.

"Which one is the minister?" one of the newcomers asked. The others, also not church members, weren't sure.

Was it the silver-haired woman who splashed a polo ball in the pool? Or how about the bearded man who flung horseshoes or the clean-cut fellow who threw darts? Was the pastor the tanned guy sunbathing in the blue bikini? Or the young mother who munched chips while her son played in the water?

The four late-comers couldn't decide. No one seemed to fit their expectations of what a minister should look like.

If Julie had overheard their question she might have responded, "All of them." Or she might have said, "None of them." Either answer would have been correct.

Christians, blessed with a variety of gifts, are all called to be ministers of the Word of God. They do that in a variety of ways.

The woman with the polo ball, a gifted artist, designs illustrations for the church publications. Gifted in music, the bearded man plays the church piano. The guy with the darts oversees church evangelism. The sunbather leads Sunday night prayer time. The watchful mother takes photos for the church scrapbook.

All are ministers, yet none of them has that title. It's not surprising that modern-day Christians sometimes fail to meet public expectations. Both John the Baptist and Jesus fell short of that mark.

By the way, the church's official minister wasn't at Julie's party. She was out of town on a well-deserved vacation.

† † †

When a trio of church workers tore away old carpet to make way for new, they found a bigger task awaited them. To their surprise, beneath the worn carpet lay tile. It was not just any tile. Years ago, thousands of one-inch ceramic squares with paper backing had been securely glued onto concrete.

The threesome's job appeared monumental. Thousands of one-inch squares had to be uprooted. Thousands of hammer strokes and thousands of beads of sweat would have to fall before the carpet could be laid.

Ruth brought her hammers and chisels. Roger and Darrell squatted at her side. And the chipping began. Church members busy with other remodeling tasks were skeptical. The skepticism grew as they saw how slowly the first tiles chipped away.

Three hammers tapped against three chisels held by three ordinary people. The trio — a telephone operator, a waiter, and a clerk — chatted as the chipping continued. For hours, it sounded throughout the church. For hours, other workers shook their heads in dismay as they walked by the squatting trio.

Still, Ruth, Roger, and Darrell chipped. Their sweat fell and their bruised fingers bled. They talked of families, romances, vacations, and the finished work. And they chipped.

By evening, thousands of one-inch tiles lay piled in a corner of the church. The work was done, completed well in time for the carpet layers. Other church workers looked at the finished job in amazement.

"Rainwater must have loosened the glue," one ventured. "Big hammers, maybe," another said. The pastor remarked, "They worked consistently. Not fast, just steadily."

Ruth, Roger, and Darrell simply thanked God the job was done. God never promised them or us an easy task. Our job is just to keep on with the chipping.

† † †

For weeks, the clerks in an office near mine were despondent. They fell behind in their filing and correspondence. Phones went unanswered. At times, the workers even wept.

My heart went out to them as I watched them grieve for a former co-worker. They had watched this friend fall in love and marry. They had shared and celebrated each milestone with her. They had been saddened a few years back when she had left her job. But they were elated later when she gave birth to a daughter.

Now this friend's young child was dying. The former co-workers felt helpless, unable to ease the burden that had befallen their friend, powerless to spare the young mother her pain.

Then an amazing thing happened. One of the clerks came up with an idea that changed their entire outlook: They would throw a community-wide festival to raise money for the young family. No longer were they helpless. The idea, a seemingly simple thing, energized them. Just as they had celebrated the good times with their friend, they would now share the hard times.

Much had to be done, but when the day of the festival came, the clerks were ready. Invitations had gone out and were read that morning at the beginning of church services throughout the community.

Like other pastors, my minister shared the news of the festival. When he finished, though, he did an amazing thing. He told his followers that the festival was bad, unholy, because it was being held on the Sabbath.

I didn't wait to hear his sermon. I took the hand of my healthy child and walked out of the church. My Jesus was at the festival.

† † †

When I look back over my life, I realize that the hardest times weren't those when I lacked money, health, or friends. I can live with poverty, sickness, and loneliness, and, like many people, I have done so. The true low points came when I lacked hope. For without it, each day becomes a bitter chore to be endured.

Such was the case during the last days of my marriage. Ignorant of the blessings that come from a knowledge of Christ's love for all people, I lived with anger, guilt, and hatred, for I believed no hope existed for a better day.

I thought myself condemned, cut off from Christ and beyond hope. Indeed, those were the worst days of my life. Worse than living on stale bread and bologna as a teen-age father, struggling to pay for an education and support a family. Worse than facing major surgery as a young adult. Worse than living alone for the first time at the age of thirty. During those times, at least I felt God was with me, and I trusted in God's love to see me through.

How foolish — and totally helpless — we are when we face life's struggles without accepting Christ. Without God, we come face to face with a world without hope.

Today's passage makes it abundantly clear, though, that we need not spend one moment in despair. The prophecy was fulfilled long ago. The Chosen One was sent into the world for all people.

Yes, the nations will place their hope in Jesus. So will all of us, as the peoples of those nations. Only then will we be able to endure life's low points.

Jesus didn't promise that we'd never be poor, sick, or lonely. He promised only to be there for us. And that is enough.

† † †

An elderly man in my home town sat with buddies at the country store and complained at length about the sad state of world affairs. But when the talk turned to the role of our national leaders in those affairs, he prefaced his complaint with the words, "Of course, I don't vote, but if I did . . . ."

The old guy wouldn't fare well in my pastor's flock. Reverend Karen tells congregation members that being part of a community requires more than pointing out problems; it also means being willing to help prevent and solve them. In civic matters that means voting.

Reverend Karen is a wise woman. She knows that if we're not part of the solution, we may be part of the problem.

Jesus told his disciples much the same thing in today's passage: He said that if they were not squarely with him, they were against him, that if they did not make a firm and clear decision to stand with him, then they would scatter and drift away from him.

There is no in-between, no such thing as an uninvolved Christian. If we are not committed to good, then we risk surrendering control to evil. And that means that inaction can do as much damage as acting maliciously.

Alice and Lynn, newcomers to the church, visited three times before deciding never to return. It wasn't that church people greeted them harshly. The problem was that no one spoke to them at all.

Because no one was committed to good, evil had a chance to assert itself. The problem won out because no one was committed to a solution. No one took a stand for what was right, so what was wrong carried the day. Reverend Karen wouldn't have been pleased.

Blessed Creator,
be with us as we act to show the world
that we are on your side. Amen.

† † †

My friend Denise, a bright, energetic woman blessed with a rare zest for life, sometimes speaks so rapidly in her excitement that strangers look at her with confusion. They simply aren't accustomed to coping with so many words spoken so quickly.

My friend Jay, on the other hand, lets words roll lazily off his Southern tongue, sometimes speaking so slowly that listeners try to fill in the blanks, often completing his sentences for him.

Whether our words flow quickly like Denise's or slowly like Jay's, they are powerful things, capable of inflicting much pain or bestowing much joy. In today's passage, Christ acknowledges the power of words, telling us they come from "the abundance of the heart." Our hearts will be judged, we're told, by the words we speak.

As humans and as Christians, we all remember times when we've said things we later regretted. How vivid the pictures are of the pained faces our careless words have caused. We can be thankful that our God is forgiving, the judgment merciful.

We can also praise God for times when we are able, through our words, to bring comfort and encouragement to others, and for the joy that others have poured out to us through kind words.

Although Denise and Jay deliver their words in vastly different ways, no two people are more capable of making me smile and, yes, even laugh out loud.

Denise and I met more than a dozen years ago when we worked together in a small South Carolina mill town. Jay and I met at church a few years back. Both friends have been there when I needed them, offering words of support, comfort, and encouragement.

Because I have heard my friends' words, I believe I know their hearts. I feel sure Jesus does, too.

† † †

Carole's neighbor simply changed her flat tire. No big deal. He didn't even bother to tell her it was flat. He just changed it, leaving a note of explanation on her windshield before pulling out of his own driveway.

But Carole was amazed nonetheless, and told others of the act of kindness. She marveled, not so much at her neighbor's deed, but at the circumstances under which he had performed it.

Her neighbor discovered the flat as he headed to his car to begin a long and tragic journey. He was on his way to a city four hundred miles away to make arrangements for the return of the body of his wife who had died earlier that day in a car accident.

Yes, Carole had reason to marvel. Her neighbor's deed went beyond what we expect of others. If anyone ever had an excuse to pass by a person in need, her neighbor surely did. But like the good Samaritan in today's parable, Carole's neighbor stopped and helped out. Certainly God was with him as he turned those lugs. The same God who would be there during his personal grief.

How easy it is for us to think of reasons to ignore people in need. We tell ourselves we're too busy, we have our own problems, or we're not good in those situations. We wonder what we really know about changing tires. Surely, someone else can do it better, we say. Surely, a mechanic is close by. And finally, we ask ourselves, is this person really our responsibility? Our neighbor?

Like the lawyer in today's passage, we look for loopholes in Christ's command to love one another. There are none. No excuses.

The next time such an excuse pops into our heads we should remember Carole's neighbor. He stopped to help. Because he fixed Carole's tire, she was able to tell others about God's love.

† † †

Preacher Dwayne, as his friends call him, grew up the eldest child in a fatherless, dirt-poor family of nine. He missed out on college and a lot of other things that are considered necessary to make a person sophisticated. The small Baptist churches of south Georgia are as far from his backwoods Florida home as Preacher Dwayne has ever been.

But he is a happy man who feels at ease with strangers and content with his life. He can boast that, although he stands more than six feet five inches tall and wears size fifteen shoes, he is the runt of his family. His brothers are all bigger and his sisters almost as big, he claims with a hearty laugh.

Preacher Dwayne works weekdays as a trainer at my neighborhood weight room. The job is an easy one and gives him a chance to do the things he loves. He spends much of his time munching peanuts, joking with buddies, reading his Bible, and witnessing about God.

Now you'd be hard pressed to find two people more different than Preacher Dwayne and I. Just physically considered, his neck is thicker than my thigh.

But a few similarities do exist. We both belong to persecuted minority groups. We both are struggling to be better Christians. We both have felt the Holy Spirit in our lives and are struggling to answer God's call.

On Monday mornings when I hear Preacher Dwayne humming a hymn and see his ragged Bible nearby, I know he, too, has felt the wonder that comes from knowing God's love.

Despite all the differences, we share a beautiful bond. We are brothers in Christ. We are family.

† † †

Church members thought the annual festival a great place to circulate newsletters, so they printed an extra three hundred copies. Within a short time, Mark and Dee had handed all of them out to festival-goers.

The church, proud of its newsletter, took seriously the call to reach out to others in spreading the good news of Christ's love. Mark and Dee were pleased with their work. They had given out copies to anyone who would take them. But as they loaded up leftover balloons and other items from the church's booth and prepared to leave the festival, they found that not all of the newsletters had been treated kindly.

Some lay crumpled in a trash bin, not far from the booth, their message never read and lost forever among discarded hot dog wrappers and soda cups. Other newsletters had been carried across the festival grounds to a picnic area where they now lay, their bright color bleaching in the sun. Their owners had forgotten to carry them home. Only a few of those newsletters had, perhaps, been read before being left behind.

The parking lot outside the festival grounds bore more newsletters. Tire tracks marred some of them; the wind had scattered others. Maybe at least a few of those, too, had been read before being dropped.

Like many of the seeds in today's parable, many of the newsletters had fallen on barren ground. Others, though, had made it into people's homes, where their message could change lives. Dee and Mark knew this. They knew their time hadn't been wasted.

What was important was that, as Christians, they had sowed good seeds.

Dear Saviour, bless our seed sowing.
And help us not to be discouraged when some
of our efforts fall short. Amen.

† † †

NOVEMBER

The Feast of All Saints

"Seeing the crowds, Jesus went up on the mountain and sat down; and the disciples came to him."

As this new month begins, I seek you out, Jesus. Leaving the crowds, I climb the holy mountain, that place within which gives a perspective on all the constituent parts of my life, where you sit waiting for the disciple who chooses to draw near to you, where you restore harmony to the crowded chaos of my life with words of beauty and of truth. Today I climb the holy mountain in my heart to sit at your feet, attentive.

"Jesus," I ask, "teach me the secret of happiness."

"It is well that you ask this, my friend," you reply, "for you have often sought happiness in the wrong places. You have learned to seek happiness in power, possessions, and self-gratification. But if you wish true happiness, you must allow yourself to experience the pain in your life. This will not overwhelm you as you fear, but at the bottom of your pain you will find a well of joy.

"You have learned to be aggressive and controlling; but this leaves no room for God's work." Then you add, with a twinkle in your eye: "If you wish to inherit the earth, you must allow God to give it to you."

And so you continue turning my world upside down, teaching me that where I am poor, sad, hungry, thirsty, harassed, and persecuted, there is precisely where I can expect happiness to break forth.

Jesus, today I remember that you sit enthroned on the holy mountain in my heart, teaching me the truth about happiness.

† † †

"Hear then the parable of the sower."

I stand with the crowd today and listen attentively as your words fall on me like seeds ready to sprout, grow, and bear fruit. Suddenly I am an expanse of land stretching north, east, west, south, with the landscape of my inner life lying open before you.

I watch as you scatter seeds on pathways worn hard by my busyness, and I see commitments, like a hundred birds, swoop down on each moment, devouring the promise of new life before it can sprout.

I watch as you scatter seeds on rocky soil, that part of me that has not yet learned to persevere, and I see that the seeds sprout quickly in the morning, but cannot endure the heat of noon.

I watch as you scatter seeds on thorn-infested soil, that part of me that is full of contradictory desires that turn my inner life into a battleground, and I see the seeds choked to death before they can mature.

A great sadness comes over me, because I understand that in my search for meaning and purpose I have left little room within me for your Word to take root and grow.

At that very moment I see you casting seeds with wild abandon on good soil. The wind carries your words to me: "Now that you are open to hear, accept, and persevere in my Word, you have become good soil, and you will yield abundant fruit."

Throughout the day, I observe the many kinds of soil in the fields I pass. With a knowing smile I scatter seeds of truth that Jesus has entrusted to me; for I know that even if some seeds are lost on hard, rocky, or thorny ground, in the end some will fall on good soil and yield an incredibly abundant harvest.

† † †

"The servants replied to the householder,
'Then do you want us to go and gather [the weeds?]'
But the householder said, 'No . . . .' "

"Jesus, I love the church, but there's just one problem."

"And what is that problem?"

Without hesitation I reply, "Some people in the church are unbearable! They bicker, criticize, judge, and gossip. They inject negative energy wherever they get involved. Jesus, if the church were a wheat field, these people would be weeds!"

Jesus responds tersely, "Nice analogy — moreover, you're right. This is a problem in the church."

"Well then," I add impatiently, "why do we put up with these people? Let's get rid of them! After all, a cardinal rule of agriculture is to stay ahead of the weeds!"

"No; let them stay," Jesus says calmly. "It is not up to you to pull out the weeds. That is my prerogative."

"If that's the case, Jesus," I answer impulsively, "you're going to have a very messy reign on this earth!"

"You're quite right; the church will always be a mixed bag, but its task is not therefore to engage in purges and inquisitions." Jesus' eyes grow bright with intensity as he continues: "We must not reject the unlovely and the unlovable, but rather let us love them to wholeness. For it is not God's will that one single soul should be lost to evil."

A strange peace settles on me at these words, as if somehow what Christ is suggesting I do for others has just been done for me. In one sense nothing has changed: judgmental people, gossips, and nit-pickers will always be in the church. Yet in another sense everything has changed: for thanks to this conversation with Jesus, I am learning not to be one of them.

† † †

"The realm of heaven is like leaven which
a woman took and hid in three measures of meal,
till it was all leavened."

"Little piece of leaven, what secrets make you a sign of God's realm?"

"My first secret is hiddenness. I do my best work when I allow my presence to work in hidden ways. This secret holds true for all creation: a seed cracks its husk and begins to grow in the dark hiddenness of the earth; a pregnancy comes to term in the nurturing hiddenness of the womb; Christ is raised from the dead in the quiet hiddenness of the grave. Therefore, create a hiddenness in your life where seeds of change can germinate and grow.

"My second secret is that I am ordinary. Paradoxically, even though the realm of heaven is hidden, it is found in the most ordinary places in your life. It is no accident that Jesus chose as a symbol of God's realm something from a place as ordinary as a kitchen! Therefore, do not imagine that you must travel to faraway shrines and monasteries to find God; rather, cultivate an openness to the presence of God that permeates everything and everyone around you.

"My final secret I call sheer grace. My friend, pieces of leaven had always been a symbol of corruption and evil. So it was revolutionary when Jesus lifted me up as an example of God's realm. For the first time in history someone called me good! Many people were scandalized, and many persist still in calling me evil, but I don't believe them any more because I know that God accepts me as I am. Hidden, ordinary, and despised, I have been transformed by Christ, who was also hidden, ordinary, and despised. Therefore, I have found self-esteem without pride, and humility without self-hatred."

"Little piece of leaven, how wonderful are your secrets. I will hide them in my heart today that they may teach me wisdom."

† † †

". . . why are you anxious . . . ?"

Today's Gospel is an invitation to childlike trust. The central question it poses is this: Who is in charge of my life? If I am in charge of my life, then it is up to me to provide for every possible contingency — an impossible task whose pursuit will succeed only in making me a nervous wreck!

The desire of Jesus is to free us from this burden of anxiety. Jesus therefore not only addresses our symptoms (". . . do not be anxious about your life . . ."), but also offers us a way out ("Instead, seek [God's] reign . . .").

To seek God's reign is to surrender control of my life to God confidently, knowing that I am the child of a provident God. To seek God's reign is to accept with humility the fact that in my humanness I cannot possibly know, anticipate, or do everything myself. To seek God's reign is to imitate Jesus when he said, "For I have come down from heaven not to do my own will, but the will of the One who sent me." (John 6:38)

This attitude of childlike trust freed God to bring Jesus to the fullness that God had in mind before Jesus was ever born. It is that same glory that Jesus desires for each of us today. Therefore, let the mantra on our lips today be: *Provident God, I trust you.*

† † †

"The righteous will shine like the sun."

In *The Ascent of Mount Carmel*, John of the Cross compares the life surrendered to God to a log placed onto the fire. Initially, the wood crackles and hisses, "crying out" as the fire destroys its outer defenses. Eventually, however, it yields to the flame; it ignites, burns, and is finally converted into the fire.

Today's Gospel describes a similar process. The Messiah enters the world with fire, and in the heat of the flames, all causes of sin and all evildoers are destroyed. The children of the heavenly realm, however, are not destroyed; they "shine like the sun," suggesting that they have been changed into fire — for what is the sun if not a huge ball of flames?

Today's Gospel therefore invites us to gather up those scattered longings of our hearts that obscure our deepest desire, the desire for union with God, and to gather up along with them the little strategies we use to avoid intimacy with God, and to surrender them all as a burnt offering to God. As we repeat this surrender each day, the fire of God's love gradually transforms us into itself until we ourselves become that same gift of fire to the world — like Moses, like Jesus, like the disciples at Pentecost.

> Abbot Lot came to Abbot Joseph and said: "Father, according as I am able, I keep my little rule, and my little fast, my prayer, meditation and contemplative silence; and according as I am able I strive to cleanse my heart of thoughts. Now what more should I do?" The elder rose up in reply and stretched out his hands to heaven, and his fingers became like ten lamps of fire. He said, "Why not be totally changed into fire?"[1]

---

[1]Thomas Merton: *The Wisdom of the Desert*. Copyright © 1960 by The Abbey of Gethsemane, Inc. Reprinted by permission of New Directions.

† † †

". . . the realm of heaven is like a merchant in
search of fine pearls, who, on finding one pearl of great
value, went and sold everything and bought it."

Sitting beside my friend, the stream, I ponder this parable.
"Obviously," I tell my friend, "like the merchant, I should
sacrifice everything to gain heaven."

The stream gently responds, "You've got it backwards."

"What do you mean, 'backwards'?"

"Read the parable again," the stream advises. "It doesn't say
you are like a merchant; it says *the realm of heaven* is like a
merchant. In other words, *God* is like a merchant in search of
fine pearls." The stream gives me time to absorb its wisdom,
then continues: "The fine pearls are the people of earth. Like
a merchant who loves pearls and wants as many as possible,
God loves people and wants to bring them all into God's realm."

"What about the price?" I ask. "What does it mean when it
says that the merchant 'sold everything'? What does God 'sell'
to 'buy' human beings?"

The stream reflects, then asks, "What is the most valuable thing
God has?"

"That would be God's unique Child, Jesus," I reply — and
immediately I see that Christ's life was what God paid to buy
humanity, and a verse of Scripture leaps into my mind: "You
are not your own; you were bought with a price." (I Corinthians 6:19-20) After savoring this insight, I say, "Friendly
stream, there's one part of the parable that I still don't understand: what is the 'one pearl of great value'?"

The stream responds gently, "My friend, it is you . . . ."

Today I sit quietly beside my friend, the stream. In my heart
I repeat as a mantra its precious gift to me: *I am a pearl of*
great value.

† † †

"Is not this the carpenter's son?"

Sitting beside my friend, the stream, I consider the unbelief of the people of Nazareth. "Why was it so hard for them to believe in Jesus?" I ask. "They had known him all their lives."

"Perhaps that was their stumbling block," the stream replies softly. "Perhaps they could imagine a Messiah emerging from Jerusalem or from some other faraway place, but not from their midst. Perhaps Jesus was too ordinary, too common, too familiar for them to believe that he was actually the Christ."

Reflecting on the stream's words, I see that I am not unlike the people of Nazareth. "It's easy for me to think of encountering Christ on a retreat or in a house of prayer or on a holy mountain," I confess, "but what about meeting Christ in the town where I live, or where I work, or on my block, or in my home? What if Christ were that ordinary?"

"You are beginning to have eyes of faith," the stream says gently. "For Christ always lives where you live. That is why Jesus said, 'The realm of God is not coming with signs to be observed; nor will they say, 'Lo, here it is!' or 'There!' for behold, the realm of God is in the midst of you.' " (Luke 17:20-21)

"But if the reign of God doesn't come with signs to be observed, how shall I recognize Christ?" I ask.

The stream says quietly, "The secret is to look for Christ in the people you encounter each day."

Today I encounter many people: friend and stranger, male and female, young and old, gay and straight, Black and White, Asian and Hispanic. I look into each one's face and within my heart I ask: *"Is not this the carpenter's son?"*

The answer always comes back: *"Yes."*

† † †

". . . he sent and had John beheaded in the prison, and
his head was brought on a platter . . . ."

Jesus, today you receive the news of the tragic death of John the Baptist, your friend and forerunner. Without a word, you withdraw to a lonely place apart. You withdraw, perhaps to reflect on the depth of evil in our world, evil that has erupted so violently in John's death. You withdraw, perhaps to contemplate the mystery of a God who would raise up a mighty prophet like John and then allow him to die so cruelly. You withdraw, perhaps to discern in this tragedy something of the pain of every human tragedy. And perhaps you see in the death of this, your forerunner, something of the tragedy of the passion and death that awaits you as the price to be paid for the healing of the evil in our world.

Today I withdraw with you, Jesus. Without a word, I find "a lonely place apart" in my heart, and I pray for the healing of the evil in our broken world.

I raise to you the tragedy of people unjustly imprisoned and murdered by the Herods of today's world, and I pray: *Christ, have mercy.*

I raise to you the tragedy of AIDS and other terminal diseases that afflict us with fear and pain, and I pray: *Christ, have mercy.*

I raise to you the tragedy of unresolved anger, pain, and fear that erupt in acts of violence in our nations, our cities, and our homes, and I pray: *Christ, have mercy.*

I raise to you the tragedy of needless pain that I have inflicted, intentionally or unintentionally, on others, and I pray: *Christ, have mercy.*

I raise to you all the unnecessary tragedies in our world today, both large and small, and I pray: *Christ, have mercy.*

† † †

". . . Jesus looked up to heaven, and blessed, and broke and gave the loaves to the disciples, and the disciples gave them to the crowds."

One day God decided to come to earth, for God had heard the people's cries of affliction. On the appointed day, God set out across the expanse of space that stretches like a sea between heaven and earth; and as the boat approached the shore there was a great throng waiting. When God saw the throng, God had compassion on them, and spent the day healing the sick.

That evening God's disciples wanted to send the crowds away to buy food for themselves; but God said, "They will not find the food for which they hunger in the nearby villages. Let them stay; I will find a way to satisfy their need."

Then God saw five loaves of bread near the disciples. God said to the loaves, "Will any of you offer yourself for these people? To satisfy their hunger is the very highest calling, but if you give yourself to this purpose, you will be broken and die. Still, I will change you into something new when it is all over."

There was a long pause as the loaves searched their hearts. Finally the smallest one said, "I will give myself to feed this great throng." The loaf trustingly placed itself in God's hands, who blessed, and broke, and gave it to the disciples to give to the crowds. When everyone was satisfied, the disciples gathered and offered to God twelve baskets of fragments — for, miraculously, those who had eaten of the sacrificial bread had become like the bread themselves!

God said, "We will invite these fragments in due time to offer themselves to feed other crowds that come hungry." And at God's right hand the risen Christ appeared and said, "Amen."

† † †

"Take heart, it is I; have no fear."

Sitting beside the Sea of Galilee, I ask, "What will you teach me today about Jesus?"

The Sea replies, "Jesus is God, 'who makes a way in the sea, a path in the mighty waters' (Isaiah 43:16), even the waters of death. Jesus is the one who answers the prayer, 'Stretch forth thy hand from on high . . . and deliver me from the many waters.' (Psalms 144:7) Therefore, 'at the name of Jesus, every knee should bow, in heaven and on earth and under the earth . . . .' " (Philippians 2:10)

"And what will you teach me about the Wind?" I ask the Sea.

The Sea replies, " 'The Spirit of God was moving over the face of the waters' (Genesis 1:2) to form a new creation when Jesus was crucified. To the disciples it seemed in their pain as if they were adrift on a storm-tossed sea, and as if the Wind was against them; but the risen Saviour was in the mighty Wind, reborn in the power of the Spirit. Therefore, give praise to the Holy Wind that blows where it will (John 3:8) to breathe new life into dead bones." (Ezekial 37)

"And what will you teach me about myself?" I ask the Sea.

The Sea replies, "Like Peter, when you fear the Wind in your life, you are like a sinking ship. Like Peter, when you trust that God is in the Wind, you walk through seemingly impossible situations. Therefore, like Peter, you must learn to recognize that the Wind is the Spirit of God revealing a new direction for your life."

Sitting in my boat I row into the Sea's deepest waters. As I watch storm clouds gather, I repeat as a mantra the promise of God to the disciples: *"Take heart, it is I; have no fear."*

† † †

"Come; for all is now ready."

Sitting beside my friend, the stream, I say, "How I long to sit down at the heavenly banquet!"

The stream replies, "The banquet is now."

"How can it be now?" I ask.

The stream says, "Every day the Spirit invites you to partake of the heavenly feast."

"Then why haven't I heard the invitation?" I ask.

"It is because it is so much a part of life that you don't notice it. It first comes in the morning when you awaken, a gentle invitation to feed on Christ before you begin your day."

"Yes, I have heard that invitation," I answer, "but I must hurry to get to work."

"Still," the stream says, "the invitation is extended throughout the day, for God longs for your presence. The Spirit therefore whispers in your heart, 'Will you take time from your day to come and enjoy the great banquet prepared for you?' "

"Yes, I have heard these words, but I have mortgaged my days with meetings, appointments, conferences, luncheons, phone calls, and dinners. I have no time left for the banquet."

"All is not lost," the stream continues, "for the invitation also comes in the quiet hours of evening when peace has settled on the earth. With gentle persistence the Spirit announces, 'Come; for all is now ready.' "

"I've heard that invitation, too," I admit, "but I'm so exhausted from the day's busyness that I have no energy to respond."

As I sit beside the stream I realize how impoverished my busy life has been and how deaf I have become. At that moment I hear in the silence the invitation that I have so often ignored: "Come; for all is now ready."

Gratefully I set aside the cares of the day and enter the heavenly banquet.

† † †

*". . . not what goes into the mouth defiles
a person, but what comes out of the mouth,
this defiles a person."*

Today's Gospel presents a moment of great significance for our spiritual life. The Pharisees ask Jesus why his disciples do not observe a particular tradition of Jewish religion. Jesus responds by saying that their tradition is itself a violation of the Scriptures. He makes this point indirectly, through an example, but his conclusion could not be clearer: "So for the sake of your tradition, you have made void the Word of God." Jesus thereby teaches us that human traditions, however good they may be, do not supersede God's Word.

But Jesus does not stop there. He goes on to contradict, explicitly, the food laws of the Hebrew Scriptures (vs. 11)! The implications of this radical position frighten the disciples, who urge Jesus to soften his message lest he offend the establishment. Jesus only gets more emphatic, and finally makes his main point: Authentic religion is a matter neither of human traditions nor of religious laws, *even the laws of Scripture*! In other words, Jesus proclaims boldly that, just as the Scriptures supersede tradition, so Scripture is superseded by Christ. This leaves us with one supreme Guide: Christ enthroned in our hearts, who gives us direction for each circumstance as it emerges. From now on, therefore, authentic religion must proceed from the heart, that interior center where Christ indwells and communicates with us.

Today's Gospel is therefore the moment when Jesus ushers in the fulfillment of the vision of Jeremiah: "I will put my law within them, and I will write it upon their hearts . . . ." (Jeremiah 31:33) Therefore, let us today return to Christ who dwells in our hearts and ask our Guide to show us the path of faithfulness.

† † †

Broader Horizons

A Play in Five Acts by Matthew

Cast of Characters:

God..........................Played by the Canaanite Woman
Jesus *and* Every Christian....................Played by Jesus
Outsiders and Outcasts............Played by the Daughter
The Church...........................Played by the Disciples

Synopsis

ACT I: (Matthew 15:21-23a) The Canaanite Woman, who loves both her unnamed Daughter and her Son, Jesus, cries out to Jesus to help his sister, for the Woman has lost her to evil influences and is desperate to have her back. Jesus, who hasn't yet learned to recognize the Daughter as his sister, ignores the cries within him and acts as if nothing is happening.

ACT II: (Matthew 15:23b-24) The Canaanite Woman persists by making her desire known to the Disciples, who become visibly irritated and discuss ways to silence her. Finally they ask Jesus to do something to make her go away. Jesus responds by declaring flatly that the Daughter is not included in his ministry.

ACT III: (Matthew 15:25-26) The Canaanite Woman changes tactics. Refusing to take "No!" for an answer, she begs Jesus on her knees to expand his vision. Jesus responds by insulting her. He calls her and her Daughter "dogs" unfit to share in the gifts of heaven! The Disciples feel righteous and the Daughter's condition worsens.

ACT IV: (Matthew 15:27-28) The Canaanite Woman uses Jesus' own words to teach him: ". . . even the dogs eat the crumbs that fall from their owners' table." Jesus finally grasps the fact that his mission is to bring everyone to the heavenly banquet, even those considered most unworthy. He says to God, "O Woman, great is your faith! Be it done for you as you desire." At that moment the Daughter is healed. The Disciples scratch their heads and wonder.

ACT V: (Today) Each of these characters lives within you. If they could speak, what would they say? Their dialogue is Act V.

† † †

"And great crowds came to him, bringing with them
the lame, the maimed, the blind, the dumb, and many
others . . . and he healed them . . . ."

Today I climb the holy mountain in my heart to be with you,
Jesus. I set aside my busyness and I seek your presence. The
journey up the mountain is steep, but my longing is great, for
"You have the words of eternal life . . . ." (John 6:68)

At the top of the mountain you are seated, receiving the crowds
that flow toward you like a river of pain seeking a place of healing. In the crowds I see friends, enemies, relatives, neighbors,
strangers, all kneeling before you as you reach out to touch,
heal, and restore them one by one.

Now I stand before you, Jesus, and you speak my name and
ask, "What do you want me to do for you?"

Seeing your compassion, I allow you to see me just as I am:
I show you my spiritual lameness, caused by my need to forgive
another and be forgiven for the hurt we have caused each other;
I let you see how I have been emotionally maimed by unresolved anger, fear, and pain turned against myself; I confess
my psychological blindness that leads me mistakenly to see my
mother or father in every authority figure; I admit my deafness
toward my body, which I treat as a machine rather than as the
temple of God.

"My need," I respond, "is for healing."

At these words, I feel and see a loving light radiating from your
presence, surrounding me, and seeking out in my body, mind,
and spirit the wounds I have shown you. One by one you touch
them with the healing light of your presence.

Today, Jesus, I will remain on the holy mountain, glorifying
the God of Israel in my healed heart.

† † †

"Do you not remember . . . ?"

Today's Gospel invites us to grow from the milk of infant discipleship that seeks signs of God's love to the solid food of mature faith that believes without seeing. It shows us the disciples, after two separate multiplications of loaves, showing up for a meal without bringing any bread at all! In response, Jesus calls them "people of little faith" whose attitude resembles that of the Pharisees and Sadducees in that they seek signs of God's favor without developing faith in God. They are like children who seek the gift and forget the giver.

To the unbelieving Pharisees and Sadducees Jesus promises only "the sign of Jonah." To the disciples Jesus asks: "Do you not remember the five loaves of the five thousand . . . or the seven loaves of the four thousand . . . ?" For these, like the sign of Jonah, are signs of his death and Resurrection, when he trustingly placed himself in God's hands to be raised on the third day. That is why at the Last Supper, when he broke the bread, he said, "This is my body which is given for you. Do this in remembrance of me." (Luke 22:19)

The point is this: there are times when, in order to lead us into a fuller life, God removes the signs of God's love which we have grown accustomed to. There may even be times when we are invited to walk in total darkness, as Jesus did in his passion and death. But no matter how deep the darkness of such times, there always remains one sign of God's abiding love that Jesus tells us to remember: a little piece of bread broken and multiplied to feed the world. Therefore, let us pray today: *"Lord, give us this bread always."* (John 6:34)

† † †

"And I tell you, you are Peter . . . ."

Today, Jesus, I climb the holy mountain in my heart to sit at your feet once again.

You look at me intently, then ask, "Who are people saying that I am in the late twentieth century?"

I reflect and answer: "Some say you are a great prophet, like Jeremiah or Elijah; others say you are a spiritual leader, like the Buddha; still others see you as a great humanitarian, like Albert Schweitzer."

Looking at me intently again, you ask, "And *you* — who do you say that I am?"

I pause and I remember the many miracles I have seen you perform: you have healed the wounds of the broken-hearted; you have taught and preached with life-changing power; you have restored outcasts to dignity and self-esteem. Remembering these and many other signs, I speak the words before they form in my mind: "You are the Christ, the unique Child of the living God."

"How blessed you are that God has revealed the truth to you," you respond. "I tell you, you are a rock on which I will build my church."

"But Jesus," I reply, "you know how impulsive I am . . . ."

But you continue: "The more you abide in me, the more your true self will emerge. You will find in time that instead of being shifting sands, you are in fact a rock. Therefore I will give you the keys of heaven, for you will lead many people to their true home."

"Who am I to be so honored?" I ask. "These are promises you made to Peter centuries ago."

You respond with a twinkle in your eye, *"I tell you, you are Peter."*

Today I treasure your words in my heart, savoring the truths they reveal to me.

† † †

"If any would come after me, let them deny themselves and take up their cross and follow me."

Today's Gospel invites us to embrace the suffering that comes into our lives as part of our faith journey. Now that the disciples recognize who Jesus is, he pierces to the core the mystery of his own identity as the one who will reveal the meaning and purpose of life through his suffering, death, and Resurrection.

The disciples are incredulous. Yesterday's "rock," full of faith, becomes today's "stumbling block," full of doubt: "God, who is good, would never raise up the Messiah and then allow him to suffer and die!"

Jesus responds: "From a human perspective, Peter, you are correct; from a faith perspective, however, you have it backwards. Perhaps God would not raise up the Messiah and then allow him to die, but God *would* allow the Messiah to die and then raise him up!" In other words, suffering and death are not ends in themselves, but means to enter into a transformation process that ultimately issues in newness of life.

We are all a little like Peter: in the face of pain and suffering we want to run. This does not mean that we are bad, it just means that we are human. And yet, Jesus invites us to believe that, just as he emerged transformed from his passion and death, so the suffering that enters our lives is a path by which we are daily transformed into a deeper expression of ourselves, until that final transformation which takes place in death. He therefore not only prophesies about his own passion, death, and Resurrection, but he invites us to enter that pattern of salvation ourselves: *If you wish to come after me, then deny yourself and take up your cross and follow me.*

† † †

"The master commended the dishonest steward for
acting shrewdly . . . ."

Sitting beside my friend, the stream, I consider the parable of the dishonest steward. "What was so shrewd about him?" I ask. "He went right on wasting his master's goods!"

After a long silence the stream replies, "His shrewdness consisted first in facing the truth that he had wronged his master and had been found out." After another long silence the stream speaks to me, asking, "And how would you respond to the words, 'Turn in the account of your stewardship'?"

The question takes me by surprise; then I recall that one day I, too, will have to render an account of my life and actions. Reflecting on this truth, I admit to my friend, "I will be in the same situation as the dishonest steward was, for my faithfulness has certainly not been perfect."

"Then learn from the parable and be as shrewd as the dishonest steward was," the stream coaxes.

"But what does that mean?" I ask. "The dishonest steward went out and cancelled the debts of his master's debtors."

"You do the same," the stream says gently. "Just as the dishonest steward averted disaster by forgiving his master's debtors, so will you. That is why Jesus taught that 'if you forgive others their trespasses, your Heavenly Parent also will forgive you; but if you do not forgive others their trespasses, neither will God your Father and Mother forgive your trespasses.' (Matthew 6:14-15) Therefore, be shrewd and learn the power of forgiveness."

Sitting beside my friend, the stream, I consider the parable of the dishonest steward. In my heart I summon my master's debtors one by one, and I say, "Take your bill, and write on it: FORGIVEN."

† † †

"And . . . Jesus . . . led them up a high mountain apart."

Sitting beside my friend, Peter, I say, "Tell me how to find the mount of transfiguration, for I am hungry for a deeper knowledge of God."

Peter replies, "You need not travel far; the mount of transfiguration is the holy mountain in your heart."

"But how shall I climb the holy mountain in my heart?" I ask. "It is high and its ways are steep and unpredictable."

"You are quite right," he responds. "There is only one who can lead you safely through them to the mountaintop, and that one is Jesus. Therefore, do not climb the mountain without Jesus as your guide."

"And what will happen at the top?" I continue.

"You will look into Jesus' face, and in its light you will be enlightened; and you will begin to know the truth about yourself, your world, and your God. Therefore, do not climb the mountain unless you are willing to know the truth."

"I want to know the truth," I exclaim. "I want to settle on the mountaintop forever and tell Jesus again and again of my love for him!"

Peter smiles, then says, "And you would be interrupted by the voice of God telling you to listen for a change! And when your words had finally ceased and you had ceased attending to the images that clutter your mind, then in the silence you would hear God's Word, and in the darkness you would see God's radiance, and the hunger in your heart would be satisfied."

Today I approach the holy mountain in my heart, hungry for a deeper knowledge of God. I take several deep breaths to prepare myself — then, following Jesus, I begin the climb to the top.

† † †

*"Then the disciples came to Jesus privately
and said, 'Why could we not cast it out?' He said
to them, 'Because of your little faith.' "*

Jesus, I have wondered why we, your disciples, have been unable to heal so many cases of cancer, AIDS, and other forms of disease and sickness. In today's Gospel you offer a five-word answer: "Because of your little faith." I resist your analysis, Jesus, but it is inescapable, for the disciples' situation described here is no different from ours today.

We say we have faith. We want to have faith. But as diseases and sickness continue, your words return to disturb us. Perhaps we do not understand what faith is, after all. Jesus, teach us about faith.

My child, faith is not primarily an acceptance of some revealed truth, although it may involve this. Nor is faith primarily the assent of your will to something you have not chosen, although it may involve this, too. Rather, faith is the knowledge of God experienced in prayer. When you open yourself to that gift, you are transformed little by little to become God's self. Through this process the powerful presence of God enters the world to heal and transform. My child, you were created to be an opening for God to heal the world. Therefore, if you wish to increase your faith and fulfill your high calling, there is only one way: you must enter more deeply into prayer.

Jesus, we Christians pay lip service to prayer, but our lives betray our words. We are more interested in programs and projects and propaganda. Perhaps that is why our world is still not healed and transformed. Help me today to set aside my frenetic busyness and to enter into the simplicity and power of prayer.

† † †

". . . the children are free."

The key to today's passage is an understanding of the half-shekel tax which every adult male was required to pay annually under the Mosaic covenant. In practice, it was used to maintain the Temple, but its spiritual purpose was that "each shall give a ransom for himself to the Lord." (Exodus 30:12)

Now the collectors of the tax ask Peter, "Does not your teacher pay the tax?" Peter replies, "Yes," and from the perspective of the Mosaic covenant his response is correct. "But when Christ appeared as a high priest . . . Christ entered once for all into the Holy Place, taking not the blood of goats and calves but Christ's own blood, thus securing an eternal redemption." (Hebrews 9:11-12) "Therefore Christ is the mediator of a new covenant . . . ." (Hebrew 9:15) There is consequently no obligation to pay the half-shekel tax, for the Mosaic covenant with all its requirements is obsolete. (Hebrew 8:13) Jesus, who is on the brink of his death and Resurrection and already anticipates its effects, therefore declares to Peter that "the children are free."

Having alluded to this new age of freedom, Jesus immediately invites Peter — and us — to be part of it. He says,

> "Peter, go to the sea of all the possibilities of your life as you would go to the sea on an early morning full of possibilities. Cast out your desire there as you would cast a hook to catch the first fish of the day; you will find that your desire has hooked onto the one who first comes up from the grave as the first fish comes up from the sea, rising in its very dying. Hook onto me, Peter! Catch me, Peter! Bring me into your boat, Peter! And when you have brought me into your life, take the spiritual currency, the truth that I am telling you with my own mouth, the good news of my death and Resurrection, the shekel of freedom, and give it to the people for me. Tell them I have paid their ransom, as I have also paid yours, when I gave myself as a ransom for all. (I Timothy 2:6) Tell them they are free!

† † †

". . . your hand . . ."

Thank you, God, for the gift of my hands. Thank you for empowering me through them to receive the gifts of life, to heal others with a gentle touch, to praise you by raising them in openness and trust.

Forgive me for the times I have used my hands to grasp and cling to power, possessions, and prestige, to touch others possessively, lustfully, or violently, or to take what belongs to another. Today I cut off these uses of my hands and throw them away.

". . . your foot . . ."

Thank you, God, for the gift of my feet. Thank you for the pleasure they give me in running, swimming, and playing, in walking about on our planet, and in standing tall and proud in your sunlight.

Forgive me for the times I have used my feet to enter places that do not glorify you, to kick or trip up others on their life journeys, or to intrude into another's space. Today I cut off these uses of my feet and throw them away.

". . . your eye . . ."

Thank you, God, for the gift of my eyes. Thank you for the way they enable me to enjoy the colors, shapes, and textures of your creation, to read and learn from the insights of others, and to communicate without words my inner life.

Forgive me for the times I have used my eyes to look at others in a depreciative way, to convey a dishonest message, or to violate another's privacy by looking at his or her words, experiences, or possessions uninvited. Today I pluck out these uses of my eyes and throw them away.

Thank you, God, for all the parts of my body.
Teach me the right use of each part and help me
to eliminate those abuses and misuses that
separate me from the fullness of life.

† † †

". . . and if your neighbor refuses to listen
even to the church, let that neighbor be to you as . . .
a tax collector."

To the Jews of Jesus' day, tax collectors were social and spiritual outcasts, lumped together with gentiles, sinners, murderers, and thieves. Pharisees would not allow even the skirt of their robe to touch one of them. And, of course, not all the tax collectors were innocent victims. Most of them were untrustworthy and exploitive participants in an unjust economic system which gave them wealth at the expense of their fellow citizens.

Yet Jesus cared deeply for these clever thieves. He called Matthew to become one of his closest disciples. (Matthew 10:3) He invited himself to the home of Zacchaeus. (Luke 19:5) The Pharisees in fact complained that Jesus ate with tax collectors (Matthew 9:11), and there were those who derided Jesus as being a friend of tax collectors. (Matthew 11:19)

In the light of Jesus' deliberate outreach to tax collectors, today's passage dealing with sinners in the church cannot therefore mean, "Three strikes and you're out!" It is, rather, as if Jesus were saying: "When someone seems to you to be the worst kind of sinner — as traitorous and dishonest as a tax collector — then treat that individual exactly as I treated the tax collector, as the very person whom I am most eager to befriend. Leave the others, if necessary, and find a way to bring him or her home. For 'I have not come to call the righteous, but sinners to repentance.' " (Luke 5:32)

It is significant that only Matthew records these words of Jesus comparing sinners in the church to tax collectors. As a redeemed tax collector, he would have understood immedately that Jesus was teaching us to see the sinner as one of us: A lost sheep in need of God's grace, one for whom Jesus goes out searching to find and bring it home.

† † †

*" . . . should you not have had mercy
on your co-worker, as I had mercy on you?"*

A popular expression says, "What goes 'round comes 'round."
Today's Gospel contains just that idea: the unmerciful servant
ends up in the same prison into which he has had his fellow
servant cast, and for the very same reason.

Jesus taught this principle on many occasions. "Judge not," he
said, "and you will not be judged; condemn not, and you will
not be condemned; forgive, and you will be forgiven . . . . For
the measure you give will be the measure you get back." (Luke
6:37-38)

It seems logical enough. But is that all there is? Is that the extent
of the good news? Is life no more than an inescapable cycle
of karmic retribution and reward?

To say "Yes" would be to miss the central Gospel message of
God's unconditional love. The good news is precisely that God
did not wait for us to earn divine mercy and forgiveness, but,
like the ruler in the parable, has had pity on us and forgiven
us everything. That is why Paul wrote, "But God shows love
for us in that while we were yet sinners, Christ died for us."
(Romans 5:8)

It is only when we, like the unmerciful servant, fail to allow
the same love of God that saved us to become the basis of our
human relationships that we fall back into the karmic cycle.
Then we are left to suffer alone in the prison of our grudges,
self-righteousness, and hard-heartedness.

Who is it in your life that you have not completely forgiven?
Your father? Mother? Spouse? Brother or sister? Son or
daughter? Co-worker?

Let your prayer today be: *"Lord, have patience with me."* God
will show you how to forgive from your heart.

† † †

". . . I was afraid . . ."

Fear is the greatest immobilizer in the world. When we are afraid, we are reluctant to take risks because we think that we will be punished for our mistakes. This is as true spiritually as it is in the other dimensions of our lives.

There are many kinds of fear, but mostly we simply fear rejection. Sometimes we are so afraid of rejection that, like the third servant, we keep the love offered to us safely hidden away where it will never require us to make ourselves vulnerable by risking a response to it.

There is only one antidote to this kind of fear, and that is love. The good news of today's Gospel is that Christ comes to give each of us a share of God's love, much as the ruler in today's parable entrusted a pound to each of the ten servants.

Sometimes, like the first and second servants, we multiply Christ's love in the world by investing it wisely.

Sometimes, like the third servant, we allow fearful images of God or ourselves to immobilize us. We think of God, for example, as "a severe man," even though God has shown us otherwise countless times. Or we think of ourselves as helpless children, even though we are full-grown adults. We cling to these old, distorted images because, even if they are painful, at least they are familiar and we know what to expect. Clinging to them allows us to play it safe and maintain the illusion of control.

Today's Gospel invites us to risk letting go of crippling and fearful images of God and ourselves and to begin experiencing and investing the currency of God's love.

Are you afraid? Then let the mantra on your lips today be: *". . . perfect love casts out fear."* (I John 4:18)

† † †

*"For there are eunuchs who have been so
from birth, and there are eunuchs who have been
made eunuchs by men, and there are eunuchs who
have made themselves eunuchs for the sake of
the reign of heaven."*

Today's Gospel represents a radical departure by Jesus from the prevailing view of his day that marriage and procreation were the sacred duty of every devout Jew. Jesus says that there are three groups of individuals for whom it is not expedient to marry.

The first group, eunuchs who have been so from birth, have been understood as people born with serious birth defects. It makes equal or greater sense, however, to understand this group as homosexual men and women. As with eunuchs, traditional marriage makes little sense for gay men and lesbians; as with eunuchs, the sexual activity of gay men and lesbians is not directed toward procreation; as with eunuchs, religious and cultural institutions have scorned gay men and lesbians. Finally, research is suggesting increasingly that gay men and lesbians "have been so from birth."

The second group, eunuchs who have been made eunuchs by men, is clearly a literal reference to eunuchs.

The third group, eunuchs who have made themselves eunuchs for the sake of the reign of heaven, are persons who choose a celibate life in order to devote themselves singlemindedly to God.

The good news of this passage is that Jesus affirms all these states of life as a gift. Some receive the gift of heterosexuality, while others receive the gift of homosexuality or celibacy. Eunuchs, too, are welcomed into God's household. (Acts 8:26-40) There is room for everyone in the reign of God.

Therefore, whatever our state of life, let the prayer on our lips today be: *Thank you, Jesus, for including me in the family of God.*

† † †

". . . come, follow me."

Today you invite me, Jesus, to follow you. You invite me to unclutter my life of all the little strategies I use to insulate myself from risk and vulnerability. You invite me to learn again what it means to need God. You invite me to enter with you into the paschal mystery by following you to Jerusalem where you will suffer, die, and rise again.

Your answers to my questions leave no doubt that accepting your invitation will cost me everything. I ask you, Jesus, to lead me to life, and you tell me to begin by dying to everything except you. I ask you, ". . . what do I still lack?" — as if I had to acquire one more thing to find life — and you tell me, ". . . go, sell what you possess . . . ." I offer to *do* more "to have eternal life," and you tell me to *be* little like a child, "for to such belongs the reign of heaven."

This is, of course, not the first time you have invited me to follow you, Jesus. Sometimes I have willingly accepted your invitation. At other times I went away sorrowful like the rich young man because I wanted the rewards of spiritual life without the cost. I was all too willing to observe the externals of religion without surrendering my heart to you.

Today I choose to follow you, Jesus. I renounce the persons, powers, prestige, possessions, and philosophies that prevent me from following you wholeheartedly. I embrace you alone as the life I long for. Today I will not walk away from you in sorrow, but like a little child I will run to you in joy. Today the prayer in my heart and on my lips shall be: *"I will follow you wherever you go."* (Luke 9:57)

† † †

> *". . . it is easier for a camel to go through*
> *the eye of a needle than for a rich person to*
> *enter the realm of God."*

Today Jesus teaches us that the pursuit of wealth and the pursuit of God's reign are incompatible.

It is not that money in itself is bad. The problem is the subtle way that wealth influences and shapes our attitudes, for wealth feeds the illusion of control, security, and self-sufficiency. We begin to think, ". . . I am rich, I have prospered, and I need nothing" even when we may in fact be spiritually "wretched, pitiable, poor, blind, and naked." (Revelation 3:17) Wealth leads us to proclaim, "Blessed are the rich;" but Jesus says, "Blessed are you poor, for yours is the realm of God." (Luke 6:20) Wealth leads us to proclaim, "Woe to you that are poor;" but Jesus says, ". . . woe to you that are rich, for you have received your consolation." (Luke 6:24) Wealth leads us to proclaim, "The wealthy shall be first;" but Jesus says, "Many that are first will be last, and the last first." It is as if wealth turns reality upside-down, on its head.

"No servant can serve two masters; for the servant will either hate the one and love the other, or be devoted to the one and despise the other. You cannot serve God and mammon." (Luke 16:13) Jesus is uncompromising on this point.

Today's Gospel is an invitation to choose God and to renounce the false values that wealth engenders. In return, Jesus promises eternal life, which is the knowledge of God. Is that not why we chose to follow Christ in the first place?

Therefore, ". . . choose this day whom you will serve . . . but as for me and my house, we will serve Yahweh." (Joshua 24:15)

† † †

"You go into the vineyard too,
and whatever is right I will give you."

I remember the day, Jesus, when you first invited me to become a laborer in your vineyard. How honored I felt! At that time the knowledge was still fresh in my mind that everything, including the call to work in your vineyard, was your gift to me.

But you did not ask me to work for nothing. Your reward, you promised, would be the gift of yourself. "I am with you always," you said, even "to the close of the age." (Matthew 28:20)

You have kept your word, Jesus. You have nourished me with yourself in prayer, in Scripture, in the Eucharist, and in encounters with other laborers in your vineyard. You have gradually shown me that "My food is to do the will of God who sent me, and to accomplish God's work." (John 4:34)

I will not pretend that it has been easy. Sometimes it has seemed impossible to bear "the burden of the day and the scorching heat," and I have felt like giving up. But Jesus, to whom would I go? "You have the words of eternal life." (John 6:68) At other times I have acted as if I had a special right to the gift of your Holy Spirit, the "denarius" you promised as my reward. How foolish to want to set limits on your generosity! Please come and change my heart into one as generous as yours, so that I may learn to give myself as you do, without exception or reserve.

As this month comes to an end, Jesus, I re-dedicate myself to working in your vineyard, confident that you will always give "whatever is right" at the end of the day.

† † †

DECEMBER

Nowhere is the revolutionary nature of the Gospel of Jesus Christ more apparent than in today's passage. Jesus reminds us that great people "lord it over" others. But, he says, "It shall not be so among you." He then goes on to explain the astonishing reality of the new order that he brings to us: ". . . whoever would be great among you must be your servant, and whoever would be first among you must be your slave."

The Greek word in verse twenty-six that is translated "servant" in the Revised Standard Version and "minister" in the King James version is *diaconos*, from which the term "deacon" is derived. This implies that every Christian is a deacon or minister called by Christ to serve others. There is no higher office in the realm of God; there is no greater title in the Christian community. We may exalt titles like priest, bishop, elder, or district coordinator, but the bold and compelling fact of Christianity is that every follower of Christ who serves is great in the eyes of God.

Sometimes we yearn for leadership, power, and fancy titles, as James and John do here; but when we do, we forget the teaching of Jesus that real power and leadership in the realm of God is not entrusted to those who lust for power, but rather to those who serve others with humility. Authentic leadership implies responsibility and often carries with it a great deal of stress and pain.

This revolutionary message flies in the face of all the world's understanding of leadership and power. It is a message of gentleness and peace, of service and love, of sensitivity and self-effacement.

Dear God, I thank you for leading us to a new understanding of leadership and power. Help me to live up to Christ's demanding example. Amen.

† † †

"Have mercy on us, Son of David!" The cry of two blind beggars to Jesus is more than just an appeal for help; it is an acknowledgement of the fact that Jesus is the Messiah. Somehow these blind beggars knew more about the Saviour they were addressing than even the disciples. They also knew that their persistent prayers would be answered. When the crowd tried to silence them, they cried out again. Jesus was moved to pity, he heard their prayer, and they were healed.

But the most crucial moment in this brief episode occurs when Matthew tells us that "they . . . followed him."

Often we cry out to God in our pain and anguish, praying in our time of need that God be with us and heal our hurts. Often God stops, takes pity on us, and heals us. And often we simply go on our way, forgetting even to thank the source of all our healing and joy, not to mention forgetting to follow Jesus as disciples.

The proof that the prayer of the blind beggars was sincere is that they became disciples of Jesus. Moreover, they became his disciples right before the crucifixion, not an easy time to begin to follow Jesus. We turn to God when we are in need, but the true test of our faith is whether we continue to follow God after our needs have been met. Jesus, who gives sight to sightless eyes, inspires us to follow, even through death, to Resurrection and new life.

Great Physician, help us to look to you
not only when we are in need, but also in those
times after our needs have been met. Help us to have the
faith of the two blind beggars, who saw you
with eyes of faith. Amen.

† † †

"Take heed that you are not led astray . . . ."

Jesus does not encourage us, in today's Gospel, to expect that the world will always affirm us in our experience of and belief in Christ. In fact, Jesus tells us that we can expect persecution, and history confirms Jesus' prediction.

Those of us who are gay Christians have had to face persecution, just as Jesus warns. Many in the world despise us for being religious, organized religion having been "the enemy" for so long. And as if that weren't enough, we are at times persecuted by the very church family we seek to belong to.

Some would say that we are victims of false prophets, that we have been led astray, that the Gospel of love is not for all people, or even that we should deny that our sexuality is a good gift from God. With so many conflicting messages, how do we know God's will in our lives? How do we ferret out the truth?

Each Christian begins to find the truth by listening to the whisper of the Spirit in the heart. God still speaks to each of us, and if we are quiet and open, God's truth will be revealed to us.

In order to test what we believe God has laid upon our hearts, we then look at the results of our beliefs, for God's truth will not result in confusion and pain, but rather in peace and joy. The fruit of the Spirit in our lives — love, joy, peace, patience, kindness, goodness, faithfulness, gentleness, self-control — will help us know the truth and will set us free.

Dear God of Truth, help me to discern the truth
in my life. Help me to separate my imperfect will from
your perfect will. Help me see the fruit of the
Spirit of truth. Amen.

† † †

If Jesus wanted to make a point with his entry into Jerusalem, it was that he came for peace, forswearing violence and force. All the details of this story illustrate the point that Jesus is a new kind of ruler, reigning in love and peace.

Jesus came meekly, on a lowly animal that was a symbol of gentleness. He relied on the anonymous assistance of his friends. An unnamed follower provided the ordinary animals for his transportation. Simple people accompanied him. He was escorted by children and common folk, armed with palm branches rather than spears, singing songs of praise rather than war chants.

Despite Jesus' intention to show what kind of ruler he was, some of his followers tried to give a different impression, perhaps trying to force him into a more political role. By spreading their garments on the road before him they echoed the actions of the followers of Jehu (II Kings 9:13), a great and powerful king of Israel who ruled by armed might. But regardless of the attempts to force Jesus into another kind of power, it is the image of Jesus as the serene, loving, peaceful ruler of our hearts that comes down to us through the years.

Sometimes I look for a Saviour who will come with sword and fury, punishing those who are especially vexing me at the moment. Sometimes I look for Jesus to come and force those who oppress me to mend their ways and do as God wills, or at least do what I want to be God's will. Then I remember and I am stilled by this image of the Prince of Peace, Jesus, sitting on a donkey, serenaded by the songs of children. As the hymn says, "*Ride on! Ride on in majesty!*"

† † †

In today's passage we see a side of Jesus that makes many of us very uncomfortable: the angry Jesus, cleansing the Temple, overturning the tables of the money-changers and merchants, cursing a barren fig tree, and causing its death. Is this our familiar Jesus, "meek and mild"?

In these stories, the God within Jesus burns brightly, an incandescent light of holy anger. Jesus is God; since the Hebrew Testament is full of stories of God getting angry, why is it so hard for us to picture Jesus angry? What are the elements of godly anger and when is anger appropriate for us?

True Christianity should be known for its anger as much as for its gentleness. Christian gentleness is not a passive quality, but one of inner, God-directed peace. When a Christian is confronted with injustice and moral decay, as Jesus was in the Temple, or a failure to fulfill his or her God-given potential, as in the case of the fig tree, then the Christian is roused to indignation. Christians should be known as much for their enemies as for their friends.

Jesus reacted to wrong with anger, it is true, but it was anger that was clothed with the authority and power of God. Similarly, our anger must be inspired by God's truth in our lives, not solely by our own convenience and need. Our anger must be righteous in nature, keeping the Gospel message constantly before us. Our anger must be assured, not extreme, but appropriate to the circumstances. And our anger must be quick to abate and ready to forgive.

Dear God of Justice, help me to know the difference between godly anger and my own selfish anger. Amen.

† † †

Challenged by the Sanhedrin in the Temple, Jesus is asked by what authority he teaches there. In asking "by what authority," they imply that he is not rabbinically ordained by the Temple authorities. Jesus affirms that both he and John the Baptist have no need of rabbinical or Temple credentials, because their credentials, confirmed by the people, have come directly from God.

Jesus' story of the two sons emphasizes the difference between religious people like the Sadducees, who claim to be obedient to God, yet are not, and the followers of Jesus and John, who though they are sinners, repent of their sin as a result of the Gospel and do God's will. "The tax collectors and the harlots go into the realm of God before you. For John came to you in the way of righteousness, and you did not believe him, but the tax collectors and the harlots believed him." Thus Jesus, while not rejecting the authority of the Temple to ordain preachers and teachers, says that ordination that truly comes from God must also involve the confirmation of the believers.

This principle is very important for people who are struggling to claim their own liberation and freedom. It is too easy to allow those who say they are called to leadership to have their way. But true leadership in the church comes as a result of God's call, which is then confirmed by the Body of Christ, the believers. We rely on a collective wisdom that we believe is imparted by the Holy Spirit. The support that true leaders receive from the community of believers is crucial in discerning those who are acting according to God's will.

Beautiful Creator, help me to discern true leadership and to know your will. Give me wisdom to make way for leaders whom I see emerging in response to God's call in their lives and confirmed by the people of God. Amen.

† † †

It is easy to think of this passage as history. The owner of the vineyard is God, the tenant farmers are the Jewish people, the fruit is righteousness, the servants sent to collect God's due are the prophets, and Jesus is the heir. Of course! It is so easy to reflect on how wicked *they* were in the past.

What is more difficult, yet more appropriate, is to apply this parable to ourselves. All that we have is a gift from God; do I remember God as the source of all life and goodness? God's messengers come before us even today to remind us of our right relationship with God; have I welcomed these "servants of the householder"? Jesus is the unique Child of God sent to bring us the Word of God; do I receive Christ without reservation into my life? We are called to be faithful stewards of all God has bestowed on us; do I render to God the fruit of my labor?

What if God's judgment began with the Church? "For the time has come for judgment to begin with the household of God; and if it begins with us, what will be the end of those who do not obey the Gospel of God?" (I Peter 4:17)

The truth is that there are times when we are less than faithful to God in the way we live our lives. Today's Gospel invites us to examine our lives and repent of such times so that we may receive God's mercy. For "mercy triumphs over judgment" (James 2:13) when judgment brings repentance.

Eternal Householder, I confess that I have not always been a good steward of all you have given me. Help me to serve you with singleness of mind and faithfulness. Amen.

† † †

Jesus says that in the realm of God "many are called, but few are chosen." This is not an elitist message, but an important teaching about the nature of spiritual life.

"Many are called": everyone is invited. God's invitation is a gift of free grace for all, without exception or precondition. Both bad and good fill the banquet hall. This is truly good news for us, especially when we don't feel good or worthy enough, because we don't have to do anything to be good or worthy — God accepts us just as we are.

"Few are chosen": the gift, to be received, requires in us true repentance. While it is true that we don't have to be righteous when we hear the invitation and that we can enter God's realm wearing sin's dirty clothes and still be welcome, it is also true that once we have come in, we are expected to put on a wedding garment, that is, to live a life that reflects the new life into which we have entered. In other words, once we are saved, we are invited to an ongoing transformation so that our everyday lives will more and more reflect our new spiritual life. Only then will we have shown that we are properly practicing our Christian faith.

Today's text invites us to reflect on this tension in the Gospel message: God's grace is a free gift that we can never deserve, and yet we can grow in grace by cooperating with it. What change in your life could you make today that would draw you closer to God?

Generous Host, thank you for inviting me to the wedding feast today. Help me to make the changes that will make your transformation of my life complete.
Amen.

† † †

Whose image is on the coin of your life? If Christ asked you to see the image stamped on the things you prize most, whose image would be revealed? The image of Christ or your own? Who ultimately owns the things you prize most?

In today's story, Jesus sets himself against fanatical allegiance to the state. He teaches us an application of the Gospel for our lives as citizens. "Render therefore to Caesar . . . ." We do, of course, have certain obligations toward the nation in which we live. As Christians, this means intelligent and conscientious participation in the political process to the end that God's will may be done.

But Christ's teaching goes beyond a political application. When we are told to "render to God the things that are God's," Christ is thereby inviting us to examine our lives and consider the source of all we have and are. It is an invitation to each of us to make God the ultimate ruler over every aspect of our lives: our bodies, lovers, money, homes, jobs, cars — everything. It is an invitation to stamp the perfect image of God on every facet of our lives, with all that implies: that we give Christ the ultimate power over our lives.

Do people look at our lives and see Christ resplendent on the coin that we prize most highly? Is Christ's image and superscription stamped on the currency of our lives? Once we have given ourselves wholly over to Jesus, then this coin will be the only true currency.

God, I give you the central place in my life.
Reign over all I say, think, and do. Stamp your
image on every aspect of my life. Amen.

† † †

"What then will this child be?"

John the Baptist was in many ways a miracle child. His mother, Elizabeth, was barren. Both she and her husband, Zechariah, were advanced in years. The angel Gabriel had appeared to Zechariah in the temple to foretell John's birth. Zechariah was struck dumb because he doubted the angel, not wanting to believe that his greatest wish was being granted.

Then Elizabeth calmly announced that the baby would be called "John," a new name, unused in their family. The relatives said, "None of your kindred is called by this name." But Zechariah, remembering the words of the angel, wrote, "His name is John." Immediately he was able to speak again; he was healed as he was obedient to God's command. The people wondered and asked, "What then will this child be?"

Name changes are not uncommon in Scripture. Abram became Abraham, Jacob became Israel, Simon became Peter, Saul became Paul — and all these changes were made to indicate that God had brought about great changes in their lives. Similarly, John's unfamiliar name was a sign that a great shift had taken place in salvation history. This child of miracles with the strange new name and God's hand upon him would be special. He would be the forerunner of the Messiah!

When we become followers of Jesus we take on the new name of Christians for ourselves. Angels and saints wonder at our new life and say, "What then will this child be?" The answer lies in how we choose to live our lives each day.

Dear Name-Giver,
you who name us in your wisdom,
help me to discern the new names, new ministries,
new tasks you lay before me. Amen.

† † †

The Sadducees must have been a real trial to Jesus! Political and social conservatives and Biblical literalists, they were legal purists who accepted only the Pentateuch, the five books of Moses. The fact that they also favored cooperation with Rome, lived off the offerings people made to the Temple, and prided themselves on being the intelligentsia, all made them folks whom it was hard to love.

In today's passage, they test Jesus about resurrection. A woman has been passed childless from brother to brother as each dies, as required by the law. All seven brothers die, and then the woman dies. Who gets to be married to her in the resurrection?

The poor Sadducees, trying to play "how-many-husbands-do-you-get-in-heaven?" It is the old game of those who read too literally, and Jesus finesses it brilliantly. Jesus begins his response to the Sadducees by saying, "You are wrong," even though they had not stated their position on the question. He is saying that their whole perspective on Scriptural interpretation is in error. They have concentrated so much on the interesting but secondary details of Scripture that they have ended up knowing "neither the Scriptures nor the power of God."

Jesus is telling the Sadducees — and us today — to keep the central message of Scripture in mind when interpreting specific messages. If an interpretation contradicts that central message, then it is probably wrong.

The central message of Scripture is God's power and love and our salvation. If we lose ourselves in theological controversies, no matter how interesting, then we, too, are wrong.

Giver of Wisdom, keep me focused on you so that the details of life make sense. Amen.

† † †

One rabbi tells how Moses gave 613 commandments. David, however, reduced them to eleven (Psalm 15:2-5), Isaiah to six (Isaiah 33:15), Micah to three (Micah 6:8), Amos to two (Amos 5:4), and Habakkuk to one (Habakkuk 2:4).

Jesus follows this tradition of simplifying the commandments to a few pithy, profound sentences. Asked what is the greatest commandment, Jesus replies with the two from which come all the law and the prophets: "You shall love the Lord your God with all your heart, and with all your soul, and with all your mind. This is the great and first commandment. And a second is like it. You shall love your neighbor as yourself."

In so saying, Jesus gives us the whole law in a nutshell: love God, love your neighbor, and love yourself.

In a way, the many laws of Moses were easier to deal with — at least you knew precisely what was required in virtually every instance. Jesus' law is more complicated, in that it implies a great deal of personal responsibility. If we stay close enough to God, who is love, we learn what love is, as well as its implications for our lives as we walk on our faith journey. This requires and presupposes a relationship with God nurtured in prayer.

Gracious Lawgiver, I give thanks that you have given us guidelines for our lives. Help me today to discern how to truly fulfill the requirements of your laws. Teach me your law of love so I can truly live a life of love. Amen.

† † †

Jesus cites three of the great sins of religious authorities in today's passage: hypocrisy, heartless lack of charity, and ostentation.

We could spend a great deal of time castigating preachers for these great sins, as familiar today as they were then, but that would be missing Jesus' point. Jesus is not addressing the religious authorities here but "the crowds" and "his disciples." The real issue is our response to the imperfections of religious authorities. Jesus gives a clear principle: Do as they say but not necessarily as they do.

It is disconcerting when those we admire and trust for bringing us the good news are revealed as being imperfect. We may be tempted at such times to give up our faith and consider it all a hypocrisy, or to condemn them, or to conclude that we are better than they. Jesus does not teach us such behavior; rather, he exhorts us to remain faithful to the truth and to persevere in our spiritual life, even though our teachers may have fallen.

Pride stands back and smugly condemns religious leaders for their sins, which are magnified because of the leaders' public position. Rather than exalting ourselves by adopting a posture of condemnation, we may need to say, "There but for the grace of God go I." That is why Jesus says, "All those who exalt themselves will be humbled, and all who humble themselves will be exalted."

Dear Creator, help me today to humble rather than exalt myself. Keep me faithful to your Word, and touch those spiritual leaders among us who need your healing touch. Amen.

✝ ✝ ✝

There was a man who followed to the letter every law he could find. He was especially scrupulous about his tithe. At the end of every week he would carefully count up all his income: salary, tips, gifts, even coins found in the road. Painstakingly he figured out exactly ten percent of the total, and with a great and obvious show, dropped it ponderously into the collection plate.

This man was careful not to tithe twice on any income. He tithed on his gross income, so that if he got a tax refund, he did not have to tithe on it. He was careful to give God exactly what God asked for, ten percent, no less, and certainly no more.

Each time he was stopped by a panhandler, he said to the poor unfortunate, "I have a job and I tithe to my church, I have nothing left for you!" Each time the March of Dimes or the Cancer Society came to his door for a contribution, he turned them down, saying, "I give my tithe to my church." Each time issues of social justice were raised at church, he looked out the window and wished the service were over. Each time there was a family in need at church, he told the pastor to find money for the family somewhere in the church budget, adding that he had no extra to give.

He died as he had lived. People came to his funeral out of obligation, but no one spoke of justice, mercy, or faith. His tithe alone, given under compulsion and with a mean spirit, was all anyone could praise him for.

Great Giver of all Gifts,
help me to tithe on my income without
neglecting "the weightier matters of the law,
justice and mercy and faith." Amen.

† † †

Jesus really knows human nature! How easy it is to read the old prophets' harangues about others and smile and nod knowingly as we apply their words to the past. How much harder it is to read the ancient prophets and apply their words of prophecy to our lives today! How much harder it is, indeed, to hear the voice of the prophet in our own time, pointing out and condemning our own faults.

Yet prophets are not solely for one time and for no other. The Biblical prophets have much to teach us about how we can live meaningful lives today. For example, the prophet Isaiah still speaks to us today when he describes the kind of fast that is preferable to God, the kind that calls us "to loose the bonds of wickedness, . . . to share your bread with the hungry, and to bring the homeless poor into your house . . . ." (Isaiah 58:6-7)

God also sends prophets to us today. Sometimes they are like the great, loud, thumping prophets of old — people who relish the gift of prophecy and boom it out to our discomfort. But often they are ordinary people, like you and me, who will on occasion quietly speak a word of truth about our world and our life. Prophecy is essentially the gift of speaking forth God's truth about a given situation.

It is hard to listen to prophets because they call attention to the things in our lives that need to be changed. They call us out of our complacency into the risks of trust in God as the source of our security. To heed their call is to admit that we are still sinners in need of God's grace.

Great Inspirer of the Prophets, I humbly ask that
you help me to hear the prophets which you send into
my life today. Amen.

† † †

Matthew was convinced that the end of the age could not come until Christ's message had been proclaimed to all nations: "And this Gospel . . . will be preached throughout the whole world, as a testimony to all nations; and then the end will come." This was a startling shift from the traditional Jewish notion that only the Jews were the children of God. Matthew, like Paul, insisted that the good news is for everyone, not just for the Jews.

Why is this true? Why must the Gospel be preached to the whole world? The answer is simple: the Gospel represents God's love offered to every person, without exception; by definition, then, every person must be given a chance to receive it.

It is clear that we haven't succeeded in preaching the Gospel to the whole world, inasmuch as the end has not yet come. The truth of Jesus must still be spread to the forgotten, the ignored, the discounted, the unloved. We still have much to do.

Jesus suggests in today's reading that the false gospels of false prophets who arise and lead many astray represent one obstacle to the spread of the true Gospel. A false gospel is one that proclaims that happiness can be attained apart from God — for example, through material wealth, individual self-fulfillment programs, or the exercise of political power without the guidance of the Holy Spirit. Such "gospels" lead directly to the chaos Jesus describes here: wars, famine, and persecution. Jesus Christ, the true Gospel, promises only one source of happiness: the love of God offered to every person on earth.

Lord of Light and Truth, for our sake and our redemption you sent Jesus into the world. You have given us the good news to tell to the nations. Help speed us on our way! Amen.

† † †

In today's reading Jesus calls forth witnesses to corroborate his claim to being the Messiah: God, John the Baptist, the Scriptures, and the prophecy of Moses. But the most compelling witness is Jesus' own miraculous actions: "For the works which God has granted me to accomplish, these very works which I am doing, bear me witness that God has sent me."

For three years Jesus ministered to the needs of his people. He gave sight to the blind, made the lame walk, healed the sick, restored hearing to the deaf, gave speech to the dumb. He multiplied loaves and fishes to feed the people, calmed storms, cast out demons, even raised the dead. As Nicodemus the Pharisee said to Jesus, "No one can do these signs . . . unless God is with that one." (John 3:2)

Just as Jesus' works were evidence of his divine mission, so today the primary evidence for the validity of Christianity is what it does. If lives are transformed; if family is created where once there was aching, empty loneliness; if hope springs up where once there was despair; if confidence, self-esteem, and dignity replace degradation — then there is no need for further proof of the power of God at work in the people. Such modern-day miracles speak for themselves, for "no one can do these signs . . . unless God is with that one."

Blessed Creator of Joy, thank you for sending Jesus into my life and miraculously saving me from loneliness, despair and degradation. I know by the works being done in my life that Jesus is my Saviour. As a grateful recipient of your bounty, I will praise you today. Amen.

† † †

Jesus predicts many false Messiahs, saying, "For false Christs and false prophets will arise and show great signs and wonders, so as to lead astray, if possible, even the elect." Indeed, the Acts of the Apostles records at least three false Messiahs, Theudas, Judas of Galilee (Acts 5:36-37), and "the Egyptian." (Acts 21:38)

We may be tempted to scoff at those who are gullible enough to follow these false Messiahs, but as William Shakespeare wrote in *Hamlet*, "The devil hath power to assume a pleasing shape." If the truth be told, we are all prone to follow false hopes.

False prophets are not only called Theudas, Judas of Galilee, and the Egyptian; they are Hitler, Stalin, Franco, Marcos, Pinochet, Duvalier, Long, and many more. Many political figures through the ages have promised peace and happiness, some even using the name of Christ to validate their claims to power.

But political leaders aren't the only false Messiahs we may follow. Sometimes we are tempted to put our hopes for salvation in charismatic religious or spiritual leaders. Sometimes we are tempted to look for salvation in stocks, bonds, real estate, or investment portfolios. Sometimes we look to movie stars, rock idols, best-selling authors, sports heroes, or spellbinding public speakers to provide us with a sense of well-being. Sometimes we see our Messiah in fads, ideas, or movements, in material possessions, positions, or power.

Today's Gospel message is clear and unambiguous: the real Messiah, the only one who can bring true happiness into our lives, is Jesus. Only Christ can guide us through those times when our heaven and earth are shaken and there is nothing to hang on to.

True Messiah, help us to follow only you! Amen.

† † †

For all our pride in our civilization's progress, human society really hasn't changed all that much from the times of Jesus or of Noah until now. Jesus prophesies that at the time of his second coming people will be behaving pretty much as they were at the time of the great flood, "eating and drinking, marrying and giving in marriage."

Jesus is not condemning people for their eating, drinking, marrying, and other ordinary pursuits. His point is that people are entirely preoccupied with their everyday activities, heedless of God in the routine of life.

Sometimes we get so caught up in everyday life that we don't stop to consider the reality of God's transcendent, shining presence all around us. Our thoughts focus on what to prepare for dinner, where to go for the weekend, whom to ask to the dance, how to impress the boss, or when to buy that new car, rather than on the presence of God permeating our lives.

In today's passage, we are told to watch and be ready for Christ's coming into our lives. What would my life be like if I were to take that command seriously? Would I ever cheat my customers or employer? Would I remain indifferent to the poverty, homelessness and hunger around me? Would my attitude toward war and conflict change? Would I treat my loved ones and friends differently? Would my relationships with my opponents and competitors be more open? Would I take more time to see God in all the circumstances of my life?

Jesus, help me to watch and be ready for your coming into my life. Help me to see what it is that you would have me do to ready myself for your advent on earth. Amen.

† † †

We could interpret today's parable as an exhortation directed to clergy and lay leaders in the church, but it is in fact directed to each of us. Each of us has been entrusted with some responsibility by God, even if it is only for our own life. Jesus urges us today, whatever our responsibilities are, to be always ready to give an account to the higher authority placed over us — and ultimately to God. Today's parable therefore invites us to examine our faithfulness in the day-to-day discharge of our service to God.

The servant of God is faithful, which means honest, trustworthy, hard-working, diligent, and competent. The servant of God is wise, which means just, compassionate, kind, caring, intelligent, and fair. The servant of God is ready to be evaluated, which means amenable to correction and discipline, as well as to praise and affirmation.

The bad servant takes advantage of the absence of the boss, is abusive and cruel to those under his or her care, wasteful and dishonest. The bad servant is lazy and shirks work whenever possible. When corrected, the bad servant blames others or tries to point out the failings of co-workers. The bad servant tries to avoid evaluation, and is unable to take criticism, correction, and discipline. Such servants think praise is their due, but do nothing to truly earn it.

One measure of our faithfulness to God is our faithfulness to others: to our co-workers, our church, our spouse, our parents, our children, our friends. Today, as I examine my relationship with God in the light of my care for others, what do I see?

Great God, help me to become
a good servant in my daily life so that I can be
a good servant to you. Amen.

† † †

There wasn't anything especially significant about the ten women in today's Gospel; they were all pretty normal. They were all ready for the wedding during the daylight hours, and they all slept when the night came.

Now, falling asleep wasn't such a terrible thing to do; in fact, it was probably a good idea to take a little nap right before the wedding celebration. Where five of these women fell short, though, was in their failure to make adequate preparation. Five were smart and had extra oil for the lamps; the other five didn't seem to think beyond what to wear.

Jesus is teaching us to watch for the second coming, to be vigilant so as to be adequately prepared for the judgment, since we cannot know when it is to come. The five who were ready with extra oil for their lamps were ready to meet Jesus at the judgment, but the five who hadn't made adequate preparations lacked the resources to enter into the celebration and meet the bridegroom face to face.

In the daytime, the wise and unwise seemed alike. It was only at midnight, when the test came, that the lack of preparation of the unwise showed.

What oil shall we prepare for *our* lamps? Prayer, faithfulness, ministry to those in need, support for the church, worship, study, and a life that reflects the Gospel — these make up the oil that will light our lamps for salvation.

Divine Host,
help me to prepare so that I will not miss
the feast that you have prepared for me. Keep me ready
and watchful for your coming. Amen.

† † †

In today's parable Jesus makes two important points: first, God has given people different talents and skills; and second, regardless of what those talents and skills may be, they are meant to be used.

Each person is talented in some way. Too often, though, people believe their abilities are inferior to others', resulting in resentment toward those whose gifts are more showy. It is tempting to think, "With my insignificant abilities, I can do nothing." Or the temptation is to envy more gifted people, and as a consequence spend time and energy criticizing God and others out of a feeling of inferiority. The fallacy in this thinking is the belief that some gifts are more important than others. The truth is that every person's unique gifts are necessary in the body of Christ. God values us just as we are.

Whatever our gifts may be, they are meant to be used, rather than buried in the garden out of fear. Refusing to utilize what God has given ultimately means the loss of the gifts, just as muscles atrophy if they are not used. If fear prevents a person from using the talents God has given, perhaps it is because that person views God as vengeful, exacting, and punishing, a view of God that leads to immobilization.

The one-talent people who use their abilities as best they can will be as appreciated, valued, and important to God's realm as will be the five- or ten-talent folks. The gifts each person brings are each important. Ask yourself today: What gifts has God given me, and how am I using them?

Beloved Provider, thank you for
the talents you have given me. Help me to use them
to your greater glory. Amen.

† † †

Jesus' image of judgment is much different from the ones we may hold. The amount of money given to our church, the power and wealth we have accumulated, the titles we have achieved, our stature in the community, our beliefs — none of these things will count for anything. Rather, each of us will be singled out in turn and challenged about our relationship with the poor, the hungry, the imprisoned, and the physically afflicted. For "as you did it to one of the least of these my sisters and brothers, you did it to me."

What would it mean in my life if I were to commit myself to the impoverished and needy, the sick and imprisoned, the helpless and homeless, the physically handicapped and the mentally disabled? Surely it would mean more than merely putting a dollar in the Christmas basket of the Salvation Army volunteer, or buying tickets to a concert to benefit the poor, or an occasional prayer for those less fortunate than we are. Charity calls on us to speak out against sinful systems that create poverty, disease, war, and injustice. It calls on us not only to feed the hungry, but to provide for their future independence from us. It calls on us to adopt a way of life that expresses our solidarity with those we seek to serve.

Christ calls us to great things, it is true, but what Jesus considers as great seems minor in the eyes of much of our society. Greatness in Jesus lies in helping "the least of these."

Just and Great Judge, help me today to recognize and serve you in "the least of these." Amen.

† † †

The Feast of Christmas Eve

The Scriptures don't tell us much about Joseph. We know that he took Mary and Jesus to Egypt to escape the wrath of Herod; we know that he was a carpenter who probably taught his trade to Jesus; we know that he took his family to Jersusalem when Jesus was twelve. Then we hear nothing more of Joseph. He probably died sometime between the trip to Jerusalem and the beginning of Jesus' public ministry.

In today's story, we perceive Joseph as sympathetic, kind, and aware of God's active presence in his and Mary's lives. He was obviously devoted to Mary; even when he believed that she had been unfaithful to him, he didn't want to cause a scandal or embarrass her. He accepted the assurances of the angel of God about Mary's unborn child.

Joseph clearly made an impression on Jesus as a devoted father. When describing his special relatonship to God, Jesus used the closest similar human relationship that he had had, that with Joseph. Jesus often called God "Father," or "Abba," which is best translated as "Daddy" — just what he probably called Joseph. The Hebrew writers of the Old Testament seldom used the word "Father" to refer to God. Jesus' use of the name "Father" for God, the same name that he called Joseph, was therefore, indirectly, a high honor that Jesus paid to Joseph. It meant that he saw something of the love of God in the love of Joseph.

In each life there are people like Joseph who make a difference, revealing something of God's nature. It may be one's mother or father, an uncle or aunt, a friend, a childhood playmate, a grandparent. Today as you prepare for Christmas, remember those special persons and open your heart to the goodness of God that they reveal.

Emmanuel, God with Us!
You are often with us through special people.
Be with us now. Amen.

† † †

The Feast of Christmas

What kind of God is born as a poor baby in an insignificant, backwater part of the world? Jesus is Emmanuel, "God with us." This God is a God for the people.

What kind of God is celebrated by giving brightly wrapped presents to each other? Jesus, who grew up to give the ultimate gift of his life for us, is God's greatest gift. This God is a God who gives.

What kind of God's birth is noted by a star in the heavens? Jesus is one with God the Creator, who made the earth, sun, moon, and stars. This God is the Creator who brought forth everything that has been made.

What kind of God is born in a stable, of poor, common parents, with only shepherds and stablehands in attendance? Jesus told us that when we minister to "the least of these" we minister to Christ. Jesus bids us heal the sick, feed the hungry, minister to the oppressed, clothe the naked, and visit those in prison. This God is the God who brings liberation to the oppressed.

What kind of God has foreign royalty come to the stable birthplace to worship? Jesus came not just for one chosen people, but that all people might become the chosen of God. This God is the God of all!

What kind of God is born a human and later dies and is raised from the dead? Jesus Christ — Saviour, Shepherd, and Friend. This is our God!

Merry Christmas!

> *Beloved Saviour, today we celebrate*
> *your birth and all that it means to us and to*
> *the world. Happy birthday, Jesus! Thank you for*
> *being our God and Saviour. We rejoice*
> *in being your people. Amen.*

† † †

Patrick was young and very little. He sat with wonder in his eyes as he listened to the Christmas story in the second chapter of Luke. Great peace and joy seemed to come over his little spirit as he listened and all tension left him. When I finished reading, I asked, "How did you like that story?"

"It's the best!" Patrick was emphatic, yet calm and at peace. The story had made such an impact that I had to ask, "What's so good about the story for you?"

"Be not afraid," Patrick answered. "That's the best part. We were afraid and the angel said, 'Be not afraid.' We don't have to be afraid ever again."

I asked Patrick what kinds of things he might be afraid of as this year draws to a close. He said, "Getting sick, being alone in the dark, not having friends, not doing good in school — stuff like that."

In his simple, innocent, unsophisticated way, little Patrick hit the nail on the head! The meaning of Jesus' humble birth in a rude stable in an obscure corner of the Roman Empire is "Be not afraid."

No matter what our fears, today's Gospel message echoes down the centuries to speak to us: "Be not afraid." Like little Patrick, we are comforted with the knowledge that Christ has come to bring "peace among those with whom God is pleased."

Blessed Saviour, thank you for coming to us with your divine message of grace and peace. Thank you for having your angels comfort and assure us, saying, "Be not afraid." Amen.

† † †

One of Ronald Reagan's favorite Russian proverbs was, "Trust, but verify." That was a favorite of these shepherds, too! Immediately after hearing the angels, they set out for Bethlehem to see for themselves and found Jesus lying in a manger just as the angels had said.

Then they did two other things: "They made known the saying which had been told them concerning this child." They testified to what they knew about Jesus. They witnessed to others about what God's angels had told them. Then they worshiped God. As they returned to their fields, they were "glorifying and praising God for all they had heard and seen."

When God confronts us with the truth, we can follow the example of the shepherds. We also can verify through prayer, reflection, and spiritual discernment that it is truly God speaking in our hearts, not the selfish needs of our own egos. Having discerned God's will as best we can, we can then testify to others what God has revealed to us. And throughout this whole process we can continue worshiping, praising, and glorifying God.

Finally, just as the shepherds returned to their fields and sheep, we can return to our lives, back to our homes and jobs, back to what we were doing before. But we go back with a difference, for when we have been touched by the wonder of God's love for us, we are changed, exalted, fulfilled, satisfied. We go back, but we will never be the same again! That is the good news of the Christmas story that is still offered to us today.

Great Revealer of Truth, guide me as I take time to discern your holy will for my life today, that I may return to my daily routine rejoicing. Amen.

† † †

The Feast of the Holy Innocents

So soon after the angels tell us, "Be not afraid," there is this sad and tragic story of the murder of innocent children. Jesus is born, his birth is celebrated, God is glorified and praised, and suddenly we read of Herod's fear of this long-heralded Messiah, a fear that leads to a horrible act of vengeance and death.

What is the point of commemorating this senseless act of evil so soon after the joy of the birth of Jesus? The point *is* the birth of Jesus! And the point of the birth and life of Jesus is not that the senseless tragedies on earth have ended, as Jesus' own death attests; the point is that there is a power greater than all the tragedies in the world that has entered the world to overcome them, as Jesus' Resurrection attests.

Therefore, even though death, injustice, oppression, murder, and all kinds of vicious acts continue in our world, the good news is that they do not have the final word. There is a God whose power has come into the world to overcome all evil.

What can we say about the slaughter of the innocents? With Paul we affirm, "Who shall separate us from the love of Christ? Shall tribulation, or distress, or persecution, or famine, or nakedness, or peril, or sword? . . . No, in all these things we are more than conquerors through the one who loved us." (Romans 8:35,37)

God of Love, be with me in times of joy
and in times of pain. I know that nothing can
separate me from your love. Amen.

† † †

Jesus' first miracle, at the wedding in Cana, sets the tone for his entire ministry and sums up what is to come in the Gospels.

Jesus understands and empathizes with our troubles, just as he understood the embarrassment of his host when the wine started to run out. Without great fanfare, he simply supplies what we need, enriching us in the process (the steward thought the host had saved the best for last, when in fact it was Jesus who provided the best). Imagine the relief the host felt after Jesus provided the wine; that is the kind of relief that Jesus always gives us.

Jesus was the kind of person who was able to enjoy himself and others at community celebrations. He had been invited to this party, he fit in, he wasn't out of his element, and he didn't make others feel uncomfortable. In other words, Jesus and his followers were not dour religious figures, frowning censoriously, but were able to enjoy life and share in the happiness of others.

Jesus allowed the servants to be co-workers with him. To this day Christ does not keep the healing, helping, and saving of the world in Christ's own hands, but offers a share in ministry to all who will join in.

Like Mary, we can be confident that Jesus will be thoughtful, dependable, and helpful. She knows, as we do, that whatever the need, Jesus can do something to help.

Sovereign Jesus, Gracious Guest, be ever present
at our celebrations, join our parties, be with us in
our joy, for you provide all we need. Amen.

† † †

Back in Cana, Jesus was met by an official who had come the twenty-five miles or so from his home in Capernaum to beg Jesus to come there and heal his son.

Jesus had begun to tire of people who clamored for more miracles. He knew that some of them were not there out of faith but out of curiosity. They didn't look at Jesus as a spiritual leader but rather as a carnival-side-show attraction who performed amusing tricks. Testing the official's faith, Jesus rebuffed him, saying, "Unless you see signs and wonders you will not believe." But the official was not dismayed at the rebuke; he merely stated his hope and his belief. His little boy was dying and he didn't care about any signs and wonders. All he wanted was help, before it was too late.

Touched and reassured by the official's faith, Jesus said, "Go; your son will live." Sure in his faith, the official did not question Jesus' reply. He did not continue to importune Jesus to come to Capernaum; he did not ask how the healing could possibly happen; he simply "believed the word that Jesus spoke to him and went his way." In the end, his faith was rewarded; the boy had been healed at exactly the time that Jesus had said the words.

Is my faith that strong? Can I deny the desire for a good show from Jesus? Can I take the word of the Saviour that, even at long distance, my needs will be met? Do I trust that the many promises Jesus has made to me will come to pass?

Great Physician, give me the faith to believe your healing promises. Help me to go on my way trusting in your promise of life. Amen.

† † †

New Year's Eve

No matter how wonderful tonight's celebrations, they cannot compare to that wonderful and miraculous new age that Simeon and Anna saw when Mary and Joseph brought the infant Jesus to the Temple in Jerusalem.

Simeon, it had been prophesied, would not die before seeing the Messiah. One look at the baby Jesus and Simeon knew that this child was to be the Christ, "the consolation of Israel." With this promise fulfilled, he was content to die, and so he prayed the prayer we call the *Nunc Dimittis*: "Lord, now let your servant depart in peace, according to your word; for my eyes have seen your salvation which you have prepared in the presence of all people . . . ."

Then Simeon uttered an amazing prophecy. He called Jesus "a light for revelation to the gentiles, and for glory to your people Israel." Jesus would be not only the Jewish Messiah long foretold, but a light to all people!

The prophetess Anna confirmed Simeon's prophecy and "spoke about the child to all who were looking for the redemption of Jerusalem." What a new year had dawned in Jerusalem that day!

As we celebrate another new year's coming tonight, consider that Jesus represents a new beginning in our lives. Jesus is a light for revelation to all. Jesus is the Saviour. Jesus is the bright morning star that announces the dawn. Jesus is the greatest new year ever seen!

Wonderful God, now let me depart in peace from this old year, secure in the knowledge that my eyes have seen your salvation in Jesus, the light for revelation to all people. Amen.

† † †

THE AUTHORS

Kathy Baker (June 19-21) is a member of MCC Baltimore. She resides in Baltimore City with her two cats, Ralph and Max, who continually teach her much about God. She is ordained in the ministry of the Church of Christ Consciousness, based in Great Barrington, Massachusetts.

Harold Joseph Burris (July 1-31 [co-author]) was born in New York City. He is a graduate of Brothers College at Drew University in Madison, New Jersey, and of Garrett Theological Seminary and the Graduate School of Northwestern University, both in Evanston, Illinois. Ordained a clergyperson in the United Methodist Church, Mr. Burris served pastorates in Chicago, Illinois, and Long Island, New York. After a long tenure at the University of Northern Iowa and as a consultant with the U.S. Department of Education's Alcohol and Drug Abuse Education Project, Mr. Burris now resides in Washington, D.C. He is a Human Services Consultant and works with a variety of projects serving persons living with AIDS.

Philip E. Carolan (August 1-5) served as Treasurer of the Board of Directors of Emmaus House of Prayer from October, 1986 to January, 1989.

Sara Case (June 18, 22 and 25-30; August 6 and 22-31) is a lesbian who lives in Mt. Rainier, Maryland, with her spouse and two ferrets. She is an intern member of the Earth Keeping Mission Group of New Community Church, Church of the Saviour, and Clerk of the Board of Directors, Emmaus House of Prayer.

R. Adam DeBaugh (December 1-31) has served the UFMCC in various capacities since 1975. He was Assistant Director and then Director of the Washington Field Office, Director of the Department of Christian Social Action, and Co-Director of the Department of Ecumenical Relations. In 1983 he was elected District Coordinator of the Mid-Atlantic District and was re-elected to a four year term in 1988. He is also Director of Chi Rho Press. He lives with his lover, Rick Ferenci, in Rockville, Maryland.

THE AUTHORS

Nancy Eichert (June 1-15) resides in Mt. Rainier, Maryland, with two ferrets, Boots and Spike, a dog, Midnight, and Sara, friend and lover. The meditations she has written, she affirms, actually belong to the folks who have allowed her to travel with them for short segments of their journeys toward eternity.

Kate Eysaman (April 1-30) lives and works in St. Paul, Minnesota. Her two daughters connect her to the earth, while projects such as this devotional connect her to the Spirit. Her experiences as a teacher and a nurse have given her rich opportunities to observe life and grow. Writing, for her, is the chance to move an everyday occurrence to a personal epiphany. She intends her poetry to be a record and report of the constantly changing reality.

Sarah K. Fershee (May 1-15), formerly a member of Emmaus House of Prayer's Board of Directors, is currently studying spiritual direction at the Shalem Institute, Washington, D.C., as she prepares for licensed ministry within the UFMCC. With sixteen years' experience in retreat ministry, Sarah co-leads contemplative retreats and workshops.

Jeannine Gramick (January 1-5, 11-15, and 21-25), a nun prominant in the Catholic women's movement, taught mathematics at the high school and university levels before 1977, when she co-founded New Ways Ministry, a social justice center working for the reconciliation of sexual minorities and the church. Among her books are *Homosexuality and the Catholic Church, The Vatican and Homosexuality,* and *Homosexuality in the Priesthood and Religious Life*.

Joseph W. Houle (June 17; July 1-31 [co-author]; November 1-30) is the founder and Director of Emmaus House of Prayer, a center of contemplative prayer and healing in the Mid-Atlantic District of the UFMCC. As a native of Minnesota, he loves the rhythm of the four seasons, things that are cold (like ice cream), and family connections. His current work involves offering workshops and retreats that integrate the insights of spirituality and psychology.

THE AUTHORS

Louis F. Kavar (August 7-21) is a clergyperson with the UFMCC and has served as Project Coordinator of Lazarus Ministries, the AIDS-related outreach of the Mid-Atlantic District. Kavar is author of *Pastoral Ministry in the AIDS Era*, has published and lectured widely on topics of AIDS and spiritual development, and holds a Master of Arts degree in Formative Spirituality from Duquesne University. He is currently a Ph.D. candidate in Counseling at the University of Pittsburgh.

Leah Maroney (September 16 and 22) is a native of Houston, Texas, and has been an EXCEL and EXCEL in Faithfulness team member for five years. An active and enthusiastic lay minister, Leah is regularly a guest speaker at area churches and organizations. Her ministry also includes spiritual and guidance counseling within the community.

Virginia Miles (May 16-31) has been the Pastor of the Metropolitan Community Church of Rockville, Maryland, since 1985. She is a graduate of Wesley Theological Seminary. Prior to beginning her theological studies, she served as an Administrative Officer with the U.S. Geological Survey, for which she received a Meritorious Service Award.

Vanessa Moore (June 16; September 1-7, 9-15, 17-20, 23, and 26-30) is a member of MCC Washington, D.C. She helped found the Capital EXCEL Team in the Mid-Atlantic District and recently served as the team's Facilitator. A writer and editor, she is currently helping to develop a manual for EXCEL in Relationship, a retreat weekend for Christian gay and lesbian couples.

Robert Nugent (January 6-10, 16-20, and 26-31) is a Catholic priest who has been involved with ministry for the church and homosexual people since 1971. He is co-founder of New Ways Ministry in Washington, D.C., and editor of *A Challenge to Love: Gay and Lesbian Catholics in the Church*. He is an author and lecturer and holds an STM from the Yale Divinity School. His most recent work is *Stations of the Cross for Persons with AIDS*.

THE AUTHORS

Jack Pantaleo (September 8 and 21; June 23-24) received his Masters of Arts in Writing from the University of San Francisco in 1988. From 1983 until 1989, he served as Co-Founder and Co-Director of the AIDS InterFaith Network of San Francisco. He is currently involved in Evangelistics Concerned/San Francisco and taking care of children with AIDS.

Carolyn "Dusty" Pruitt (March 1-31), raised in the Baptist tradition, served six years as a U.S. Army Officer. Leaving the Army to become a clergyperson, she attended the Iliff School of Theology in Denver, Colorado, where she received her M. Div. degree, and the School of Theology at Claremont, California, where she received her D. Min. degree. She has pastored MCC-Long Beach from 1980 to the present. Her published doctoral thesis, a study of authoritarianism, religiosity, and child sexual abuse, is entitled, *But Thou Shalt Not Forget the Shame of Thy Youth*.

Andy T. Sidden (October 1-31) lives in Valrico, Florida, and is a student pastor at MCC-Tampa. A graduate of the University of North Carolina at Chapel Hill, he works as a reporter for *The Ledger*, a daily newspaper in Lakeland, Florida. He and his spouse, Kevin Dove, recently celebrated their sixth anniversary.

Larry J. Uhrig (February 1-28) has served as pastor of MCC Washington, D.C., since 1977. He is the author of *The Two Of Us*, 1984, and *Sex Positive*, 1986, both published by Alyson Press. He has been published in newspapers and magazines throughout the United States.

Claire Vasilioy (September 24-25) has been an active member of MCC-R in Houston, Texas, since 1983. She has also been active in EXCEL since the movement came to Houston in 1983. When invited to contribute writings for this publication, she asked herself, "Are you sure you want me?" And when the answer returned to her was "Yes," she believed that God was calling her to share of herself in an unexpected way. She hopes you enjoy her writings.

INDEX OF SCRIPTURE REFERENCES

INDEX OF SCRIPTURE REFERENCES

INDEX OF SCRIPTURE REFERENCES

INDEX OF SCRIPTURE REFERENCES

EMMAUS HOUSE OF PRAYER

Each person has a unique experience of the holy. Some experience God most deeply in the simple beauty of nature. Others sense God more readily in the human community. Still others find God most real as the transcendent Other whom we can never fully know, but whom we encounter in silence and solitude. All of us, however, even though we may differ in the way God touches us most profoundly, share the longing of the human heart to know God.

Emmaus House of Prayer has been called into being to serve as a resource for those who have awakened to that longing and therefore seek a deeper walk with God. The purpose of this book, *The Road to Emmaus*, is accordingly to provide food to satisfy people's hunger for God. Also, Emmaus House currently offers a mini-retreat series, *Spirituality and Emotionality*; a New Year's retreat, *Experiencing Emmanuel*; and workshops on prayer. In 1990, Emmaus House plans to open a house in West Virginia, where the contemplative rhythm of prayer, work, and leisure will be kept alive in a small community which people may join for brief periods of retreat.

As a Special Work of the Mid-Atlantic District of the Univeral Fellowship of Metropolitan Community Churches (UFMCC), Emmaus House welcomes all people, regardless of race, gender, sexual orientation, or economic condition. If you would like to know more about Emmaus House, you may write to the Director at: Emmaus House of Prayer, P.O. Box 70434, Washington, D.C. 20024.